NUTRITION
PRESCRIPTION

Also by Brian L. G. Morgan

The Lifelong Nutrition Guide
The Food and Drug Interaction Guide
Brain Food

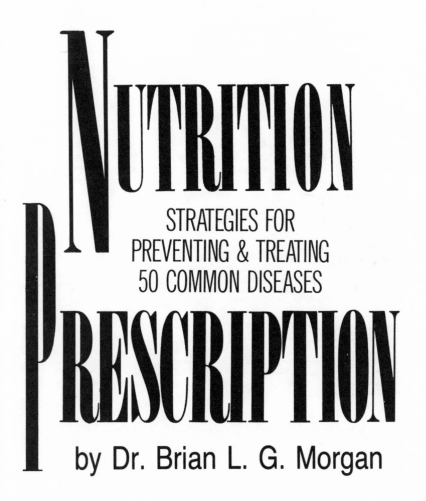

NUTRITION

STRATEGIES FOR
PREVENTING & TREATING
50 COMMON DISEASES

PRESCRIPTION

by Dr. Brian L. G. Morgan

CROWN PUBLISHERS, INC.
NEW YORK

TO BINKY:

My prescription for
health and happiness

I should like to thank warmly the following people who gave generously of their time and expertise to help me write this book: My friends and partners John Gallagher and Hugh Howard, for aiding me at every stage of the conception, planning, and writing of *Nutrition Prescription*—it really was a team effort; my editor, Barbara Grossman, who believed in the book from the start; my agent, Glen Cowley, for his continuing support and friendship; my wife, Roberta (Binky), for her patience through the long hours that I spent working on the manuscript, and for her unfailing support and encouragement; and, last but not least, my parents, for their understanding last summer when I spent most evenings working on the book during my visit with them.

Publisher's Note: This book contains recommendations within the context of an overall health program. The composite case histories are designed to illustrate prototypical health situations and are drawn from interviews and research. They are not intended to depict any actual persons, and the instructions are not intended as a substitute for professional medical advice. Before commencing any health program a physician should be consulted.

Published by Crown Publishers, Inc., 225 Park Avenue South, New York, New York 10003 and represented in Canada by the Canadian MANDA Group.

CROWN is a trademark of Crown Publishers, Inc.

Manufactured in the United States of America

Library of Congress Cataloging-in-Publication Data

Morgan, Brian L. G.
    Nutrition prescription.

    1. Diet therapy. I. Title. [DNLM: 1. Diet—popular works. 2. Diet Therapy—popular works. 3. Preventive Medicine—popular works. QT 235 M847n]
RM216.M542 1987   615.8'54   87-6808

ISBN 0-517-56302-9

10 9 8 7 6 5 4 3 2 1

First Edition

Contents

Introduction

Mankind spent the first half of this century making remarkable gains in life expectancy and overall health. Crucial to those gains were a number of nutritional adjustments that reduced the chances of contracting a variety of diseases caused by nutritional deficiencies. We now routinely add vitamin D to milk in processing; we add iodine to our table salt; we add vitamin A to margarines; we add B vitamins to flour; we enrich breakfast cereals.

Today, however, we are confronting a new onslaught of nutrition-related diseases; in fact, six out of ten of today's leading causes of death in the United States (stroke, heart attack, cancer, atherosclerosis, cirrhosis of the liver, and diabetes) are inextricably linked to our diets. In response, nutrition education in this country is changing, and the best hospitals have more than 100 patient protocols to meet the differing nutritional needs of patients with different problems. In short, nutrition has become an integral part of patient care.

More important, nutrition is at the forefront of preventive medicine. At the Institute of Human Nutrition, my colleagues and I teach nutrition to doctors. The focus is increasingly upon the relationship of nutrition to specific health problems. Rather than talking about, say, the value of eating breakfast, we talk about the role of dairy products in osteoporosis and of vitamin C as a factor in the prevention of a wide variety of illnesses. Our intent is to teach nutrition in terms of doctors' professional concerns rather than as an abstract discipline to which doctors have paid little or no attention for too long.

In the same way, it is the purpose of this book to alert its readers to the link between diet and disease. The fact is that our diets are quantifiable risk factors related crucially to our chances of contracting—or surviving—a great variety of diseases. Until now there has been no practical, comprehensive guide for the layman to assess his or her own diet and help make dietary changes for overall health to avoid disease. *Nutrition Prescription* is intended to help you take advantage of the best knowledge available today of the interactions between food and disease.

Although medicine may be relatively unsuccessful against a multitude of diseases, sensible dietary practices can be effective indeed in reducing your chances of contracting those diseases or in mitigating their effects. *Nutrition Prescription* will help you determine which of the more than 50 common, nutrition-related diseases discussed here you may have or be likely to get, and to avoid or to minimize their consequences through comprehensive nutritional strategies.

The Diseases

Many researchers believe that a number of the degenerative diseases have periods of latency: they may be developing in your system for 20 or even 30 years before any symptoms are observable.

By adjusting the environment in which a disease develops, the course of the disease can be altered. It is not possible to change one's genetic makeup, but it is increasingly apparent that dietary changes—that is, the practice of preventive nutrition—can contribute to improved health and the prevention of disease.

The evidence is overwhelmingly in favor of an orderly, sensible approach to the nutrition-and-disease link. To cite but one instance, consider the Multiple Risk Factor Intervention Trial (MRFIT) conducted by the National Heart, Lung, and Blood Institute. This six-year investigation was conducted at 20 different clinical centers to determine the effects of high cholesterol, hypertension, and smoking on the chances of a coronary event occurring among a randomly chosen group of men representative of one risk group. In this case, almost 13,000 white males between the ages of 30 and 59 were selected to participate.

The data gathered have produced, and will continue to produce, innumerable scholarly papers and reports. But one representative finding effectively makes the point: 1 in 50 of the white males in the study who controlled their cholesterol intake and their blood pressure, and did not smoke, had a heart attack; those who failed to control one of the three risk factors saw their chances of heart attack ascend to roughly 1 in 20; those with two risk factors had almost a one-in-ten chance of a coronary event; those with all three had nearly a one-in-five chance. Given the fact that proper dietary measures enable cholesterol and hypertension to be controlled, the benefits of doing so are obvious: you decrease your chances of having a heart attack *ten times* by controlling those factors.

The promise of this book, then, is to help you assess your chances of contracting more than 50 common diseases. Some, like cancers and heart disease, are major killers; others, like migraine headaches and insomnia and dental decay, are pesky, inconvenient ailments; yet others, like colitis, anemia, and hypoglycemia, fall somewhere in between. But each of the diseases discussed in this book has a clear nutritional component that can be used to decrease the risk of a disease or to ameliorate its symptoms or severity.

Fact vs. Fiction

People in this country spend billions of dollars on vitamins, minerals, and health foods, some of which are said to have health-giving or curative powers. In some cases the consumer is looking for a magical cure for a dread disease, in others the desire is simply for the healthiest and longest life possible. The reality, however, is that many claims made for so-called health foods are unproven or false.

In the same way, many unqualified "nutritional consultants" pander to people's needs to feel better, look younger, and lose weight quickly. There is often considerable salesmanship involved, too, but little genuine science or medicine. Sometimes the advice of opportunists masquerading as health experts can even prove dangerous in the long run. In Appendix 3 you will find a list of substances claimed by faddists to be essential components of the diet, but which are, in fact, not essential to health—and some of which are potentially hazardous.

Nutrition Prescription is not about miracle cures; it is about using nutritional strategies as adjuncts to sound medical care and proper treatment. You will find many vitamins and minerals discussed in this book, and some supplements are recommended. But you will not find an elaborate litany of all the "miracle cures" being sold; the ineffectual ones are absent, the dangerous ones indicated. And, of course, you will find in these pages the instances in which the nutritional treatments are, according to today's best medical knowledge, effective.

A Balanced Diet

Frequently, the best possible nutritional approach is that old standard, the balanced diet. A balanced diet is one that supplies all the essential nutrients required to keep your body functioning perfectly well. In practical terms, this means consuming the following on a daily basis:

• Two servings of protein-rich foods
• Four to six servings of vegetables and fruit
• Four to six servings of bread and cereals
• Two servings of milk and dairy products

A diet consisting of this mix of foods will supply all the essential nutrients at the level of the Recommended Dietary Allowances.

How to Use This Book

You may elect to read this volume from cover to cover; if you do, you will gather an immense quantity of information and guidance on some diseases for which you are at risk, but also about others you are unlikely to contract.

To facilitate both occasional reference use and cover-to-cover review, each chapter opens with a summary of the information that is to follow. First, the disease to be discussed is described. Second, the warning signs are identified, along with the portion of the population that is most likely to contract the ailment. From this information you will be able to locate yourself with respect to the disease. A listing of the nutritional strategies one can use to combat or prevent the disease comes next.

Each chapter also features a case history of a prototypical patient. Though based on facts, these composite cases have been assembled to illuminate in as personal a way as possible the nature and course of each disease. The remainder of each chapter is devoted to comprehensive "Dietary and Life-style Recommendations" for avoiding and/or treating the disease.

In essence, I believe that by arming yourself with a liberal mixture of knowledge about the disease, some information about its statistical probability, and a substantial body of knowledge about the relationship of the food eaten to the development of the disease, you can determine whether you or anyone in your family fits the profile. There can be no guarantees, but by following the recommendations contained in each entry, you may succeed in reducing your risk of contracting certain diseases or be able to live with them better.

1
Acne and Other Skin Problems

Acne develops when the level of *androgens* (male sex hormones) increases in the body at puberty due to the increased production of the hormones in the testes and ovaries. This disrupts the skin's normal processes, causing the *sebaceous glands* to grow and produce excess oil.

The sebaceous glands are fat-producing glands at the base of the hair follicles. Ordinarily they produce just enough oil to keep the skin slightly lubricated, but under the influence of androgens, the cells lining the hair follicles are produced at a rapid rate. These are then shed, and become stuck together with oil. They clog the follicles, causing "pimples." Dermatologists refer to these as *comedones*.

Whiteheads are comedones in which the opening of the follicle is tightly closed. Blackheads are comedones that are open enough for the plug of oil and cells to push up to the surface. The black coloration is not dirt but results from the exposure to air of the pigment-containing cells that are over-produced with other cells lining the follicle.

Acne most commonly affects areas of skin containing a lot of sebaceous glands, such as the face, forehead, scalp, neck, chin, shoulders, and chest.

Acne is not caused by particular foods, by getting too much or too little sleep, or by any sexual practice (thinking of the opposite sex, masturbating, having sexual intercourse, or being celibate). Bacteria are also not a cause of acne, although they do help it to develop. Bacteria that are normally present in the hair follicles set off a chemical reaction that damages the wall of the follicle. It breaks and the fat and other substances in the infected follicle spill out into the surrounding tissue, causing a red skin lesion.

1

Noninflammatory acne is characterized by blackheads, whiteheads, and a few *papulae* (which are larger lesions), and is usually treated conservatively. The person is told to wash the infected area two to three times a day, and the hair at least once a day (to keep oil off infected follicle heads). This helps to keep the area dry, as do over-the-counter drying agents containing *benzoyl peroxide* or *sulfur salicylic acid*. *Exfoliates* keep open the follicles to allow the oil and shedded cells to ooze out, and the follicle to heal. Sometimes a prescription drug made of an acid form of vitamin A called *tretinoin* is used.

Inflammatory acne is more serious, with deep pustules and cysts. This will be treated with antibiotics or another prescription drug, *Accutane*, which is a toxic derivative of vitamin A.

A variety of other skin problems are discussed below, including dermatitis, eczema, and psoriasis.

Warning Signs

DERMATITIS   Commonly referred to as *eczema*, dermatitis is a reddening and swelling of the skin, causing itching. These symptoms are followed by blistering, oozing, and eventually crusting and scabbing on the skin. If the condition becomes chronic, the skin may peel or chap or become thickened, or may even become darkened in color. Dermatitis may be caused by allergies, toxic reactions to drugs and other substances, irritations from clothing (especially wool or silk), or infections. An inherited predisposition may also be a factor in its occurrence.

DERMATITIS HERPETIFORMIS   This has a gradual onset and usually occurs between the ages of 15 and 60. It is characterized by tiny, blisterlike, burning and itching hives that are found on the elbows or knees, at the base of the spine, on the buttocks, or at the back of the head. It is usually found on both sides of the body in a symmetrical fashion and is caused by a sensitivity to wheat protein.

SEBORRHEA DERMATITIS   Scaling of the scalp (dandruff), eyelids, and eyebrows, or of the skin around the nose, behind the ears, under the arms, around the anal and genital areas, and in the body folds of the obese. There may be redness and oozing, or hard, dry, and crumbly crustiness of the skin.

PSORIASIS   This skin problem is characterized by small, silvery, scaly lesions that cover round or oval red patches. The cause of psoriasis is not known, although it is believed by some to be caused by a genetic defect that affects the growth of the top layer of the skin. That layer is usually replaced every 26 to 28 days, but in the psoriasis sufferer it is replaced every three to four days.

Psoriasis usually affects the back, knees, elbows, scalp, buttocks, palms, or soles. Less frequently, it affects the nails, eyebrows, anogenital regions, and armpits, as well as the folds of skin in the obese (although in these warm and damp areas, no scales of skin are likely to be found).

Psoriasis often first reveals itself between the ages of 10 and 40 and appears often on injury to the skin or after a generalized infection. After that, it may be brought on or exacerbated by stress, drug reactions, or a strep throat. When it starts after a strep throat, it usually looks like a red, bumpy rash. When the nails are affected, they become pitted and dry, and scaly material builds up underneath, separating them from the nail beds.

Psoriasis is usually chronic, erratic, and unpredictable. Outbreaks may last for weeks, months, or years, and when the condition goes into remission, nobody can predict whether or when it will return again.

HIVES   An itchy swelling that comes and goes. It may be the result of an insect bite if found as a single lesion; if it occurs as multiple lesions, it is probably an allergic reaction.

Epidemiological Data

Four out of five teenagers have acne. Some suffer for a few weeks, some for a year, but most for ten years or more into early adulthood. If your parents had acne, the chances are that you will also.

A few women who escaped acne in their teens develop it in their twenties and thirties. This is rarely the case with men.

People with oily skin are likely to have a bigger problem with acne than those with dry skin.

Women who take birth-control pills that have a high progesterone content sometimes develop acne. When they switch to a pill higher in estrogen, the acne goes away.

DERMATITIS   Seborrheic dermatitis is more common in people with Parkinson's disease and other neurological problems than it is in the rest of the population.

Seventy to ninety percent of people with dermatitis herpetiformis have it as a result of sensitivity to wheat protein.

PSORIASIS   More than one percent of the American population suffers from psoriasis; 30 percent of them have a blood relative with the disorder. Psoriasis is more common in whites than in blacks.

One in twenty of all psoriasis sufferers will develop *psoriatic arthritis*, a variety of arthritis that is most likely to affect the hands.

Two-thirds of patients with psoriasis have significant periods of remission.

Prevention and Treatment

ACNE   Foods and beverages do not cause acne; although neither zinc nor vitamin A supplements can cure acne, a deficiency of either nutrient may make an outbreak more likely; be sure to get the Recommended Dietary Allowances of both.

DERMATITIS   Scaly dermatitis may be caused by a lack of vitamins C, A, and perhaps E; be sure to consume the Recommended Dietary Allowances of them.

Greasy, scaly dermatitis can be caused by zinc or essential fatty acid deficiencies, so be sure to get 15 milligrams of zinc in your diet, and cook with vegetable oils.

The variety of dermatitis known as *infantile eczema* can be due to a hypersensitivity to milk, egg protein, or wheat; consult your doctor.

DERMATITIS HERPETIFORMIS   Sufferers from this skin problem should avoid food products containing wheat.

SEBORRHEA DERMATITIS   The skin disorder can be caused by a vitamin B_6 deficiency, so be sure you get ample vitamin B_6 in your diet.

PSORIASIS   Reduce your consumption of seafood and animal protein for a trial period; also try reducing your intake of citrus fruits, nuts, corn, and milk for a trial term.

CASE HISTORY: Phil Jenkins

Phil started to develop very bad acne when he entered puberty. As if he were not already self-conscious about it, his schoolmates made derisive remarks about his skin problems. Even at home, he was berated for his unsightly complexion. His older brother chided him about not washing his face often enough, although his problem certainly had nothing to do with cleanliness, since from the time he learned to dress himself, Phil had been fastidious about his appearance.

His mother, too, had been less than helpful, believing as she did that it was the "junk food" Phil ate that gave him acne. His ravenous teenage appetite led him to consume chocolate, pizza, and a lot of cake, as well as just about anything else put before him.

However, even after he eliminated what his mother regarded as the "guilty foods" in Phil's diet, his complexion problem remained the same. His mother then tried another home remedy, this one involving life-style changes. Phil was to stop staying up late listening to loud music, and start getting a full eight hours of sleep a night. Phil followed his mother's advice, but this treatment also failed.

Finally, Phil went to see his doctor, who prescribed Accutane. He told him to wash his face three times a day with a special medicated soap. Over a period of twenty weeks, the treatment brought Phil's condition under control.

In his early twenties, though his acne trouble was behind him, he was left with badly pitted skin. He decided to be treated with a series of *collagen* injections (collagen is a body protein), which didn't eliminate the scarring entirely but helped enough to please him.

Dietary and Life-style Recommendations

In Dealing with Acne, Be Sure You Are Getting Sufficient Vitamin A and Zinc

Vitamin A and zinc deficiencies may exacerbate an acne condition, in that they are very much involved with the health of the skin. Zinc is critical for the growth of new cells, and vitamin A helps produce the "cement" that joins the cells together.

Strategy Be sure to get at least 15 milligrams of zinc and 5,000 international units of vitamin A in your diet. Foods rich in vitamin A include apricots, broccoli, cantaloupe, carrots, liver, peaches, pumpkins, squash, and tomato juice; zinc-containing foods are most meats and grains. (See tables on pages 318 and 323 for listings of a variety of foods rich in these nutrients.)

Consuming doses well in excess of the recommended amount will not cure acne. In fact, large doses of either of these nutrients are extremely toxic. Zinc will prevent your absorption of other essential nutrients like iron and copper and make you anemic. Vitamin A will cause hair loss and give your skin a "sandpaper" appearance. Excessive amounts of this vitamin taken over a period of many years can even be fatal.

What Foods Should I Avoid in Dealing with Acne?

Over the years, many foods and beverages have been accused of causing acne. At present, chocolate, fatty foods, and soft drinks are commonly assigned the blame. However, there is absolutely no proof that any food or drink can cause any kind of acne flare-ups.

Dermatitis Patients Should Be Sure to Get Sufficient Vitamins A, C, and E

A lack of vitamin A or C in the diet reduces fat secretion from the sebaceous glands and can cause dry skin. It has also been suggested that a deficiency of vitamin E is to blame for similar problems in some people.

Strategy Be sure you get the Recommended Dietary Allowances of these vitamins in your diet (5,000 international units, 60 milligrams, and 10 milligrams of vitamins A, C, and E respectively). Include foods rich in these nutrients in your daily menu. Vitamin A–rich foods include broccoli, cantaloupe, carrots, apricots, liver, peaches, squash, and tomato juice; foods rich in vitamin C are citrus fruits and juices and green vegetables such as kale, mustard greens, parsley, and broccoli; vitamin E is found in a variety of nuts and oils. (See tables on pages 318, 321, and 322 for more foods rich in these nutrients.)

If You Suffer from Seborrhea Dermatitis, Get Sufficient Vitamin B₆

A classical sign of vitamin B_6 deficiency is seborrhea dermatitis. Many people in America have an inadequate intake of this nutrient, especially premenopausal women taking oral contraceptives.

Strategy Be sure to consume plenty of foods rich in vitamin B_6. These foods include bananas, fish, Grape-Nuts cereal, liver, and peanuts. (See table on page 320 for other B_6–rich foods.)

For Greasy, Scaly Dermatitis, Be Sure to Consume Sufficient Zinc and Essential Fatty Acids

This type of dermatitis usually occurs on the forehead, face, chin, scalp, shoulders, and chest. It can be the result of a zinc deficiency or of an inadequate consumption of the essential fatty acid linoleic acid.

Strategy Linoleic acid is best found in vegetable oils (see table on page 311). Cook with vegetable oils and be sure to get 15 milligrams of zinc in your diet from such foods as meats and grains (see table on page 323).

If You Suffer from Dermatitis Herpetiformis, Eliminate Wheat-Containing Foods from Your Diet

Up to 90 percent of people with this disorder can be completely cured by removing all wheat-containing foods from their diets.

Strategy Be sure to read all food labels to avoid consuming gluten (wheat protein). Make careful selections in restaurants, too.

If Your Child Suffers from Infantile Eczema, Milk, Eggs, and/or Wheat May Be the Cause

Very often the culprit is a sensitivity to one of these foods. However, if you removed all of these foods from a child's diet, you would run the risk of malnourishment, as these foods contain nutrients essential to normal growth and development.

Strategy Consult with your child's doctor before experimenting with the elimination of foods.

In the Psoriasis Sufferer, Should Taurine Be Eliminated from the Diet? What About Citrus Fruits, Nuts, and Other Foods?

The answer is that nobody knows. Some clinicians claim that *taurine* (an amino acid or component molecule of protein), which is found commonly in seafood and animal proteins, can exacerbate a psoriasis-type condition. The simplest way to take advantage of this possible benefit is to cut down on seafood and animal protein in your diet for a trial period. A month is generally thought to be a suitable time. If you benefit from this approach, you might want to pursue a vegetarian diet, which means combining proteins as shown in the chart below.

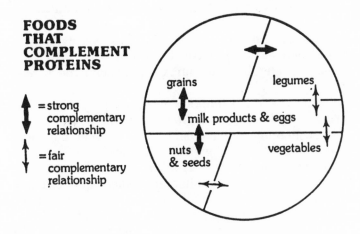

Apart from soy protein, all proteins from plant foods are of poorer quality than those found in meat, fish, poultry, and dairy products. But by eating plant foods that complement one another—as shown in this chart—at the same meal, the mixture of their two proteins is as good as protein from animal foodstuffs.

Some clinicians suggest that citrus fruits, nuts, corn, and milk should also be avoided by the psoriasis sufferer. You may want to try eliminating them one at a time for a two-week period. If your condition seems to improve, this might well be a useful approach for you. But remember that citrus fruit is most people's primary source of vitamin C, and milk their main dietary source of calcium. If you cut down on these foods or eliminate them from your diet, take a daily supplement of 60 to 100 milligrams of vitamin C and 1,000 milligrams of calcium as calcium carbonate (2½ grams of calcium carbonate). Half the calcium should be taken in midmorning, half at bedtime.

Other Advice

The following drugs are often prescribed for the treatment of skin problems:

TETRACYCLINE   This antibiotic should be taken on an empty stomach one hour before or two hours after meals. Avoid dairy products and iron-rich foods for an hour before and after taking tetracycline. Take a one-a-day vitamin supplement containing vitamin C and the B-complex vitamins.

ANTIHISTAMINES   Do not take these drugs with milk or alcoholic beverages.

ISOTRETINOIN   Sold under the brand name Accutane, this generic drug should be taken in two equal portions with breakfast and the evening meal. Do not take vitamin A supplements concurrently with Accutane.

METHOTREXATE   Consumption of this drug by psoriasis sufferers (methotrexate is sold as *Folex* and *Mexate*) should be accompanied by a supplement containing 400 micrograms of folic acid, 6 micrograms of vitamin B_{12}, and 1,000 milligrams of calcium.

CORTICOSTEROIDS   *Prednisone*, taken orally, should be consumed with milk or meals. A 1,000-milligram supplement of calcium should also be taken, as should 15 milligrams of zinc, 100 milligrams of vitamin C, and 2 to 3 milligrams of B_6. You should also include lots of potassium-rich foods while taking prednisone (see table on page 313).

IBUPROFEN   Sold under the brand names *Motrin* and *Rufen*, ibuprofen should be taken with meals or milk.

If you would like further information on acne or other skin problems, contact the National Health Information Clearinghouse, P.O. Box 1133, Washington, D.C. 10013-1133, phone (800) 336-4797; in Virginia, phone (703) 522-4797. If you suffer from psoriasis, contact the National Psoriasis Foundation, Suite 200, 6415 Southwest Canyon Court, Portland, Oregon 97221, phone (503) 297-1545.

2
Alcoholism

Although it is true that an occasional drink is not normally harmful, any form of regular drinking is a potential health hazard. The liver is the organ most susceptible to the noxious effects of alcohol, and the end result of 20 years of alcoholism could be cirrhosis. Even from the time you take your first drink, however, alcohol impairs liver function and puts you in a high-risk group for high blood pressure, heart disease, cancer, gastric irritation, pancreatitis, malnutrition, fatty liver, mineral deficiencies, and even an impairment of sexual performance in men.

Epidemiological Data

One out of every ten American adults who drink has a drinking problem, yet only 15 percent of them seek formal help. (Since many professionals believe there is no meaningful distinction between the terms *problem drinker* and *alcoholic*, I will use them interchangeably. It is said that alcoholism exists when the individual is physically dependent upon drinking alcohol. If someone "must" drink each and every day, he or she is an alcoholic.)

For every alcoholic, there are four people who are directly affected by his or her problem.

Alcohol has some part to play in 95,000 deaths a year in this country. Drunk driving accounts for the largest number of deaths in the 15- to 24-year age group, and alcohol is involved in half of all traffic fatalities.

Alcohol abuse is one of the leading causes of nutritional deficiencies among American adults.

Fetal alcohol syndrome is one of the three major causes of infant mental retardation. Less severe defects resulting from consumption of alcohol during pregnancy affect 36,000 infants born each year.

Thirty-one percent of high school students are "alcohol misusers," defined as having at least six episodes of drunkenness per year. Alcoholism among students from 12 and 13 years of age and up is a growing problem throughout America.

Alcoholics are more likely to suffer from depression, suicide attempts, death in fires, and are more likely to be perpetrators or victims of violent crimes. Alcohol is a factor in 45 to 68 percent of spouse-abuse cases and up to 38 percent of child-abuse cases.

Warning Signs

This test may used to identify the warning signs of alcoholism.

1. Do you occasionally drink heavily after a disappointment or a quarrel, or when the boss gives you a hard time?   __YES __NO

2. When you have trouble or feel under pressure, do you always drink more heavily than usual?   __YES __NO

3. Have you noticed that you are able to handle more liquor than you did when you were first drinking?   __YES __NO

4. Did you ever wake up on the "morning after" and discover that you could not remember part of the evening before, even though your friends tell you that you did not "pass out"?   __YES __NO

5. When drinking with other people, do you try to have a few extra drinks when others will not know it?   __YES __NO

6. Are there certain occasions when you feel uncomfortable if alcohol is not available?   __YES __NO

7. Have you recently noticed that when you begin drinking you are in more of a hurry to get the first drink than you used to be?   __YES __NO

8. Do you sometimes feel a little guilty about your drinking?   __YES __NO

9. Are you secretly irritated when your family or friends discuss your drinking?   __YES __NO

10. Have you recently noticed an increase in the frequency of your memory "blackouts"? ___YES ___NO

11. Do you often find that you wish to continue drinking after your friends say they have had enough? ___YES ___NO

12. Do you usually have a reason for the occasions when you drink heavily? ___YES ___NO

13. When you are sober, do you often regret things you have done or said while drinking? ___YES ___NO

14. Have you tried switching brands or following different plans for controlling your drinking? ___YES ___NO

15. Have you often failed to keep the promises you have made to yourself about controlling or cutting down on your drinking? ___YES ___NO

16. Have you ever tried to control your drinking by making a job change or moving to a new location? ___YES ___NO

17. Do you try to avoid family or close friends while you are drinking? ___YES ___NO

18. Are you having an increasing number of financial and work problems? ___YES ___NO

19. Do more people seem to be treating you unfairly without good reason? ___YES ___NO

20. Do you eat very little or irregularly when you are drinking? ___YES ___NO

21. Do you sometimes have the "shakes" in the morning and find that it helps to have a little drink? ___YES ___NO

22. Have you recently noticed that you cannot drink as much as you once did? ___YES ___NO

23. Do you sometimes stay drunk for several days at a time? ___YES ___NO

24. Do you sometimes feel very depressed and wonder whether life is worth living? ___YES ___NO

25. Sometimes after periods of drinking, do you see or hear things that aren't there? ___YES ___NO

26. Do you get terribly frightened after you have been drinking heavily? ___YES ___NO

Patterns of "yes" answers to questions in the following sections may indicate stages of alcoholism:

Questions 1 to 8:   Early stage: You are developing a problem.
Questions 9 to 21:   Middle stage: You have a problem.
Questions 22 to 26:   The beginning of the final stage: You have a problem that is seriously affecting your life.

(Reproduced with permission of the National Council on Alcoholism.)

Prevention and Treatment

- Limit your drinking as much as possible, and certainly to no more than one or two drinks a day.
- Do not drink alcohol during pregnancy or prior to breast feeding.
- Never drink alcohol on an empty stomach.
- Dilute liquor with ice and water and drink slowly, in a relaxed, comfortable setting; do not drink if you are depressed, nervous, or tired.
- Do not drink and drive.
- Do not mix alcohol and drugs.
- Anyone who drinks two or more drinks a day should take a multi-vitamin supplement containing the RDA along with some calcium and magnesium.
- Do not try to sober someone up by giving him black coffee or a cold shower.
- To combat a hangover, eat bland foods such as toast or a soft-boiled egg; drink soup for thirst or bloating; take a hot shower for muscle aches or fatigue; drink orange juice or some other fruit juice for dizziness.
- If you are suffering from alcohol withdrawal, eat a high carbo-hydrate diet.
- If your father or mother is an alcoholic, be wary of abusing alcohol.

CASE HISTORY: Jean Pomerantz

From Jean's earliest memory, her mother and father were known as people who loved to throw a party, and they did so frequently. On the weekends when she got up, her parents were always still in bed, "recovering from last night's party." When she was in high school the parties seemed to stop, because her mother wanted her father to cut down on his drinking. But when she came home from a date, her father was usually in the kitchen having a nightcap while he "waited up for her." She went to college out of state and came home only for the holidays. It was during these infrequent visits that she noticed that her father's "ceremonial" drinking now began before noon. Still, it was only many years later that she came to realize he was an alcoholic.

In the same way, Jean took years to recognize her own alcoholism. She went to New York City after college and worked in advertising. She became a copywriter, and a good one, but as she neared thirty, her dreams of becoming the best and most innovative creative director faded.

Her personal life wasn't perfect, either, not least because she gave so much of herself to her work. But when she wasn't dating married men or bringing someone home from the local singles bar, she went drinking with some friends from the office. Once she admitted that she drank to feel better about herself, she found it easy to justify coming home from work and drinking alone until she fell asleep on the living room couch.

As she moved into her thirties, Jean developed a weight problem and suffered from premenstrual syndrome. This depressed her and contributed to the cycle of drinking to get "up," which only served, in time, to bring her further "down." She found that she sometimes awoke in the morning after a long evening of drinking at a local bar unable to remember whole conversations of the night before. Sometimes, too, she remembered too clearly things she had said that she wished she had not. Her clever way with words, when her tongue was lubricated with a couple of drinks, lost her more than a few friends.

She was thirty-five when the accident happened. She had decided to drive out with a friend to his weekend home late one Friday night. As was her habit, she had had a couple of Bloody Marys at lunch, and several cocktails after work. She and her weekend host had split a bottle of wine over dinner before getting in the car. The worst of the Friday-night traffic had dissipated, so they anticipated clear sailing.

The drive was uneventful until she misjudged an exit ramp off an expressway. The car went into the woods and struck several trees before finally coming to a halt.

The good news was that both Jean and her friend sustained only minor injuries. But Jean found herself in court, charged with driving while intoxicated. She could no longer deny that she was a drunk. It was a tough time for her, because she did not immediately understand the degree to which alcohol had taken over her life. But once she realized the extent of her disease she accepted the fact that her recovery was going to be a slow process.

Today, Jean is a grateful recovering alcoholic. She credits her sobriety to the work of friends, and most of all to Alcoholics Anonymous.

Dietary and Life-style Recommendations

Limit Your Drinking to No More than One or Two Drinks a Day

There is a linear relationship between the amount of alcohol consumed and the risk of contracting cirrhosis of the liver. If you were to consume a pint of liquor a day for 25 years, you would have a 50-percent chance of developing cirrhosis. This disease results partly from the direct effects of alcohol on the liver and partly from the malnutrition common to heavy drinkers. The risk of developing liver disease starts to climb when a man consumes more than three daily drinks, and a woman one and a half.

The lower figure for women is a result of the fact that women tend to be smaller than men; the smaller the body, the greater the effect of alcohol. A 160-pound man would need four to five drinks over the course of an hour or two to reach the blood alcohol level of .1 percent, the point at which most states consider a person to be legally intoxicated. But it would take less than four drinks to achieve the same level in a 120-pound woman. Alcohol also has a greater effect on women immediately before the onset of menses. The rate of metabolism of alcohol is reduced owing to the hormonal changes that occur just prior to menstruation. Oral contraceptives also slow down the metabolism of alcohol and accentuate its effects. The slower the metabolism, the longer the alcohol stays in your system and the greater the chance of a buildup in the body.

Twenty percent of the alcohol we drink goes directly from the stomach into the bloodstream. Most of the remaining alcohol is absorbed through the small intestine. The body begins to eliminate the alcohol once it reaches the bloodstream. About 3 percent leaves the body in an unchanged form in the urine, perspiration, and expired air. The rest is processed mainly in the stomach and small intestine immediately after it is consumed. Since the intestine can only process roughly seven grams (one-quarter fluid ounce) of alcohol an hour, the alcohol starts to accumulate in the blood and to affect other organs such as the brain and liver if it is drunk at a faster rate.

In the brain, alcohol acts just like a narcotic and anesthetizes the areas of the brain that control normal behavior. This tends to eliminate inhibitions that prevent us from acting antisocially. As the blood alcohol levels rise, other areas of the brain become depressed, resulting in slurred speech, blurred vision, and poor coordination. The table that follows indicates how the consumption of various quantities of alcohol affect the body:

THE EFFECTS OF ALCOHOL

Quantity of whiskey consumed	Result
2 fluid ounces in two hours	Euphoria, minor movement disturbance
2.4 fluid ounces in two hours	Problems with vision
3 fluid ounces in two hours	Impaired driving ability
4 to 6 fluid ounces in two hours	Complete lack of coordination
8 to 12 fluid ounces in two hours	Loss of memory
12 to 14 fluid ounces in two hours	Coma
14 to 16 fluid ounces in two hours	Possible death

One gram of alcohol is equivalent to 7.1 calories, one ounce to 71 calories, one drink to 100–150 calories, one pint to 1,141 calories, and one liter of wine to about 673 calories. Hence, you can see that it is very easy to consume a large quantity of energy in this form. Unfortunately, alcohol has little nutritional value other than its energy content and is simply a form of "empty calories." If a person satisfies his appetite with alcohol by taking, for example, 1,000 calories in this form, it is unlikely that he will obtain the nutrients he needs from the rest of his diet.

ALCOHOL AND CALORIE CONTENT OF ALCOHOLIC DRINKS

Beverage (alcohol percentage by volume)	Serving Size (oz.)	Alcohol (grams per serving)	Calories (per serving)
Wine (11.5%)	5	14	110
Light wine (6–10%)	5	7–12	65
Wine cooler (3.5–6%)	12	10–17	220
Sherry (19%)	3	14	125
Beer (4.5%)	12	13	150
Light beer (3.7%)	12	11	100
Gin, vodka, rum, whiskey (rye, Scotch) 80 proof (40%)	1.5	14	100
Cordials, liquors 15–100 proof (7.5–50%)	1	3–16	50–100
Martini	2.5	22	156
Bloody Mary	5	14	116
Tom Collins	7.5	16	121
Daiquiri	2	14	111

Alcohol consumption leads to gastric irritation and to a loss of part of the lining of the intestines. This loss impairs the process of absorption of lactose (the sugar found in milk) and leads to an intolerance of milk and other dairy products, as well as decreasing the absorption of folic acid and thiamine.

Alcohol also causes pancreatitis, which leads to impaired production of digestive enzymes and malabsorption of nutrients, including fat and the fat-soluble vitamins A, D, E, and K. Even beer, with a 5-percent alcohol content, will cause gastric irritation if consumed regularly. On the other hand, pancreatitis is more usually found in drinkers of hard liquor.

If it were the malnutrition arising from the consumption of alcohol that caused the liver disease, one would expect that a good diet designed to counteract the effects of the alcohol would eradicate the problem. Unfortunately, this is not the case. Although a good diet is beneficial in limiting the damage, all the evidence shows that the alcohol itself has a direct toxic effect. Alcoholics consuming a good diet would simply be expected to take longer to develop cirrhosis. It should be mentioned that not all alcoholics contract cirrhosis. However, there seems to be a genetic predisposition to the disease, and at least 50 percent of all drinkers have been shown to have such a tendency.

As mentioned before, alcohol contains only empty calories, and excessive indulgence can lead to high caloric intakes. Unlike most sources of energy, alcohol is mainly broken down in the liver. In addition, it cannot be stored in the body. Hence, it must all be disposed of as quickly as it enters the body. This means that the liver must divert most of its activity to this process. As a result, other nutrients, especially protein and fat, will not be metabolized to any extent—which will lead to their being stored in the liver. This storage leads to swelling of the liver, which in turn impairs its function. Eventually, inactive fibrous tissue replaces the metabolically alive liver tissue. This is the condition known as cirrhosis.

Inability to handle dietary protein leads to its storage in the liver. This protein absorbs ten times its volume of water and so causes swelling of the liver and eventually *ascites* (the liberation of fluid from the liver into the digestive cavity).

The protein that is digested is often only broken down to substances called *amines*, and ammonia. These substances, which are harmful to the brain, can build up to quite high concentrations in the blood if the alcoholic eats a mixed diet. An inability to break down *nucleic acids* (RNA and DNA), which are found in all cells, leads to high levels of *uric acid* in the blood. They can be deposited as small crystals in the joints, causing pain. This condition is known as *gout*, an ailment that is extremely painful and, if left untreated, can lead to erosion of the joints.

The liver of the heavy alcohol consumer is unable to metabolize fat. Hence, fat collects in the liver, producing a "fatty liver," which further impairs its function. It also means that high levels of fats in the blood occur, with their accompanying high risk of cardiovascular disease.

Alcohol also acts as a diuretic and increases the amount of urination. This increases the loss of minerals from the body, especially zinc, calcium, and magnesium.

Alcohol is broken down in the liver to produce *acetaldehyde*, which in turn is broken down to nontoxic substances. Acetaldehyde is toxic both to the heart and to the brain. It is broken down by a group of enzymes *(microsomal enzymes)* that are also responsible for degrading just about every kind of drug and toxic substance that enters the body during your lifetime. When you consume alcohol, this group of enzymes increases its activity. This means that not only will a chronic alcohol user be able to get rid of alcohol from his system more quickly than a nondrinker, but that his system will also remove drugs faster, which may make a drug prescribed by your doctor last a shorter period of time and be less effective.

The increased ability to break down toxic substances possessed by the chronic drinker can often lead to more serious problems. He may put himself in a high-risk group for cancer. Many substances in our food and the environment have the potential to cause cancer if they are partially degraded. This degradation takes place in the liver as a function of the same microsomal enzymes that degrade alcohol. *Tobacco pyrolyzate* is one such substance, *dimethyl nitrosamine* (found in some beers) is another, and *tryptophan pyrolyzate* (formed when you cook meat) is a third.

Under normal circumstances, your ability to degrade these substances is minimal, and so they are relatively harmless. However, if you drink heavily, significant amounts of them are converted to cancer-causing substances by the stimulating effects of alcohol. For instance, a person who takes four or five drinks and smokes ten cigarettes a day has five times the chances of getting lung cancer as compared with a nondrinker smoking the same number of cigarettes a day.

Hormones are also broken down more quickly in a heavy drinker. In a man, *testosterone* (the male sex hormone) is broken down more rapidly than normal in a heavy drinker. Furthermore, alcohol decreases the production of this hormone by the testes. Hence, one could say that alcohol impairs a male's sexual performance.

No matter how you look at it, moderation is the key word when it comes to alcohol. A little alcohol (one or two drinks a night) is not necessarily a problem, but if your consumption rises above this, you will compromise your health in a very serious way.

Do Not Drink Alcohol During Pregnancy

Drinking alcohol, especially during the first three months of pregnancy, can sometimes lead to fetal alcohol syndrome, which causes fetal abnormalities including brain damage; mental retardation; deformities of the limbs, joints, fingers, face, and heart; cleft palate; and poor coordination. Sometimes fetal alcohol syndrome does not show up until adolescence, when it may appear for the first time in the form of hyperactivity and learning and perceptual problems. No one knows how much alcohol is a "safe" amount for a pregnant woman to consume.

Alcohol reaches the unborn baby's blood at the same concentration as in the mother's blood within fifteen minutes of her taking a drink. Six or more drinks a day or occasional binge drinking is definitely harmful and can cause fetal alcohol syndrome. But even moderate drinking may be linked to miscarriages, stillbirths, and low birth weight.

Contrary to popular belief, it is not a good idea to drink a glass of wine or a beer to relax before nursing. In fact, alcohol inhibits the "letdown" reflex that leads to milk secretion. The alcohol also passes into the mother's milk. The level of alcohol in the milk is lower than in the mother's blood, but the infant can become intoxicated, even if his or her mother nurses after having only a couple of drinks. A breastfeeding mother is better off not drinking, but if she should take a drink, she should make sure it is well before nursing time.

Strategy   As little as one or two drinks a week might even be harmful, so, to be on the safe side, you should avoid all alcohol if you are pregnant, trying to get pregnant, or not using any form of birth control.

Never Drink on an Empty Stomach

Alcohol is very rapidly absorbed. On an empty stomach, 95 percent of the alcohol a person drinks is fully absorbed through the walls of the stomach and small intestine into the bloodstream within 20 minutes. Foods, especially fatty foods, delay absorption because they slow down the emptying of the stomach into the small intestine, where the alcohol is absorbed most quickly. Food also acts as a barrier between the alcohol and the stomach wall, decreasing absorption there. In addition, food appears to stimulate enzymes in the stomach and intestine that help to break down alcohol.

Strategy If you drink, it is advised that you consume alcohol only after eating or with snack foods. Incidentally, the older people become, the better they can tolerate the alcohol they drink.

Dilute Liquor with Ice and Water

Watery drinks, such as beer or mixed drinks, are absorbed more slowly and take much longer to intoxicate you. Light wines typically have less alcohol than the real thing. Nonalcoholic beers and de-alcoholized wines contain no more than .5 percent alcohol. By alternating nonalcoholic drinks such as alcohol-free beers and fruit juices with alcoholic ones also serves to dilute the alcohol in the stomach and slows down its absorption. Beware of carbonated beverages, as they speed up the emptying of the stomach.

Other factors that can affect absorption include the emotional and/or physical state of the drinker, and the person's individual body chemistry. If you are tired, under a lot of stress, depressed, or nervous, you will absorb the alcohol you drink more rapidly.

Strategy Use ice and mixers when drinking liquor. Whatever your choice of alcoholic beverage, drink slowly, in a relaxed and comfortable setting. Don't drink if you are depressed, nervous, or tired.

Don't Drink and Drive

Studies show that just two drinks (three ounces of alcohol) taken in a two-hour period seriously impair a person's driving ability.

Strategy Avoid driving after drinking.

Do Not Mix Alcohol and Drugs

Alcohol depresses the brain, and if you are taking drugs that have the same side effect, the combined effect can be extremely dangerous, even lethal. For example, sleeping pills and tranquilizers are relatively harmless in the sober state, but if you drink heavily, the same dose can be lethal in combination with the liquor you drink.

Serious side effects also can occur from over-the-counter medications. Another dangerous interaction is with blood-pressure-lowering medication. Alcohol also lowers blood pressure, and the combined effects can cause blood pressure to drop to dangerously low levels. Drug-and-alcohol interactions are some of the most frequent causes of drug-related medical emergencies in the United States.

Strategy Always check with your doctor about alcohol when he prescribes a medication.

Drinkers Who Consume Two or More Drinks a Day Should Take a Multivitamin Supplement

Chronic drinking leads to nutrient deficiencies in one of two ways. First, heavy drinkers would rather have a "liquid meal" than eat regular food. Heavy drinkers can easily consume 1,800 calories a day in the form of alcohol alone. Second, alcohol impairs the absorption and metabolism of many nutrients, including amino acids, vitamins B_1, B_2, B_6, A, and D, folic acid, calcium, magnesium, zinc, and glucose.

People who drink heavily are especially deficient in thiamine (vitamin B_1) and magnesium. Alcohol decreases the absorption of thiamine and increases the excretion of magnesium. Both are needed by the body for carbohydrate metabolism, and carbohydrate is the brain's main fuel source. Deficiency of thiamine can lead to *Wernicke Korsakoff's syndrome*, the symptoms of which are amnesia, loss of short-term memory, disorientation, hallucinations, emotional outbursts, double vision, depression, anxiety, aggressive behavior, and loss of muscle control. A lack of magnesium exacerbates all these symptoms.

Alcohol dehydrogenase, the main enzyme involved in detoxifying alcohol in the body, requires the presence of zinc in the body to be active. Hence, a zinc deficiency further reduces the body's limited ability to rid the body of alcohol. Anyone who drinks two or more drinks a day would benefit from taking a supplement containing the Recommended Dietary Allowances for the vitamins affected by alcohol, and should consume a diet that includes good food sources of calcium, magnesium, and zinc. (See tables of calcium-, magnesium-, and zinc-rich foods on pages 301, 311, and 323, respectively.)

Do Not Try to Induce Sobriety with Black Coffee and Cold Showers

Because you can metabolize only one-quarter fluid ounce per hour, and no food or beverage can significantly affect this, trying to sober someone up by giving him black coffee or a cold shower or walking him around is useless.

Strategy There are, simply, no shortcuts to sobriety for a person who has consumed quantities of alcohol. Caffeine does not speed up the degradation of alcohol in the body; all it produces is a wide-awake drunk who may be deluded into thinking he can drive his car home. The chronic use of alcohol does result in an increased capacity to metabolize it more rapidly and does enable the chronic drinker to function with a much higher level of alcohol in his or her blood. However, if a person stops drinking for a few weeks, both the increased capacity to degrade alcohol and to perform under its influence is gone.

How to Combat a Hangover

Nobody knows exactly what causes a hangover. But the probable reason for the headaches, nausea, fatigue, and gastrointestinal distress so characteristic of the condition are a buildup of the alcohol itself and its metabolic product, *lactic acid*. Thirst is the result of alcohol's diuretic effect. Brandy, red wine, rum, whiskey, white wine, and gin, in descending order, seem to cause the worst hangovers. The more impurities the beverage contains, the worse the hangover.

Many of the symptoms of a hangover may be eased but not prevented by eating the right foods.

STRATEGIES

FOR HEADACHES   These are caused by the alcohol's dilation of the blood vessels in the head. Coffee is the best remedy for this, as caffeine is a *vasoconstrictor*. So is aspirin. For some people, hot showers also seem to relieve head pain.

FOR NAUSEA AND GASTRIC DISTRESS   Coffee and aspirin (if not buffered) should be avoided, as they tend to irritate the digestive tract. Toast, soft-boiled eggs, and other bland foods are the best bet.

FOR THIRST AND BLOATING   Slightly salty liquids, like chicken soup, work wonders.

FOR MUSCLE ACHES OR GENERAL FATIGUE   Coffee and a hot shower are suggested.

FOR THE DIZZINESS AND WEAKNESS CAUSED BY LOW BLOOD SUGAR   Drink orange juice to boost these depleted sugar levels.

If You Are Suffering from Alcohol Withdrawal, Eat a High-Carbohydrate Diet

Alcoholics suffer from serious symptoms when they stop drinking. The chronic maintenance of high concentrations of alcohol in their blood causes a state of physical dependence. Withdrawal symptoms most commonly appear from 12 to 72 hours after the last drink. However, even a relative decline in blood concentrations may cause the same symptoms; this kind of change can be caused by a reduction in the total daily intake or by a change in the pattern of drinking.

If the level of dependence is low, withdrawal may amount to disturbed sleep, nausea, weakness, anxiety, and mild tremors that last less than a day. If the dependence is severe, the symptoms can be life-threatening. They include insomnia, visual and auditory hallucinations, disorientation, convulsions, epileptic seizures, severe shaking, acute anxiety and fear, agitation, a fast pulse, fever, and excessive sweating, all of which can last for five to seven days.

Strategy   A high-carbohydrate diet seems to help alcoholics through this withdrawal period. It is believed that the powerful effect produced in the pleasure centers of the brain by the sweet foods can help offset the desire for alcohol.

Other Advice

If one of your parents is an alcoholic, keep in mind that alcoholism as a disease seems to run in families. Statistical studies have shown that people who have alcoholics in their immediate families run a risk of alcoholism four times greater than the offspring of nondrinkers. The pattern of electrical activity in the brains of the offspring of many alcoholics shows differences that suggest genetic influences on the development of the disease.

Alcoholism can result in hypoglycemia. Some researchers suggest that hypoglycemia itself is a cause of alcoholism, though the theory remains as yet unproven. However, if you have the warning signs of hypoglycemia, avoiding alcohol is recommended (see chapter 31).

One often-heard theory is that vitamin C or selenium protects against liver damage or other long-term effects of alcoholism. There is no evidence to prove that either of these nutrients has such protective affects.

If you would like further information on alcoholism, contact the National Clearinghouse for Alcohol Information, P.O. Box 2345, Rockville, Maryland 20852, phone (301) 468-2600.

3
Alzheimer's Disease and Senile Dementia

Senile dementia is characterized by one or more of the following symptoms: memory impairment, slowness of movement and thought, confusion, amnesia, feelings of disorientation, extreme lethargy, paranoia, inflexibility, and resistance to any sort of change. People with this disease lose brain cells at a much faster rate than normal. It is important to note, however, that dementia is not the natural result of aging and that some causes are preventable.

There are many different types of senile dementia, and each demands a different type of treatment. About half of the elderly people with senile dementia are victims of *Alzheimer's disease.* Twenty to thirty percent may be suffering from a combination of Alzheimer's disease and another type of senility, called *multi-infarct dementia,* or from multi-infarct dementia alone.

In multi-infarct dementia, a series of minor strokes destroy large amounts of brain tissue. Patients with high blood pressure are most at risk for this problem. Hardening of the arteries, which limits the flow of blood and oxygen to parts of the brain, is another way in which vascular disorders can result in dementia.

The remaining 20 to 30 percent of senile patients could be suffering from any one of a number of reversible physical conditions that result in serious, but usually temporary, changes in memory or intellect such as fevers, infections, metabolic disorders, adverse reactions to drugs, deficiencies of vitamins B_1, B_{12}, folic acid, or niacin, or alcohol and drug abuse. If left untreated, such ailments can cause permanent brain damage.

23

Alzheimer's disease is perhaps the most prevalent form of senility. Recent evidence shows that it is probably genetically determined, but there is some evidence to indicate that large amounts of aluminum may worsen the condition.

One characteristic of all of these forms of senility is the reduced ability of the brain to produce *acetylcholine*, the neurotransmitter in the brain responsible for memory.

Warning Signs

- Avoidance or fear of change (an early warning sign)
- Forgetfulness
- Failure to remember words
- Loss of learned motor movements such as writing, telephoning, dressing, or using a knife and fork
- Confusion
- Difficulty in doing simple additions

Epidemiological Data

Fifteen percent of the U.S. population over 64 years of age has senile dementia.

Senile dementia is the fourth leading cause of death in this country. One hundred thousand people die from it each year.

Between 1.5 and 2 million people get senile dementia annually.

If you have a parent or sibling with Alzheimer's disease, you have a 50-percent chance of contracting the disease if you live to age 90; if no immediate relative has suffered from Alzheimer's, your chances of developing the disease are about one in six.

Eleven percent of the U.S. population over the age of 85 have Alzheimer's disease.

Prevention and Treatment

- Reduce your intake of salt and raise potassium and calcium consumption.
- Reduce your saturated fat intake (animal foods) and raise your polyunsaturated fat intake (vegetables and fish).
- Increase the fiber in your diet, specifically of pectin, anything made from oats, and beans.
- Take a B-complex vitamin supplement.
- Do not use aluminum cooking utensils or containers.
- Take 1 to 2 grams of choline or 30 grams of lecithin daily.

CASE HISTORY: Emma Parkins

Emma's father had been diagnosed as having Alzheimer's disease eight years before his death, and he suffered its gradual, debilitating effects before he died in a rest home.

Emma, seeing her father lose touch with his surroundings and the people he loved, feared that she, too, would get Alzheimer's.

She was fifty-two when it became apparent to her and her family that her memory was failing. She misplaced her keys while shopping one day, and her husband had to drive nearly fifty miles to the shopping mall to bring a second set. She had always handled the family accounts, but after bouncing several checks and having some other problems with the bank, she admitted that she could no longer balance the checkbook. She had to leave her office job with a local construction firm because she could no longer handle the responsibilities she had found routine for nearly twenty years. It wasn't really necessary to tell her family what her problem was, as they'd seen it with her father. She, too, had Alzheimer's, and her doctor confirmed it.

She began to fear leaving the house after a trip to the local drugstore when she got confused and lost for several hours. By age fifty-four, she could no longer dress herself, and her family made the hard decision to put her in a home that specialized in patients with Alzheimer's.

Today she is not yet fifty-six and appears to be in vigorous health. However, her communication is limited to only a few short phrases, and she angers easily. She is generally unaware of where she is or what day it is.

Dietary and Life-style Recommendations

Reduce Salt Intake; Increase Potassium and Sodium Consumption

Patients with high blood pressure are the most susceptible to multi-infarct dementia. To guard against hypertension, you should limit the salt you eat and increase your intake of potassium and calcium.

Strategy This means that no salt should be added to meals, but up to one teaspoon per day can be used during cooking. Pickled foods such as sauerkraut, and extremely salty foods like luncheon meats, snacking chips, and processed cheeses should also be avoided.

Foods rich in potassium and calcium should be emphasized. Potassium is contained in good amounts in citrus fruits, spinach, raisins, and almonds (see table of potassium-rich foods on page 313) and calcium in dairy products (page 301). If you have an intolerance of milk, make sure you take a 1,000-milligram supplement of calcium daily.

Reduce Saturated Fat Intake; Increase Polyunsaturated Fat Consumption

Animal fats tend to raise blood cholesterol levels, which speeds up the hardening of the arteries, whereas vegetable fats tend to reduce blood cholesterol levels.

Strategy   As outlined in chapter 6, you should aim to get a balanced ratio of fats and limit your cholesterol intake to no more than 300 milligrams per day.

Fish contain an added advantage in the form of *EPA*. This lowers *blood triglyceride* levels (see page 54) and reduces *platelet stickiness* (platelets are small blood cells that stick together and help to clog blood vessels).

Increase Dietary Fiber

Certain types of dietary fiber have been shown to lower blood cholesterol by as much as ten percent.

Strategy   Incorporate into your diet pectin, oats, and beans (see page 303 for table of foods rich in dietary fiber). For a detailed discussion of the role of fiber in lowering blood cholesterol, see chapter 6.

Take a B-Complex Vitamin Supplement

Many of the symptoms of a B-complex vitamin deficiency are the same as those of senile dementia.

Strategy   By taking a one-a-day vitamin containing the Recommended Dietary Allowances for the B vitamins, you will rule out this deficiency as a cause of the problem.

Do Not Use Aluminum Utensils or Containers in Food Preparation

Some researchers have implicated aluminum as an aggravating factor in Alzheimer's disease. Israeli studies have shown that the changes seen in brain cells in Alzheimer's patients can be mimicked in tissue cultures by incubating brain cells with aluminum.

Strategy   Avoid cooking in and eating out of aluminum pots and using aluminum utensils. As a precaution, this is true for everyone, not merely those with or at evident risk of Alzheimer's. Abuse of aluminum antacids should also be avoided.

Aluminum foil is thought not to pose the same potential risk, as long as it is the dull side of the foil that is in contact with the food.

Take Choline or Lecithin Supplements

Evidence suggests that *choline* or *lecithin* may help people who have had Alzheimer's disease for less than three years. The compounds increase the levels of *acetylcholine* in the brain. However, there are drugs such as physostigmine that are much more effective in raising brain acetylcholine levels. Acetylcholine is the chemical messenger or *neurotransmitter* in the brain that is responsible for allowing us to remember new information. More needs to be known about why acetylcholine appears to be in short supply in some people's brains, but there is no evidence to support the notion that lecithin bought from a health-food store will improve memory, mood, or behavior in normal people.

Strategy   Alzheimer's sufferers should take 1 to 2 grams of choline or 30 grams of lecithin daily. Be sure that the lecithin you use is 100-percent *phosphatidylcholine* (the label will indicate what percentage it is; products labeled only "lecithin" may contain other products, such as *phospholipids*).

Other Advice

If you would like further information on Alzheimer's disease, contact the Association for Alzheimer's and Related Diseases, 360 North Michigan Avenue, Chicago, Illinois 60601, phone (800) 621-0379.

4
Anemia

1. Folic Acid Deficiency*

Anemia results from an inability to supply the tissues with the oxygen they need. The red blood cells, which carry the oxygen around the body, have a normal life span of 120 days, and some cells must be replaced every day. If complete cessation of red-cell production occurs it results in roughly a 10-percent reduction each week in old cells. A deficiency in any of the essential nutrients for red cell production (folic acid, protein, copper, iron, vitamins C and B_{12}) will cause anemia. The most common nutritional deficiencies leading to anemia are folic acid, iron, and vitamin B_{12} deficiencies.

Warning Signs

- One or more of the following: tiredness, general feelings of malaise, irritability, decreased attention span, pale complexion, rapid heartbeat, headaches, loss of concentration, breathlessness on exertion, vertigo, ringing in the ears, spots before the eyes, irregular menstrual periods, loss of interest in sex, and gastrointestinal discomfort.
- A sore, shiny tongue; sores in the corners of the mouth; diarrhea; and sore gums.

*See subsequent sections of this chapter for *vitamin B_{12} deficiency anemia (pernicious anemia)* and *iron deficiency anemia.*

28

Epidemiological Data

One-third of all American women currently in their menstruating years have less than optimal folic acid intakes.

Chronic drinkers require more folic acid than the recommended daily allowances, as alcohol decreases its absorption.

Pregnant women and infants both require higher than normal folic acid intakes, as all growing tissues need folic acid to enable them to grow; lactating women have increased folic acid needs.

Patients on dialysis and anybody with chronic hemolytic anemia or psoriasis also have increased demands for *folate*.

Anticonvulsants *(primidone, phenytoin, phenobarbital)* interfere with the body's use of folic acid and increase need.

Folic acid antagonists (*methotrexate*, used in the treatment of cancer and arthritis, is one such agent) affect the body's use of folic acid.

Oral contraceptives decrease the body's ability to use folic acid.

Prevention and Treatment

• Increase the folic acid in your diet to alleviate folic acid anemia.
• Include at least one raw fruit or green vegetable in your diet each day.
• Drink fruit juice with meals.
• Take a daily 400-microgram supplement of folic acid.

CASE HISTORY: Nora Epstein

Nora Epstein is a graduate student in English literature. She lives and works in a college town in eastern Pennsylvania, where she divides her time between teaching freshman English and pursuing her studies of an obscure medieval poet.

Ms. Epstein (soon to be Dr. Epstein, when she completes her thesis) generally feels tired. She gets lots of headaches, and refuses to believe it is from reading all that Middle English verse. Lately also she has had some problems concentrating, and finds herself losing her train of thought when teaching her classes.

She is married to another scholar, and though they would like to have a child, they feel that their limited income does not allow for the expense of a baby at present. As a result, she continues to take oral contraceptives, as she has for nearly five years. Her husband has also complained that she is not as interested in sex as she used to be, and though she denies his accusations, she does feel that her libido is lower than it used to be. "It's not you," she insists to him. "But maybe it's me," she says to herself. Her periods have become irregular, and her gums bleed from time to time.

She went to her doctor, who gave her a complete medical examination and a number of blood tests. These revealed that she was in a folic acid deficiency state but that her body levels of vitamin B_{12} were normal (had they been deficient, that too could have caused her problem). As it was, her doctor diagnosed her condition as *megaloblastic anemia*, caused by a deficiency of folic acid.

Her doctor advised Nora to take a folic acid supplement; within less than a month she was feeling well again, with her usual energy, concentration, and healthy sexual enthusiasm.

Dietary and Life-style Recommendations

Increase Your Dietary Intake of Folic Acid

All green vegetables are rich in folic acid (otherwise known as folacin). In fact, its name is derived from the Latin *folium*, meaning "leaf."

Strategy   Increase your consumption of dark green vegetables, especially spinach, kale, parsley, brussels sprouts, and broccoli, as well as fruit such as oranges and cantaloupe. To a lesser degree, folic acid is also found in almonds, lima beans, corn, parsnips, green peas, pumpkins, sweet potatoes, bran, peanuts, rye, and whole-grain wheat (see table of folic acid–rich foods, page 307). Approximately one-half of the folic acid you consume is absorbed by your body.

Eat at Least One Raw Fruit or Vegetable Each Day

Normal cooking temperatures (230 to 250 degrees Fahrenheit for ten minutes) destroy up to two-thirds of the folic acid in foods.

Strategy   Your diet should include at least one raw fruit or vegetable every day. Cooking utensils made of copper speed up the destruction of folic acid, so you should avoid their use when preparing foods high in folic acid.

Drink Fruit Juice with Your Meals

Vitamin C helps your body absorb folic acid from the foods you eat.

Strategy   Drink juices high in vitamin C with your meals.

Take a Daily Supplement of Folic Acid
Most multivitamin preparations do not contain the vitamin.

Strategy You may need to take a separate folic acid supplement. Take 400 micrograms daily. If no improvement is seen after a two-week period of taking the vitamin, check with your doctor, as a folic acid deficiency may not be the reason for your symptoms. The supplement could be masking a vitamin B_{12} deficiency (see below). A B_{12} deficiency can lead to serious neurological problems.

If you eat very few animal products or are over the age of 60, you should check with your doctor before taking folic acid supplements, as you are in a high-risk category for a deficiency of vitamin B_{12}.

Be Sure to Consume the Other Nutrients Your Body Requires for Manufacturing Red Blood Cells
Your diet must contain sufficient protein, copper, iron, vitamin C, and vitamin B_{12}.

Strategy The best way to ensure that you get enough of these nutrients is to eat a balanced daily diet of two servings of protein, four to six portions of vegetables and fruit, four to six of bread and cereals, and two of milk and dairy products. (See page 326 for amounts of foods needed per day for a balanced diet.)

2. Vitamin B_{12} Deficiency (Pernicious Anemia)

A deficiency in vitamin B_{12} will cause anemia to develop over a prolonged period. Decreased absorption owing to a lack of *intrinsic factor* (a substance produced in the stomach that transports the vitamin across the wall of the intestine), or an inadequate B_{12} intake sometimes found in vegetarians, can cause a deficiency.

Most people have stores of vitamin B_{12} in their livers. That store should sustain their needs for a three- to five-year period, so few people who consume foods rich in B_{12} (meats, fish, and poultry) should be at risk of this problem.

Warning Signs

- Lack of appetite and accompanying weight loss
- Intermittent constipation and diarrhea and poorly localized abdominal pain
- A sore, shiny tongue
- Numbness and tingling in the fingers and toes, loss of coordination, confusion, memory loss, paranoia, apathy, tremors, or hallucinations
- Listlessness, fatigue (especially on exertion), palpitations, lightheadedness, and a pale complexion

Epidemiological Data

Vegetarians who eat absolutely no animal food products are at high risk.

The elderly are at higher risk than young adults, as some elderly people produce little intrinsic factor.

Pernicious anemia develops after surgery to remove the stomach, unless vitamin B_{12} is administered. It can also occur in patients who have only a portion of the stomach removed and in some patients who have had part of their small intestine taken out (because this is where the vitamin is absorbed).

Prevention and Treatment

- Elderly people or those who have had operations on their gastrointestinal tracts may require vitamin B_{12} injections; if you fit into one or both of these categories, consult your physician.
- Vegetarians should take a six-microgram supplement each day.
- A diet rich in animal proteins, particularly liver, will act as a preventive or treatment for pernicious anemia.
- Avoid large supplements of vitamin C, copper, and thiamine; do not take any supplements of folic acid while in a B_{12} deficiency state;
- Do not use baking soda in cooking, and do not cook meats on a hot griddle.

CASE HISTORY: Anna Carter

One of Anna's uncles took her and her brothers on a field trip to the slaughterhouse where he worked. The adolescent boys thought it was "neat," but for preteen Anna it was a jarring experience.

For the next few years, Anna flirted with vegetarianism, but as she lived in the heartland of agricultural America, many people thought she was crazy.

When she went east to college, she found a more congenial atmosphere for the development of her philosophical opposition to meat-eating. She soon became a full-time vegetarian. She was pleased with the weight loss it produced (she had always felt that her hips were too fleshy, but trimming down hadn't been easy), and she often said she felt less "weighed down" after eating and more energetic.

After graduating from college she got a job in Boston, and lived in Cambridge. Her eating habits tended to be rather inconsistent, as the demands of her work limited the time she could devote to food preparation.

Although she didn't connect her vegetarianism with the change, she began to feel tired all the time. She had been a full-fledged vegetarian for nearly eight years when she began to experience such discomforts as a sore, beefy-red tongue. Her toes and fingers were sometimes numb, which she found a hindrance to the typing that her work involved. Occasionally she felt a pain in her abdomen, and her appetite was smaller than ever.

Anna Carter had a textbook case of pernicious anemia. When she went to a nutritionist that a friend recommended (she distrusted doctors, and the nutritionist seemed to her more likely to understand her vegetarianism and other philosophical attitudes), he diagnosed her problem in a matter of minutes. He advised that she take a B_{12} supplement daily. Today she is feeling energetic again, and her other symptoms are gone. She still conscientiously avoids eating meat.

Dietary and Life-style Recommendations

For the Elderly and Postoperative Patients, a B_{12} Injection May Be Necessary

Consult with your physician first, but if your stomach has been totally removed, or if the areas known as the *fundus* and *body* have been taken out, no intrinsic factor can be produced by your body, and so no B_{12} can be absorbed. Similarly, the vitamin is absorbed in the upper portion of the small intestine, and so if it has been removed, the vitamin also passes out of your body unabsorbed.

Strategy By injecting the vitamin into the muscle, the absorption stage is bypassed. Since the vitamin is stored in the liver and used at the rate of three micrograms a day, once the anemia has been corrected infrequent injections are needed to prevent the problem from recurring.

Vegetarians Should Take a Supplement Each Day

Vegans are complete vegetarians; they eat no animal food products at all, including eggs and dairy products.

Strategy Because only animal products, including dairy foods, fish, and shellfish, contain natural vitamin B_{12}, vegans should either take a six-microgram-per-day supplement or make sure that they eat one portion or more of a supplemented food product daily. Some vegetable products are supplemented with vitamin B_{12}, including soy products, to safeguard vegetarians.

Nonvegans Should Include Liver or Liberal Amounts of Animal Protein in Their Diet

Everyone should consume liberal amounts of animal protein, especially liver, in his or her diet.

Strategy Vitamin B_{12} is stored in the liver, so one meal that includes calf's liver will fulfill your body's need for this vitamin for two or more weeks (one three-ounce serving of calf's liver contains 100 micrograms of vitamin B_{12}). If you dislike liver, then the foods listed on page 320 containing B_{12} should be included prominently in your diet.

Avoid Large Supplements of Vitamin C, Copper, and Thiamine; Do Not Take Folic Acid Supplements in a B_{12} Deficiency State

People who use significant amounts of vitamin C should be aware that vitamin C supplements of more than 500 milligrams degrade vitamin B_2 and contribute to a B_{12} deficiency. Copper and thiamine also seem to decrease its availability when they are consumed in amounts greater than ten times the Recommended Dietary Allowances.

Strategy Some of the symptoms of pernicious anemia (tiredness, pale complexion, and lightheadedness) usually occur before the neurological problems. If you take a folic acid supplement, the less serious problems may disappear while the neurological troubles may continue. These involve a breakdown in the brain membranes (called *myelin*). If not caught early on, the myelin breakdown can cause irreversible damage that manifests itself as movement disorders, poor memory, and psychotic behavior.

Other Advice
The presence of baking soda in cooking will destroy vitamin B_{12}, and so should be avoided whenever possible. Vitamin B_{12} degrades at high temperatures, such as when meat is placed on a hot griddle. The pasteurization of milk also causes loss of some B_{12}.

3. Iron Deficiency Anemia

Iron deficiency is the most common cause of anemia, and may be due to increased iron requirements, decreased absorption of iron, blood loss, or repeated pregnancies. When caused by an inadequate diet, it takes several years to produce symptoms when there are adequate body stores of iron to begin with. The body reuses its iron stores over and over, and only 10 percent is lost through perspiration, feces, and urine. Menstruation increases iron loss by about 30 milligrams per month.

Oxygen is carried in the red blood cells by *hemoglobin*, which is made from protein, iron, and copper. An iron shortage that reduces the level of hemoglobin in the blood cells and reduces the blood's oxygen-carrying capacity results in anemia.

Warning Signs

- Tiredness, general feelings of malaise, irritability, decreased attention span, pale complexion, rapid pulse, headaches, loss of concentration, breathlessness on exertion, vertigo, ringing in the ears, spots before the eyes, loss of interest in sex, and gastrointestinal complaints
- Brittle nails
- In severe cases, cracked lips, a smooth, sore tongue, and spoon-shaped nails
- *Pica*, a craving for nonfood substances (a craving for dirt is called *geophagia;* for ice, *pagophagia*); sometimes a craving for nonnutritious food substances, such as excessive amounts of Life Savers, lettuce, celery, snack chips, or chocolate
- Tarry and black stools

Epidemiological Data

About one-third of all menstruating women have less than optimal body stores of iron, and one-tenth have a severe deficiency of iron.

Other individuals most at risk for iron deficiency include teenage boys and girls, women who have had repeated pregnancies, and the elderly.

Elderly people produce less acid in their stomachs, which makes it more difficult for them to absorb iron from nonmeat sources.

People who take large quantities of aspirin or other anti-inflammatory drugs are also at risk for iron deficiency.

Prevention and Treatment

- Consume a diet high in iron, one that includes liberal portions of red meat.
- Increase your intake of vitamin C (foods such as citrus fruits, tomatoes, broccoli, spinach, cabbage, and bananas are high in C).
- Reduce your consumption of coffee, tea, and cola beverages at mealtimes.
- Steam your vegetables (rather than boiling them) and cook your food in iron pots.
- Take 300 milligrams of a *ferrous sulfate* or *ferrous gluconate* supplement three times a day with meals and preferably with a rich source of vitamin C.
- Do not take calcium or zinc supplements or antacids when you are taking iron supplements. Foods rich in *phosphate*, *phytate*, and *oxalate* should also be avoided when taking iron supplements.
- Do not take the antibiotic *tetracycline* at the same time of day as you take your iron supplement.

CASE HISTORY: Cary Becker

Cary never ate very much meat. Even as a baby, she paid more attention to vegetable foods, try as her parents might to persuade her to eat some of everything. By the time she was twelve, she had stopped eating meat altogether.

When Cary began menstruating, she found that she had to use large sanitary napkins. Like many women, she had a particularly heavy flow. At first it worried her, but soon she simply accepted it as a reality of the way her particular body functioned.

The bad news was that over time she began to develop a number of the symptoms of an iron deficiency. She didn't realize it at first, of course, but her unusually pale complexion was one symptom. When she was seen with the rest of her family, she said that she looked like Goldilocks posing with the three bears. She also found that she had trouble concentrating in school, and that her early fascination with sports faded. She found that she got too tired to keep up with the other athletes, and that in contact sports she was always breaking her nails.

However, it was her tendency to chew ice that led her physician to diagnose her problem almost instantly when her mother finally made her go to the doctor.

As her doctor tells it, Cary actually brought her paper cup of Coke into his office with her. She proceeded to eat the remaining ice, making loud (and irritating) crunching sounds. At first he thought her rather impolite, but when he remembered a reported characteristic of some patients with iron deficiency anemia, he was rather glad she had so dramatized her ailment.

He prescribed several dietary changes and iron supplements, and Cary is back on the playing fields.

Dietary and Life-style Recommendations

Eat a High-Iron Diet Rich in Meat

There are two kinds of iron in food sources: *heme iron* in meat, and *ionic iron* in vegetables. Up to 40 percent of the iron from meat, fish, and poultry is absorbed, but less than 10 percent is absorbed from eggs, whole grains, nuts, and dried beans and other vegetable sources, with as little as 2 percent being absorbed from spinach.

Strategy Those at risk of iron deficiency should consume a diet rich in meat, chicken, and fish. Other foods rich in iron include apricots, green beans, berries, bread, broccoli, carrots, eggplant, cooked peas, raisins, and soy bean curd. (See table on page 309 for foods rich in iron.)

Take Iron Supplements

To enhance your body's available supply of iron, take supplements of the mineral.

Strategy Take a 300-milligram supplement of iron three times each day. The supplement should be ferrous sulfate or ferrous gluconate, as ferrous iron is better absorbed than other iron supplements. All iron supplements upset the gastrointestinal tract and, on occasion, can cause stomachache, nausea, diarrhea, or constipation. These discomforts can be reduced or eliminated by taking the supplements with meals.

Increase Your Consumption of Vitamin C

Rich sources of vitamin C such as citrus fruit juices increase the absorption of iron from vegetables by two to three times *if taken simultaneously* with the vegetables.

Strategy Consume foods high in vitamin C, or take vitamin C supplements. (See table on page 321 for vitamin C–rich foods.)

If you take a vitamin C supplement each day, take it with one of your iron supplement dosages.

Reduce Your Consumption of Caffeine and Tannin

The tannin in tea and the caffeine in coffee and tea reduce your body's ability to absorb the iron in the food you eat.

Strategy Avoid drinking beverages and tea containing caffeine, especially when simultaneously consuming foods containing iron. (See page 300 for table of caffeine-containing foods.)

Avoid Calcium or Zinc Supplements or Antacids with Your Iron Supplements

The absorption of iron supplements is decreased by antacids and calcium and zinc supplements, as well as by foods rich in phosphorous, phytate, and oxalate.

Strategy Antacids and calcium and zinc supplements should not be taken at the same time as the iron supplement.

In addition, foods rich in phosphorous, phytate, and oxalate should not be eaten with iron supplements. Phosphorous-rich foods include almonds, dried apricots, brains, Brazil nuts, whole-grain cereals, cheese, chocolate milk, cocoa, fish, kidneys, liver, milk, peanuts, peas, and walnuts.

Foods rich in phytate include wheat germ, wheat bran, rye or whole wheat breads, cereals (including All-Bran, granola, shredded wheat, wheat flakes or corn chips), oatmeal, almonds, Brazil nuts, coconut, hazel nuts, peanuts, walnuts, sesame seeds, and raw beans and peas.

Oxalate-rich foods include coffee and tea, raw blackberries, gooseberries, or plums, whole-wheat bread, beets, cooked carrots, green beans, rhubarb, spinach, and cocoa.

Other Advice

In preparing food, steam your vegetables, and cook your foods in iron pots whenever possible. Because iron can be leached from vegetables if they are cooked in large amounts of water, it is preferable to steam them. Also, the acids in foods being prepared in the kitchen leach iron from iron pots and pans, which then becomes available as dietary iron.

A few people may be at risk of an iron overload, however. People who have been taking iron supplements for several weeks should check with their doctors before continuing to do so. Men in particular, since they do not lose iron through menstrual bleeding, are more likely to retain high levels of iron.

Symptoms of too much iron usually appear after the age of 40. Often the first sign is a bronze cast to the skin, but pancreas malfunction, liver trouble, and heart problems can result from too much iron in the body.

If you are taking the antibiotic tetracycline, do not take it at the same time as you take your iron supplement. Iron binds to the tetracycline and reduces its absorption, decreasing its effectiveness.

If you would like further information about folic acid, iron, or vitamin B_{12} deficiencies or other blood disorders, contact the National Heart, Lung, and Blood Institute, National Institutes of Health, Room 504, Federal Building, 7550 Wisconsin Avenue, Bethesda, Maryland 20205, phone (301) 496-6931.

5
Anorexia Nervosa

Anorexia nervosa is a psychological condition in which the sufferer drastically reduces food intake and, as a result, experiences substantial loss of body weight. This loss of weight in anorexics is not related to any other disease process.

Most sufferers are teenage girls, and it is thought that the fear of puberty, peer and parental pressures, an exaggerated accent on one's appearance, and academic pressures or marriage—all particularly stressful events—can trigger the onset of the disease. In older women, the birth of a first child, career changes, divorce, or even menopause can cause the condition.

The prevalence of this illness has increased rapidly over recent years and possibly caused the popular notion that "thin is in." Most anorexic patients have been overweight at some point in their lives, and initially lost weight in order to get back to an ideal weight. But this reduction in body weight becomes an obsession, and the patients live in irrational fear of regaining the lost weight. The dieting can go to such extremes that some anorexic patients weigh as little as 70 pounds.

Warning Signs

- Weight loss of at least 25 percent of original body weight, with no known illness to account for the loss
- Distorted perception of body image (when asked to estimate the width of their hips, anorexic patients often overestimate the dimen-

sion by as much as 50 percent, and select clothes that are many times too big for them)
- Refusal to maintain minimal normal body weight
- An intense fear of becoming obese, perhaps accompanied by the habitual consumption of diet foods, despite the loss of weight
- Cessation of menstrual periods
- Intolerance of cold
- Constipation
- Dizziness owing to low blood pressure or a low heart rate
- Growth of fine, fair hair over the entire body
- Tendencies to eat the same foods day after day and to be preoccupied with food, health, and exercise (anorexics also often eat very slowly and tend to avoid foods high in carbohydrates)
- The average anorexic is a perfectionist with a high IQ, but while suffering from the disease will perform poorly in school

Epidemiological Data

One out of every 200 American girls between the ages of 12 and 18 develop anorexia nervosa to some degree. Ninety-six percent of anorexics are between the ages 12 and 30; nine out of ten are female.

As a result of treatment, 49 percent of anorexics achieve normal body weight but usually develop other psychological problems; 31 percent gain some weight; 18 percent gain no weight.

Eight percent of anorexics die, 6 percent as a result of complications of the disease, and 2 percent by suicide.

Prevention and Treatment

- Attractive, palatable meals should be offered in small servings, with foods selected with special regard to food preferences.
- In the early stages of treatment, bulky food should be avoided.
- At the beginning of treatment, the diet should supply the basal metabolic needs, which is the number of calories equal to the ideal weight times ten.
- Food intake should be gradually increased by 300 to 400 calories per week until caloric intake is sufficient for the patient to maintain daily activity and ideal body weight.
- The sufferer should be assured that the diet is low in calories and will not result in her becoming "fat"; she should be encouraged to

measure and record how much food she consumes, and when she has a realistic idea of portion size, the emphasis on counting calories can be gradually lessened.

• Be sure the sufferer is not zinc-deficient.

CASE HISTORY: Jane Gross

Jane was the perfect child. She had always done exactly as she was told. She performed well in school (she was second in standing in her sophomore class). She was captain of the tennis team.

She lived in an upper-middle-class suburb in northern New Jersey. The town was within easy commuting distance of New York City, where her father was a corporate lawyer. Her mother had been a model in her youth, and the three of them seemed a happy and complete family unit.

Then her father was offered and accepted a job in another city. The opportunity was one that they all agreed couldn't be refused, so the family sold the house and moved.

In her new town, Jane found herself in a strange environment without her familiar circle of friends—and the attendant respect and popularity. She felt insecure, and tried to fit in as best she could academically, athletically, and socially. She even began to lose that extra five pounds she had carried without particular concern in her old life. She hoped to make herself as attractive as possible to her new acquaintances.

She succeeded in losing the weight she wanted, but unfortunately she didn't stop when she reached her goal. She lost nearly thirty pounds. She failed to win a spot on the tennis team when she fainted twice in practice matches, and the doctors determined that her heart rate was abnormally low. Her mother, a professional cook with a small catering business, despaired of her daughter's eating habits when she refused to eat the gourmet foods put before her, but seemed constantly to consume bland crackers with cottage cheese.

Jane had long since ceased to menstruate, and her dizzy spells were increasing. Her weight had dropped so that she looked skeletal and she was unable to go about even the simpler rituals of her life because her energy was so low. Finally, Jane had to be hospitalized.

In the hospital, she was fed intravenously for the first week. A psychologist worked with her and her family, and a dietician introduced her to a new and disciplined way of thinking about her foods. It took a year, but she gradually regained most of the weight she had lost.

Dietary and Life-style Recommendations

Serve Attractive, Palatable Meals in Small Servings

The first objective is to get the patient to consume some kind of food. The crucial concern is not *what* she consumes, but that she eat something; you are trying to get her used to eating again and want her to consume as many calories as possible.

Strategy To encourage her to eat, give her the foods she likes, and make them look as attractive as possible. The chances are she will not like carbohydrate and fat-rich foods but will go for high-protein foods. (See table of protein-rich foods, page 313.) Smaller servings are also more likely to seem palatable to anorexics.

Avoid Serving Bulky Foods

Anorexia nervosa patients feel very bloated after eating, and commonly suffer from severe constipation. By consuming foods high in indigestible fiber, they may find that these problems are exacerbated.

Strategy Once again, in the early stages of treatment, a key concern is to make the sufferer feel as comfortable as possible with food and eating; anything that will dissuade her from eating should be avoided.

Avoid foods high in fiber while the constipation lasts. (See table of foods rich in dietary fiber on page 303.) When the constipation lifts, you should incorporate into the diet liberal amounts of these same bulky foods. Tell the sufferer that this is the plan after the constipation lessens.

The Diet Should Supply Basal Metabolic Needs

The patient should consume a diet that provides for the basal metabolic needs; this is the number of calories equal to their ideal weight times ten.

Strategy The ideal weight for women is 100 pounds for the first five feet of height, plus five pounds for each additional inch; for men it is 106 pounds for five-footers, plus six pounds for each inch thereafter. So that if ideal weight is 100 pounds, then the calories required are equal to ten times that weight, or 1,000 calories.

Make the Sufferer a Partner in the Dietary Program

Initial weight gain is often twice as rapid as the average weight gain overall, owing to water retention, replacement of carbohydrate stores in the liver and muscle (*glycogen* stores) and replenishment of muscle tissue.

Initially, it takes about 2,250 extra calories over and above what the body needs for normal activities to increase body weight by one pound. For a sedentary person, calories for normal activities equal the ideal body weight times ten, plus 30 percent. After ideal weight has been achieved, 3,500 extra calories are required to increase weight by one pound.

Any weight gain, particularly a sudden increase, may worry the patient, as she may feel that it will make her obese. A low-calorie diet should minimize the chances of a sudden weight gain. Also, it should be emphasized that the rapid weight gain is only temporary.

The following is an example of a 900-to-1,000-calorie diet that would be suitable to initiate an anorexic's weight-gain program.

Breakfast   1 poached egg; coffee or tea and milk; toast (1 slice); butter (1 pat)

Lunch   Coffee or tea and milk; ½ cup tuna (2 oz.); 1 piece of fruit

Dinner   Potato (baked) and butter or sour cream; coffee or tea and milk; 3 oz. of meat or fish (4 oz. before cooking); broccoli; salad (lettuce, cucumber, endive, celery, low-calorie dressing)

Snack   1 piece of fruit

How you distribute the foods through the day is up to you, but the best diet plans include a breakfast of at least 200 to 300 calories, with the other foods being distributed through the other meals in the day.

Strategy   It is possible to control the weight gain and food consumption carefully. The anorexic should be encouraged to measure and record how much food she consumes. Anorexic patients have a very misguided idea of how much they eat, and often will eat a stick of celery or a carrot and state that they have consumed a lot. By measuring what she actually eats and rewarding how much she eats each day, the anorexic can be educated as to what a real portion is and how much must be consumed to prevent further weight loss.

Anorexics are usually obsessed with food. They may enjoy preparing food for others, usually know a great deal about nutrition, lead active lives with a great deal of exercise in their daily regime, and often take vitamin and mineral supplements. Of course, in the long run, the preoccupation with food should be deemphasized. Once the anorexic develops a realistic idea of just how much she must eat, the emphasis on counting calories should be gradually lessened and the activity of recording food consumption abandoned.

Gradually increase food intake by 300 to 400 calories per week, until sufficient calories are consumed to maintain ideal body weight. This process usually takes about eight months.

Establish that the Sufferer Is Not Deficient in Zinc

There are a few reported cases where zinc deficiency has been mistaken for anorexia nervosa. A zinc deficiency impairs the sense of taste and reduces appetite.

Strategy Be sure that zinc-rich foods are well represented in the diet. (See page 323 for table of zinc-rich foods.)

Other Advice

If you would like further information on anorexia, contact the National Association for Anorexia Nervosa and Associated Disorders, Box 271, Highland Park, Illinois 60035, phone (301) 831-3438.

The Anorexia Nervosa Aid Society's advisory phone number is (201) 836-1800.

6
Atherosclerosis

Atherosclerosis—hardening of the arteries—is the cause of most heart attacks and strokes. When the arteries supplying the heart become narrowed, they are unable to supply adequate blood to the heart in times of increased need, such as during exercise or stress. Heart pain, or *angina*, can result.

The narrowed artery also facilitates the formation of blood clots that can suddenly cut off the blood supply to a part of the heart muscle (causing heart attack) or brain (resulting in a stroke). In both cases the blockage prevents the flow of blood to the tissues and results in the death of some—or all—of those tissues.

Warning Signs

- Blood pressure greater than 130/80
- Being 20 percent or more overweight
- A tendency to belch a great deal
- Close relatives who developed heart disease before 60 years of age
- Blood cholesterol levels above 180
- A total blood cholesterol-to-HDL level greater than 4.5 to 1
- The appearance of hard yellowish pimples in the eyelids, elbows, knees, and/or other areas of the body
- Blood triglyceride levels over 250
- Type-A personality

Epidemiological Data

Heart disease is the most common cause of death in the United States, accounting for 50 percent of all fatalities, or some 1 million people per year.

Approximately 350,000 heart attack victims per year die before reaching the hospital.

Deaths from cardiovascular disease are about two and a half times as prevalent as those from the second leading cause of death, cancer.

The relative importance of cardiovascular disease, in terms of percentage of all deaths for a given age group, rises steadily with age.

Prevention and Treatment

- If you are obese, begin a weight-reduction program.
- Reduce your intake of salt to no more than three grams per day to reduce blood pressure.
- Reduce blood cholesterol levels by limiting amount of dietary cholesterol and consumption of saturated fats.
- Raise the level of HDL as compared to total cholesterol.
- Increase your consumption of fish.
- Increase your intake of dietary fiber.
- Limit your intake of zinc supplements to no more than 15 milligrams per day.
- Take one aspirin every two days.
- Limit your consumption of alcohol to no more than two drinks per day, and coffee to no more than two cups per day.
- Reduce your blood triglyceride levels by reducing sugar intake.
- Establish a regular exercise regimen.
- Stop smoking, especially if you take oral contraceptives.

CASE HISTORY: Jim Smithson

Jim Smithson was fifty-two years old. He had always enjoyed good health but had developed something of a spare tire in recent years. He saw himself as a moderate smoker, consuming something less than a pack a day. Having been brought up in Kansas City, he grew accustomed early to eating well-marbled red meat fresh from the stockyards, and prided himself on knowing a great steak from an average one.

He had been a pretty good athlete in college and as he felt his middle go soft, he decided that he would start an exercise program. He felt he knew enough from his jock days not to require conditioning advice before he started.

Jim began slowly. And he enjoyed the feeling of a kind of refreshed tiredness after his jog. The only untoward reaction he had was a frequent tendency to belch, but he half-consciously wrote that off as another of his body's ways of cleansing itself.

One day about two weeks into his program, he experienced what he called "a little discomfort" in his chest and pain in his left arm. It passed almost as quickly as it came, and by the time he had showered and dressed for work, it was gone. However, upon arriving at work he found himself in a heated argument with a co-worker and experienced more chest pains. This time they didn't go away; he did, instead, in an ambulance to the hospital.

His condition stabilized quickly, and, suddenly forced to confront the gravity of his situation, he sat down with his internist and a cardiologist. The EKG revealed he had had a small heart attack. The next test they conducted on him, an arteriogram, revealed that he had a 50 percent occlusion in two of his coronary arteries (that is, two of his coronary arteries were 50 percent blocked). A blood workup revealed he had a blood cholesterol level of 250, with something called a *high density lipoprotein (HDL)* level of 35. This meant that his blood cholesterol was significantly above the ideal of 150, and the HDL level was within the normal range.

Under the guidance of his physician, he changed his diet. Without completely altering his lifetime dietary habits, he managed to reduce his intake of animal fats and increase his consumption of fish and high-fiber foods. As a result, he was able to lower his total cholesterol levels to 205, but he was told that he was still at high risk of another heart attack because his HDL remained at 35, which was too low. It was at this point that he began an exercise program under the supervision of a physiotherapist. After six months of swimming thirty minutes a day, he learned that his HDL had risen to 49. This was critical to Jim's future risk of a coronary because his ratio of total cholesterol (205) to high-density lipoproteins (49) had been reduced to a safe 4 to 1. Clinical studies show that if the total-cholesterol-to-HDL ratio is greater than 4.5 to 1, a person is in a higher than normal risk category for a heart attack.

Jim Smithson was lucky; he survived. But there is still a tragedy here: his heart attack and its by-products of pain, his family's anguish, the expense, and his reduced life expectancy possibly all could have been avoided.

Dietary and Life-style Recommendations

Limit Your Fat and Cholesterol Intake

One of the highest risk factors for heart disease is high blood levels of fats, particularly cholesterol; and blood cholesterol levels are often dependent to some degree on diet.

Compare your blood cholesterol reading to the low- and moderate-risk levels in the table on page 333. (If you do not know what your cholesterol level is, check with your doctor, as your last physical examination should have involved a blood workup.)

Stated boldly, the lower your blood cholesterol level, the lower your risk for heart attack. Some experts suggest that we should all reduce our cholesterol levels to below 180 milligrams per 100 milliliters of blood serum. However, provided your cholesterol level is close to the figure given on page 333, you are in a fairly low-risk category in this respect.

Cholesterol is a soapy-looking yellowish substance. It is essential for life, as it is a building block of all cell membranes. Cholesterol also plays essential roles in such tasks as the manufacture of bile (which helps you absorb fat), sex hormones (*estrogen, progesterone*, and *testosterone*), vitamin D, and *myelin* (the fatty sheath that insulates the nerves).

Despite its importance, however, cholesterol does not have to be present in the diets of most adults, as it is made in the liver and the intestines at a rate sufficient to meet body needs. In most people, the more cholesterol consumed, the less the body makes, a system that seems to work very well up to a dietary intake of 150 to 300 milligrams of cholesterol.

More than this will lead to an increase in body and, more important, in blood cholesterol levels: it is the cholesterol in the blood that becomes deposited in the walls of the arteries. Since, according to recent research, most American men consume an average of up to 700 or even 800 milligrams per day, you can see how an overabundance of cholesterol has become commonplace.

Your intake of dietary fat should be reduced to no more than 30 percent of your total caloric intake. Fats are composed of substances called *fatty acids*. These are a simple group of chemicals that may be either *saturated, mono-unsaturated,* or *polyunsaturated*. Saturated fats are generally hard at room temperature; mono-unsaturated fats are soft at room temperature and harder when refrigerated; polyunsaturated fats are liquid at both room and refrigerator temperatures.

What this means in terms of heart disease can be summarized simply: saturated fat is damaging, and *raises* the level of blood cholesterol; mono-unsaturated fat seems to have a small reducing effect on blood cholesterol; polyunsaturated fat tends to *lower* blood cholesterol significantly.

The average American eats a diet with a polyunsaturated-to-saturated fats ratio of approximately 1 to 7. Given that the chief source of saturated fats is meat, and meats are favorite foods of Americans, this disproportionate consumption of saturated fats is hardly surprising. In addition, Americans have a demonstrable preference for whole milk and whole milk products that further increases the ratio of saturated fats in the diet.

In an ideal world, one would avoid saturated fat and emphasize mono-unsaturated and polyunsaturated fats. However, we don't live in a perfect world. All natural fat-rich foods contain mixtures of all three fats, but these mixtures vary widely in composition. For example, butter contains an average of about 66 percent saturated fat. In contrast, soybean oil contains about 15 percent saturated fat and 55 percent polyunsaturated fats. Similarly, safflower oil contains about 70 percent polyunsaturated fat.

Most polyunsaturated fats are derived from liquid vegetable oils; corn, cottonseed, safflower, and soybean oils are good examples. Walnuts, almonds, filberts, fish, and margarine are other good sources. Because the hardening process for margarine (called *hydrogenation*) lowers the polyunsaturate content of the oil by bubbling hydrogen through vegetable oil, soft margarines are better than hard margarines because they contain less hydrogen and more polyunsaturated fats.

Strategy   Try to balance your intake of polyunsaturated, saturated, and mono-unsaturated fats. The fats in your diet should constitute no more than 30 percent of your total intake; that 30 percent should be divided equally among saturated, polyunsaturated, and mono-unsaturated fats.

To establish a dietary polyunsaturated-to-saturated-fats ratio of one-to-one, it is necessary to reduce or eliminate fatty and untrimmed meats, fatty and untrimmed poultry, whole milk and whole milk products, butter, and solid cooking fats.

Do not buy canned or frozen cooked meat dishes, because you cannot know how much fat they contain.

Reduce your consumption of cholesterol-rich foods. In the average American's diet, the principal dietary sources of cholesterol are eggs (42 percent); meat, poultry, and fish (38 percent); dairy foods (15 percent); and fats and oils (5 percent).

As cholesterol is found in all animal cell membranes, it is distributed throughout the meat, lean as well as fat. It cannot be trimmed off like visible fat, although consumption of lean cuts (those with more muscle than fat, such as round, rump, and tenderloin) will help you cut down on your total consumption of fats. You should avoid cuts such as rib roast and steaks in which the fat is generously distributed throughout and cannot be removed in chunks. It is estimated that there are approximately two grams of fat per ounce of meat consumed (an ounce is approximately 30 grams).

Remember, because a food is not directly derived from an animal source, it is not necessarily cholesterol-free. For example, a cake is thought of as non-animal food, but the addition of eggs, butter, and whole milk to that product contributes significant amounts of cholesterol. A slice of yellow cake contains 36 milligrams of cholesterol. (See page 302 for a list of cholesterol-rich foods.)

In cooking, use a rack when broiling, roasting, or baking, so that the fat can drain off. Don't baste, because that returns some of the fat. When you make stews, boiled meat, soup stock, or other dishes in which fat cooks out into the liquid, do your cooking a day ahead of time, because after the food has been refrigerated, the hardened fat can be removed easily from the top. Also make your gravy after the fat has hardened or congealed and has been skimmed from the liquid.

Vegetable oil in the proportions shown in the table on page 304 should be added to the diet, and can be used in cooking in a number of ways: as an ingredient in barbecue and marinating sauces and salad dressings; in stir-fry cooking vegetables or as a seasoning for them containing herbs; in browning or pan- or oven-frying meats; in sautéing onions; in cream sauces; in browning rice or popping corn.

An excess of polyunsaturated fat, however, may be as bad as an excess of saturated fat. Studies have linked such an excess to an increased incidence of various forms of cancer and to the formation of gallstones. As usual, therefore, the golden rule of nutrition is moderation in all things. See pages 304 and 305 for a comparison of the fatty acid content of different foods.

Increase Your Dietary Fiber Intake

Several types of fiber lower cholesterol levels. Fiber is indigestible and is not absorbed from the digestive system. It binds to the cholesterol in the gastrointestinal tract and carries it through in the fecal matter. *Pectin*, which forms the pith of oranges and the major portion of the flesh of apples and root vegetables like turnips, and the fiber found in oats and beans may reduce blood cholesterol levels by up to 10 to 20 percent. When you consider that a 1-percent drop in serum cholesterol reduces the risk of coronary heart disease by 2 percent, fiber-rich diets can reduce the risk by a very significant 20 to 40 percent.

Strategy   Eat oatmeal, oat bran, and beans regularly. Two servings a day can reduce blood cholesterol levels.

One to two ounces of pectin can reduce some people's cholesterol by up to 10 percent. To get this amount of pectin, you would have to eat five good-sized apples each day. Hence, it is easier to buy the pure compound in the pharmacy and add it to desserts. Do not take more than one-half ounce at any one time, as it may upset your stomach in larger quantities.

Limit Zinc Supplements

Zinc supplements tend to raise blood cholesterol levels. Many people take zinc supplements because they are under the misapprehension that these will slow down the aging process or increase sexual prowess. A supplement of 15 milligrams a day can, however, perk up the immune system and may prevent acne.

Strategy Limit your intake to no more than 15 milligrams per day.

Ensure Adequate Vitamin C in Your Diet

The ability of vitamin C to help your body fight infection is much discussed; it is also true, however, that if your body is lacking in vitamin C, your blood cholesterol level may rise.

Strategy Be sure to include lots of foods rich in vitamin C in your diet, such as citrus fruit, berries, and cantaloupe (see table on page 321) or take a 100-milligram daily supplement.

Adopt an Exercise Program

Cholesterol circulates in the blood attached to specific blood proteins, the two main ones being *low-density lipoprotein (LDL)* and *high-density lipoprotein (HDL)*, as mentioned above.

LDL carries cholesterol from the liver to the tissues. It is the LDL levels that indicate the risk of atherosclerosis: the higher the levels, the greater the risk. HDL carries cholesterol from the tissues, including the lining of the arteries, back to the liver. The net effect is that the HDL, as it removes deposits from inside the arteries, reduces the risk of heart disease and can also partially reverse the process of atherosclerosis once it has begun.

The ratio of total cholesterol to HDL cholesterol in a person's blood seems to be the best single predictor of a future heart attack.

Based on recent studies, if your ratio of total cholesterol to HDL cholesterol is higher than 4.5 to 1, you should be treated to lower that ratio. Let's look at two examples: one person with an "alarmingly" high total cholesterol level of 250 but an HDL reading of 75 (for a ratio of 3.3 to 1) is in a category with those whose risk is only half the usual for heart disease in this country; however, another person with a lower total cholesterol level of 200, but also with a significantly lower HDL level of 35 (for a ratio of 5.7 to 1), is in a very high risk category.

This ratio seems to go a long way toward explaining why men have so many more heart attacks than women. Men and women have the same cholesterol levels until puberty, at which point men experience a

20-to-25-percent drop in protective HDL. This difference is believed to be the reason why there are 60 percent fewer deaths from heart attacks in women than in men in the United States.

How does one raise his or her HDL levels? Runners, skiers, and other individuals who are very active have been found to have very high HDL levels. Thus, one of the benefits of exercise seems to be to increase the levels of this protective substance. But it needs to be strenuous exercise—at least twenty minutes of vigorous aerobic exercise every other day. If you are overweight, another means of increasing your HDL levels is to decrease your weight, because studies have shown that people who are overweight tend to have low levels of HDL, and weight loss in their case has raised their HDL levels.

Strategy   Three sessions of vigorous exercise three times per week is recommended, after consulting with your physician. A walking regimen for healthy people might be as follows:

Week of Program	Distance (miles)	Time (minutes per mile)
1–2	1–2	15
3–4	2–2.5	12–15
5–6	2.5–3	12
7–8	3–4	12
9–10	4–5	12

But as the story of the running writer Jim Fixx suggests, you must be careful. He ignored a family history of heart disease (his father died young of a heart attack). Fixx ran ten miles per day but did not undergo an exercise test or cardiovascular workup. Anyone over the age of 35 who is sedentary should undergo an exercise tolerance test before starting an exercise program. This should also be done if you experience chest pain, irregular heartbeat, shortness of breath, high blood pressure, elevated cholesterol, are a smoker or overweight, or have a relative who had a heart attack before the age of 50.

People who have heart disease or who have had a heart attack should follow a specific exercise prescription that involves starting with a walking program and building up from there in duration and intensity. This should be done in a supervised setting, such as a YMCA program or other postcardiac exercise class.

Stop exercising if you experience any of the following: chest pain; pain or discomfort in jaws, arms, mouth, or ear; shortness of breath; dizziness, lightheadedness, or a faint feeling; unusual headache; irregular heartbeat; sustained increased heart rate following exercise.

People with a history of heart disease may find the following chart useful for establishing a walking regimen:

Week of Program	Distance (miles)	Time (minutes per mile)
1–2	1	20
3–4	1	17–20
5–6	1	15
7–8	1.5	15
9–10	1.5	14

If you stop exercising for more than two weeks, start again at a lower level and build up in the usual way.

Swimming is especially good for developing cardiovascular fitness, especially if you already have a heart condition.

Increase Your Consumption of Fish

Some dietary changes can also deliver considerable benefits. In fact, we can reduce our blood cholesterol levels 10 to 20 percent by using diet alone. Fish, especially saltwater varieties and shellfish, contain the omega-3 fatty acids *docosahexaenoic acid (DHA)* and *eicosapentaenoic acid (EPA)*, which raise HDL levels and lower LDL levels. EPA and DHA also lower blood *triglyceride* levels, which is another risk factor for heart disease. Hence, the more fish you eat the better, particularly fattier fish, which tend to have even a higher EPA content.

DHA and EPA may also prevent the platelets from sticking to the walls of the blood vessels at the sites of cholesterol deposition, which makes the atherosclerosis worse. Taking one aspirin every two days will have the same anti-sticking effect.

Strategy The moral here is that it might be very healthy to develop a taste for fish—the fattier the fish the better. Mackerel is especially rich in EPA and DHA. The much-maligned shellfish has also come out on top. Original analysis showed it to be rich in cholesterol and hence off limits for heart patients. However, newer analytical methods suggest that though it contains some cholesterol, its DHA and EPA content more than compensates for it, and consumption of fish actually lowers cholesterol levels. See page 307 for a list of fish and their omega-3 fatty acid content.

Beware, however, of fish-oil supplements bought in health-food stores. People on high doses of fish-oil supplements have sometimes experienced blood-clotting difficulties that lead to bleeding problems.

Limit Your Sugar Intake

When you have had the blood test that is given with a complete physical examination, your doctor may tell you in reviewing the results that your triglycerides are too high. Elevated levels of triglycerides are associated with a number of problems, such as underactive thyroid, diabetes, obesity, and the development of atherosclerosis.

Triglyceride is the technical term for fats or oils. The body stores fat as triglycerides, and although the bloodstream always contains some triglycerides, their levels are especially high after one has consumed a fatty meal. But if they stay above 250 milligrams per 100 milliliters of blood between meals, and you have a poor ratio of HDL to LDL levels and high blood pressure, it could denote high risk for a heart attack. Diet alone rarely causes very high levels of triglycerides (in excess of 500 milligrams per 100 milliliters of blood), but if you do have a tendency to higher triglyceride counts, the same changes in diet used to lower cholesterol levels will help lower triglyceride levels also.

Strategy Avoid eating a lot of foods containing simple sugars, such as candy, cake, sweet desserts, and cookies. Increase starchy and high-fiber foods such as whole-grain breads and cereals, unsweetened fruits, and vegetables. Satisfactory control of triglycerides can sometimes be achieved by reducing your weight to your ideal body weight and by increasing your physical activity.

Reduce Your Salt Intake if You Have Hypertension

High blood pressure, called *hypertension*, is so major a health issue for Americans that an entire chapter of this book is devoted to it (chapter 30). However, hypertension is also a major risk factor for coronary artery disease.

Any blood pressure reading in excess of 130/80 should be regarded as putting you at risk for a heart attack; when the reading reaches 140/90, you have doubled your chances of dying from a heart attack in the next five years. The sad fact is that some 60 to 70 million Americans have blood pressure in excess of 140/90. High blood pressure is the main risk factor in stroke, as it has seventeen times as great an impact on the threat of stroke as cholesterol or smoking.

Hypertension is a risk factor in developing not only stroke, atherosclerosis, and heart attack, but also congestive heart failure, kidney failure, and *angina pectoris* (heart pain). It also increases the deadliness of a heart attack when it does occur, as about 50 percent of all hypertension victims have been shown to have enlarged and hence weakened hearts. Hypertension has also been identified as an important cause of loss of vision.

Strategy Reduce your salt intake to no more than one half teaspoon per day. Avoid obviously salty foods like potato chips, pretzels, and salted peanuts. Read food labels to be sure not to consume foods with a high sodium content. The higher on the label sodium is listed, the more salt the food contains. Include foods rich in calcium and potassium (see tables on pages 301 and 313), which tend to counteract the effect of sodium.

Limit Your Alcohol Consumption

Excess alcohol consumption tends to raise blood pressure. Many people who drink heavily also tend to be overweight, which exacerbates the problem. However, a very important consideration of which most people are unaware is that when your consumption goes over two drinks a day, alcohol may very well begin to depress the "good" HDL levels, elevating your risk further. One or two drinks per day, however, are not likely to contribute to this problem.

Strategy Do not consume more than two drinks per day.

Reduce Your Consumption of Coffee

Some recent data show that drinking coffee increases your risk of heart attack, especially if you have a history of heart disease in your family.

Strategy Restrict your coffee consumption to no more than two cups per day.

Beware of the Side Effects of Common Drugs

Cardiovascular preparations such as *digitalis, Lanoxin,* and *digoxin* should be accompanied by a diet containing adequate potassium to avoid toxicity. Excessive licorice and calcium should be avoided.

Lipid-lowering agents such as *Atromid-S* may lead to nausea, diarrhea, and loss of appetite as well as vitamin B_{12} and iron deficiencies. *Colestid* necessitates the taking of supplements of folic acid. People taking *Questran* need an increased fiber intake to prevent constipation. *Folate,* otherwise known as *folic acid,* the fat-soluble vitamins, and vitamin B_{12} may need to be added to the diet. *Nicotinic acid* tends to cause nausea, abdominal cramps, itching, and flushing.

Strategy Take appropriate supplements as advised by your physician.

Other Advice

There is a plethora of supposed nutritional treatments for heart disease on the market. For example, vitamin E is said to inhibit platelet aggregation and hence blood clotting; there is, however, insufficient foundation for this claim, though at doses of up to 500 international units daily, the vitamin is not harmful.

It has not been adequately demonstrated that chromium (brewer's yeast being the best supplemental source) decreases LDL, that it increases HDL, or that it causes atherosclerotic plaque to regress. And lecithin does not reduce blood cholesterol levels.

If you would like further information on heart disease, contact the American Heart Association, 7320 Greenville Avenue, Dallas, Texas 75231, phone (214) 750-5300.

7
Breast, Endometrial, and Cervical Cancer

Cancer of the breast is the most common cancer striking American women, and a leading cause of death among women in the United States. In other countries, however, the incidence of breast cancer is much lower. The bad news is that the statistics suggest a pattern indicating that the more highly developed the country, the higher the incidence of breast cancer. However, the fact that certain Westernized countries, such as Japan, do not show a high incidence of breast cancer gives us possible clues as to its cause.

When Japanese people migrate to California, their children have the same incidence of this cancer as other Californians if they adopt a Western eating pattern. On the other hand, if they continue to eat as their parents did in Japan, relatively few develop cancer of the breast. Thus it appears that the food we eat contributes to the high incidence of the disease.

The etiology of the disease is unknown, but it may be caused by a sexual hormone substance. The disease is most prevalent in women after menopause. It is a very rare phenomenon in men. Because of the proximity of a large number of lymph nodes around the breasts and in the armpit, it can readily spread to the bones.

Early detection and treatment are the key to curing breast cancer. Ninety percent of localized breast cancer is now curable. As most breast cancers are discovered by the patient, by carrying out monthly breast self-examinations (BSE) you increase the likelihood of detecting any changes in your breast that could indicate a malignancy. (But

58

BSE is no substitute for a thorough medical examination.) If not caught early, the disease will spread through the lymph system and often metastasizes in the bone, with fatal consequences.

Both *endometrial* and *cervical* cancers are cancers of the uterus, which seem to follow the same pattern as breast cancer: in developed countries the incidence is high, but in Third World countries it is low.

Warning Signs of Breast Cancer

- A lump in the breast that does not go away
- Any change in the breast shape or contour
- Blood discharge from the nipple
- A thickening of the breast tissue
- Retraction or scaliness of the nipple
- Extremely tender or painful breasts
- Indentation of the skin

Warning Signs of Endometrial or Cervical Cancer

- A change in menstrual habits, especially unusual bleeding or discharge

Breast Cancer Epidemiological Data

There are 115,000 new cases of breast cancer in the United States each year. The odds are that one in every eleven women will have breast cancer, but early detection can save the lives of up to 90 percent of that number.

Approximately 37,500 American women die each year of breast cancer.

The disease is most common in women over 50 years of age, though one-third of all cases occur in women between the ages of 39 and 49.

The risk is higher in women whose mothers, sisters, or other close relatives have had the disease. You are at two to three times the risk if your mother or sister developed the disease before menopause; if both developed breast cancer premenopausally, your risk is 50 percent. If either or both developed the disease after menopause and in only one breast, your risk is only a little over one in eleven.

The risk is higher in women who have never had children, had their first baby after age 30, or reached sexual maturity early.

The risk is also higher in women with a history of cystic breast disease.

If you have had cancer in one breast, your risk of developing it in the other is increased.

Endometrial and Cervical Cancer Epidemiological Data

Endometrial cancer is most common in women between the ages of 50 and 64, while cervical cancer is most common in women under the age of 50.

Endometrial cancer has a 92-percent cure rate; the rate of cure for cervical cancer is 85 percent.

The risk of endometrial cancer seems to be increased by infertility, failure to ovulate, late onset of menopause, obesity, and prolonged estrogen therapy after menopause.

The risk of cervical cancer is greatest in lower socioeconomic classes, and is increased by a history of viral genital infections such as genital warts and perhaps herpes, becoming sexually active at an early age, and having multiple sex partners.

Prevention and Treatment

- Reduce your dietary fat intake to no more than 30 percent of dietary calories.
- Reduce your protein intake.
- If you are past menopause and overweight, reduce your weight.
- To guard against breast cysts, reduce your caffeine consumption and increase your vitamin E intake.
- Increase your intake of *beta-carotene, cruciferous vegetables* (such as cabbage and Brussels sprouts), vitamin C, and selenium.
- Make sure you consume a balanced diet.
- Visit your gynecologist regularly for Pap smears and breast examinations, and examine your own breasts each month.
- Get aerobic exercise three to five times weekly for 30 to 45 minutes.

CASE HISTORY: Margaret Filmore

Margaret Filmore's mother died of breast cancer, and her younger sister, Hannah, had already had a radical mastectomy. Since hers was a closely knit family, Margaret felt (with all her trips to the hospital and nursing duties) as if she herself had had the disease.

For more than thirty years, Margaret had been finding small knots of tissue in her breast. She is a careful person and, upon finding the lumps, quickly made appointments to see her doctor. With fear and trepidation she awaited the results of his examination and the biopsies, and in each case the lumps were identified as cysts.

One month when she was fifty-five years old, she conducted her monthly self-examination in the shower, and found the new lump in her left breast. It was hard and immobile. When she first felt it, she was on vacation in Maine for two weeks. She checked it daily, and since it showed no signs of shrinking, she called her doctor immediately upon her return.

His tests revealed that it was indeed breast cancer, and he referred her to a surgeon, who, immediately upon completing his examination, scheduled surgery. After some discussion, it was decided that he would do a "modified radical" mastectomy, which means removal of the breast, the lymph nodes in the armpit, and some muscle tissue. Her doctor told her he thought that taking more than just the breast, as is the case in a "simple" mastectomy, was warranted, given her family history.

She had the operation to remove the breast, and her surgeon deemed it a success, advising Margaret that he felt they had gotten all the cancer. To be on the safe side, however, he advised following the operation with a combination of radiation and chemotherapy.

She followed his advice. She completed the additional treatment cycles in sixty days. Before the mastectomy, she had considered breast reconstructive surgery, but after the fact, she decided against it.

Today, Margaret is fifty-eight and still careful to conduct her monthly examination. She has found additional cysts, but the cancer has not recurred. Her doctors are hopeful she will not have any further problems.

Dietary and Life-style Recommendations

Reduce Your Intake of Dietary Fat

The strongest correlation between breast cancer and diet appears to be with the amount of fat in the diet. National studies suggest that the more fat consumed by the population of a particular country, the higher the incidence of breast cancer. The United States, with its high-fat diet, ranks high, but certain countries in which even more fat is consumed, such as Finland, rank even higher. A diet high in fat is believed to result in an imbalance of the female sex hormones, which in some way promotes the occurrence of cancer of the breast. For the same reason, a high-fat diet is also believed to increase a woman's risk for other cancers of the reproductive system.

If you have an average American diet, you consume 40 percent of your calories as fat. This should be reduced to below 30 percent.

Strategy You can reduce your fat intake by making a few simple changes in your diet. An average woman consumes about 2,000 calories a day; reducing the proportion of fat from about 40 to 30 percent of total calories would require cutting about 22 grams per day, or 660 grams per month. (See the table on page 306 for reducing dietary fat.)

Strategies for reducing fat include the following:

• Select lean meats and low-fat products when you shop (see also the tables on pages 304, 305, and 306 for foods high in fat to be avoided).
• Trim excess fat from meat.
• Change to skim milk products.
• Check labels of prepared foods for fat content.
• Add more salads, low-fat soups, and bean, fish, and vegetable dishes to your weekly menu.

Reduce Your Protein Intake

Young women are reaching sexual maturity earlier and earlier, and unfortunately, the statistics show that those who reach sexual maturity early have a higher risk of breast cancer. There is research that suggests that a high-protein diet seems to accelerate the arrival of sexual maturation.

Strategy Try to keep your daughter's consumption of protein to that shown in the table of Recommended Dietary Allowances (see page 324). This means limiting her protein intake to no more than two to three portions from foods high in protein (see table of protein-rich foods, page 313).

If You Are Past Menopause and Overweight, Reduce Your Weight

Research has indicated a correlation between obesity (defined as being 20 percent overweight) and breast cancer in postmenopausal women.

Strategy If you are overweight, make every effort to reduce your weight by following the guidelines in chapter 37.

To Guard Against Breast Cysts, Reduce Your Caffeine Intake and Increase Your Consumption of Vitamin E

Women who have cystic breasts are at higher risk for breast cancer.

Strategy To help eliminate breast cysts, take 400 milligrams of vitamin E a day. Also, avoid all *xanthines* as much as possible. Xanthines (like caffeine and *theobromides*) are found in coffee, tea, chocolate, and cola beverages (see pages 300 and 317 for tables of foods containing caffeine and theobromides).

Increase Your Intake of Beta-Carotene

Beta-carotene seems to provide protection against breast, endometrial, and cervical cancer. The mechanism by which beta-carotene works is not known, but one leading theory suggests that, like vitamins E and C, beta-carotene may also help to prevent the damaging activities of substances called *free radicals*, which are thought by many researchers to be one cause of cancer.

Strategy Consume foods containing beta-carotene. It is found in dark green and deep yellow vegetables such as cabbage, spinach, carrots, broccoli, and Brussels sprouts, as well as in tomatoes. Some people advocate taking a 30-milligram supplement of beta-carotene every other day, but take care not to overdo this (or to overeat foods rich in beta-carotene), as in larger doses beta-carotene is stored in the skin in sufficient amounts to give it a yellowish discoloration.

Although beta-carotene is converted to vitamin A in the body, you should not take vitamin A supplements. Unlike beta-carotene, which is harmless (because the body can only convert a limited amount of it to vitamin A), vitamin A is dangerous at doses in excess of 10,000 international units taken over a prolonged period (five to ten years).

Eat Plenty of Cruciferous Vegetables

Cruciferous vegetables, like Brussels sprouts, cabbage, broccoli, cauliflower, and other members of the cabbage family, are good sources of vitamins, minerals, and fiber, but in addition they contain *dithiothiones*. These are substances that protect against cancer by eliminating the destructive properties of cancer-causing agents.

Strategy Eat cruciferous vegetables at every opportunity.

Increase Your Vitamin C Intake

Vitamin C has been shown to be beneficial in a variety of animal cancer studies. This could be because it is important in the maintenance of the immune system, which helps to resist cancer invasion, and because of its effects on cell-damaging agents such as free radicals.

Strategy You should incorporate quantities of good food sources of vitamin C into your daily diet. They include citrus fruits, berries, peaches, melons, green and leafy vegetables, tomatoes, green peppers, and sweet potatoes (see page 321 for table of vitamin C–rich foods).

You may also elect to take a supplement of vitamin C, but keep in mind that megadoses of the vitamin are of no proven benefit over that derived from moderate intakes of 100 to 500 milligrams per day.

Be Sure You Consume Adequate Dietary Selenium

Selenium, like beta-carotene and vitamins C and E, is a powerful antioxidant that blocks cancer-causing substances in cells. Studies in humans have shown that cancer mortality rates are higher in areas where there is little selenium in the diet. The amount of selenium in food depends on where the food is produced, as the quantities of the nutrient present in soil determine how much will be found in plants and in animals that eat plants.

Strategy   A safe and adequate dose of selenium is 50 to 200 micrograms per day, which is the range normally found in our daily diet. Good food sources of selenium include wheat germ, bran, tuna fish, onions, tomatoes, and broccoli.

Though selenium tablets are popular as a supplement, they are not recommended. Selenium is toxic, and no more than 200 micrograms a day should be taken as a supplement.

Make Sure You Eat a Balanced Diet

A balanced diet will ensure that you get all the nutrients you need for an efficient immune system to protect you against cancer-causing agents. All nutrients have an impact on the immune system, and any excesses or deficiencies reduce its effectiveness. For instance, too much vegetable fat in your diet significantly impairs the immune system, as does a daily intake of more than 2,000 or 3,000 milligrams (two or three grams) of vitamin C. On the other hand, too little of any of the vitamins and minerals can also compromise your natural defenses.

Strategy   Eat a well-balanced diet that contains two servings of protein, two to six of vegetables and fruit, four to six of bread and cereals, and two of milk and dairy products per day (see page 326). Be especially careful to include plenty of folic acid–rich foods in your diet to give added protection against cervical cancer (see page 307 for table of foods rich in folic acid).

Take Part in Intensive Physical Exercise

Exercise tends to promote irregular menstrual periods and longer menstrual cycles, which may protect against the development of breast cancer.

The latest evidence shows that women who have shorter menstrual cycles are at greater risk for breast cancer. The shorter cycle means that they have fewer days between menses and ovulation, which is the time when the breast tissue is least active and least at risk for cancer development. Longer cycles mean more days in the low-risk interval.

Strategy Exercise three to five times weekly for one-half to three-quarters of an hour. Aerobic exercises such as walking, running, bicycling, or dancing are best.

Other Advice

Female marathon runners are also at increased risk for breast cancer because intensive training alters the ratio of female sex hormones. If you are in a high-risk family, avoid such training.

Early detection is the key to being cured of any cancer, but this is especially true of female reproductive organ cancer. To this end, make regular visits to your gynecologist; at such annual visits, your doctor will check for endometrial cancer by examining the endometrium. He or she will also take a Pap smear, in which a small sampling of cells is examined microscopically for the appearance of abnormal cells that could indicate cervical cancer.

Be sure to examine your breasts at a specific time each and every month, especially if you are premenopausal. The preferred time is a few days after menstruation, when hormonal activity is at a minimum and your breasts are not so full. If you are menstruating, this procedure should be done mid-cycle.

Since studies show that perhaps only 18 to 20 percent of the female population habitually and regularly perform breast self-examinations (BSEs) and a substantial number of those who do perform them do so incorrectly, it is advised that you receive proper instruction from your physician.

BSE alone is not sufficient for early detection. After you have reached the age of 35, your doctor should also annually do a *mammography*, a very sensitive X-ray procedure. High-risk women should systematically enroll in health-screening programs and faithfully follow up on a regular basis.

For additional information about breast examination or anything else related to cancer, contact the American Institute for Cancer Research, 803 West Broad Street, Falls Church, Virginia 22046.

8
Bronchitis and Emphysema

Bronchitis is caused by inflammation of the air passages. It occurs in acute and chronic forms. The acute type usually follows a cold or a bout of flu, producing sore throat, runny nose, slight fever, cough, and pain in the back and muscles.

The chronic variety of bronchitis usually results from heavy cigarette smoking and can produce breathing problems, wheezing, fits of coughing, and phlegm.

Emphysema may develop from chronic bronchitis. Here the lungs lose their elasticity, making it impossible for the patient to exhale fully. Emphysema is life-threatening and cannot be cured.

Warning Signs of Acute Bronchitis

• Nasal catarrh, malaise, chilliness, slight fever, back and muscle pain, and sore throat
• A dry cough, which, in a few hours or days, develops into a cough where small amounts of thick phlegm are brought up
• Phlegm gradually becoming more and more abundant

Warning Signs of Chronic Bronchitis and Emphysema

• A mild smoker's cough
• Bronchitis that continues for months and returns each year, lasting longer each year
• Difficulty in getting enough air during physical exertion

• Wheezing, coughing, and frequent respiratory infections
• Weakness, weight loss, or lack of libido

Epidemiological Data

Chronic bronchitis and emphysema are the second greatest cause of disability in the United States (heart disease is number one).

The incidence of chronic bronchitis and emphysema doubles every five years.

Fifteen percent of American males are affected by emphysema and chronic bronchitis.

Chronic bronchitis and emphysema are eight to ten times more frequent in men than in women.

A smoker increases his risk of chronic bronchitis and emphysema by a factor equivalent to half the number of cigarettes smoked per day; thus, if you smoke 20 cigarettes a day, you have ten times the chance of developing these ailments compared to nonsmokers. People with emphysema are primarily men between 50 and 70 who have been heavy smokers for many years.

Half the people in the United States with emphysema are over 65; nearly all the rest are between 25 and 65.

Prevention and Treatment

• Stop smoking.
• Consume a balanced diet if you are a person of normal weight, and a high-protein/high-calorie diet if you are underweight.
• If milk tends to thicken the mucus, limit its intake and that of other dairy products.
• Get plenty of vitamins C and A.
• Increase your intake of fluids.
• Avoid very hot or very cold meals.
• Patients with emphysema should consume a soft diet containing no foods that cause regurgitation or gas; dry foods in particular may be hard to swallow.

CASE HISTORY: Fred Hopkins

Fred Hopkins was a carpenter working on the railroad. At fifty-two, he had been smoking a pack or more of filterless cigarettes a day for thirty-four years.

In recent years he had found it necessary after the first cigarette in the morning to "clear his chest." More than just a smoker's cough, it involved rapid, sharp exhalations to bring up the accumulated phlegm. His wife, Edith, told him the process was "just plain grotesque."

In the months just past, Fred had suffered a particularly bad respiratory infection. It had put him in bed for more than a week before finally clearing up. Being so ill was new to him, but the real shock was that the infection left him with a chronic cough and a problem in catching his breath whenever he exerted himself on the job. He also found that even after his recovery he didn't regain his fondness for his wife's—or anyone's—cooking. Having lost several pounds while sick in bed, he continued to lose weight in the months that followed.

After several months, he went to see his doctor. The diagnosis was chronic bronchitis. The doctor suggested that he stop smoking, and prescribed tetracycline and *bronchodilators*, which caused the passages in the lungs to open. He also prescribed a high-calorie diet to help Fred regain his ideal body weight.

An uncle of Fred's had died of emphysema. "It'll be emphysema for you too, Fred, in the long term, if you don't quit smoking those things," his doctor warned him. Fred remembered all too well the little oxygen tank his uncle had carried about with him the last years of his life, and the bluish tinge of his oxygen-starved complexion.

It was a struggle, but living with the threat of that oxygen bottle, Fred managed to quit smoking. He took the bronchodilators his doctor prescribed, and gradually regained the weight he had lost.

Five years later, he still has occasional bouts with respiratory infections, but they seem to be less severe. He still occasionally uses bronchodilators, but rather than taking them as tablets, he uses an inhaler. His problem hasn't disappeared, but Fred continues to work, and Edith no longer has to complain, because the morning "throat clearing" is now more of a dry, uncomfortable cough.

Dietary and Life-style Recommendations

Stop Smoking

Cigarette smoke irritates the airways in the lungs, which causes them to narrow and paralyzes the little hairs, or *cilia*, in the airways that help to sweep phlegm out of the lungs. Once a person quits smoking, there is some immediate benefit. However, it takes a year or longer for a longtime smoker to clear the lungs completely. Unfortunately, once the lung tissue has lost its elasticity to any degree, it can never be restored.

Strategy The long and the short of it is: QUIT SMOKING. Cutting down may help some, but the key is in quitting altogether.

There are a great many methods of quitting, including behavior modification, hypnosis, support groups, and plain, old-fashioned willpower. Only you can tell which is best for you, but adopt whatever method suits you, and stick to it.

If You Are of Normal Weight, Consume a Balanced Diet; if Underweight or Overweight, Try to Get to Your Ideal Weight

It is very important to have a balanced diet to ensure the maximum protection against respiratory infections and to provide adequate protein and other nutrients to repair damaged tissue in the lungs.

Strategy   Those who are underweight should gain weight by following the procedures outlined in chapter 50; it sometimes helps to eat six smaller meals rather than one or two larger ones if breathing is a problem. A lack of appetite and reduced ability to digest food can be caused by inadequate oxygen reaching the cells of the digestive system. Being overweight makes it more difficult to breathe, and so anyone with bronchitis or emphysema should lose weight as outlined in chapter 37.

If Milk Tends to Thicken the Mucus, Avoid It

Eating dairy products sometimes results in a thickening of the mucus associated with colds or other respiratory infections.

Strategy   If this is true in your case, cut down on your consumption of these foods. If you have chronic bronchitis, take a 1,000-milligram calcium supplement daily to replace the calcium from the milk (500 milligrams should be taken in the morning and 500 milligrams before bedtime); taking four Tums a day is an ideal way to get your calcium, but other brands of calcium carbonate are just as good. Two and a half grams of calcium carbonate contains 1,000 milligrams of calcium.

Get Plenty of Vitamins A and C

Vitamin C is important to the proper functioning of the immune system, and also cuts down the symptoms associated with respiratory infections by as much as one-third. Both vitamins A and C promote healing of the lung tissues.

Strategy   Take a 100-milligram vitamin C supplement each day for maximum protection. Be sure to get 5,000 international units of vitamin A each day. (See pages 318 and 321 respectively for tables of vitamin A– and C–rich foods.)

Increase Your Fluid Intake

Drinking lots of fluids can help to thin the phlegm and make it easier to clear the airways.

Strategy Drink at least two quarts of fluids per day, such as water, carrot juice, fruit juice, or any other beverage.

Avoid Very Hot or Cold Foods or Beverages

The consumption of hot or cold foods or drinks may have a tendency to bring on coughing spells.

Strategy Take care to avoid temperature extremes in your foods.

If You Have Emphysema, Consume a Soft Diet

It is difficult to chew when you have shortness of breath, and so the less chewing necessary, the better. Foods that are difficult to swallow, such as dry crackers and nuts, and those that cause gas (page 308), tend to cause coughing and poor appetite.

Other Advice

Several drugs used in the treatment of these lung problems have some nutritional side effects, including the following:

THEOPHYLLINE   This can build up in the body and become toxic if a high-carbohydrate, low-protein diet is eaten. It is a stimulant, as are beverages containing caffeine like coffee, tea, cocoa, and cola drinks, so you should avoid drinking them as much as possible while taking theophylline.

METAPROTERENOL SULFATE   This drug should be taken with fruit juice after a meal to avoid gastrointestinal disturbances and to prevent the bad taste of the drug from affecting your appetite.

TERBUTALINE   Take with food to avoid gastrointestinal disturbances.

TETRACYCLINE   Take on an empty stomach, one hour before or two hours after meals; if severe reactions occur, however, take the drug with meals as long as the meals do not contain any dairy products.

If you would like further information about these or other lung problems, contact the American Lung Association, 1740 Broadway, New York, New York 10019, phone (212) 889–3370.

9
Bruising

A *bruise* is an accumulation of blood under the skin, in which the skin is discolored but not broken. Bruises that are of a tiny, pinhead size are called *purpura;* larger, more extensive bruises are termed *ecchymosis.*

Warning Signs

• A discoloration of or swelling under the skin

Epidemiological Data

Bruises that appear all over the body are often symptoms of other diseases. Scurvy, meningitis, and diseases that involve high temperature, such as scarlet fever and typhus, are frequently accompanied by extensive bruising.

Purpura may occur as a result of chemical or X-ray poisoning.

Purpura may occur *idiopathically* (of unknown origin). In such cases, women between 12 and 25 years of age are most often affected.

Bruises can be caused by vitamin deficiencies, and *steroid* or *anticoagulant* drug therapies; leukemia patients often have extensive bruising; and the elderly sometimes have what are known as senile purpura.

Prevention and Treatment

• Be sure you are getting adequate vitamin C.
• Be sure you are not deficient in vitamin K.

71

• If you are not nutrient-deficient and constantly have a lot of bruises, check with your doctor.

CASE HISTORY: Annie Smith

Annie Smith was a widow. Now seventy-eight, she had spent the last ten years alone.

Since her husband had died, she hadn't had the old desire to prepare a full range of balanced meals. She almost never ate fresh fruit and vegetables; it seemed to her children she ate exclusively from cans.

She went to her doctor complaining of extensive bruising on her legs. He gave her a thorough physical examination, and determined that overall she was in good shape for a woman of her age. But when he talked to her about her diet, her doctor began to suspect that the cause of the problem was a vitamin C deficiency.

He told her to take a daily vitamin C supplement of 100 milligrams. He advised her to incorporate fresh citrus fruit, potatoes, and green vegetables in her diet. When she returned for a follow-up visit three weeks later, her bruises were much improved, and her doctor's diagnosis was confirmed.

Dietary and Life-style Recommendations

Consume Plenty of Vitamin C

Without vitamin C in the system, blood vessels become leaky and bruising occurs. If you are deficient in vitamin C, you may also experience such symptoms as acne on the forearms, legs, and thighs; hardening and scaling of the skin around the hair follicles; hemorrhages around hair follicles; broken and coiled hairs; weakness, fatigue, restlessness, and neurotic behavior; aching bones, joints, and muscles; sore mouth and gums.

Strategy   If you take a 100-milligram supplement of vitamin C daily, or include two or more portions of vitamin C–rich foods in your daily menu, a vitamin C deficiency and hence the bruising should disappear in a matter of a week or two. (See page 321 for table of foods rich in vitamin C.)

Make Sure You Are Not Deficient in Vitamin K

Vitamin K is required for blood clotting; without it, hemorrhaging and bruising can occur. A deficiency is rare, as the vitamin is made by the intestinal bacteria and is commonly available in such foods as green leafy vegetables, liver, egg yolk, vegetable oils, wheat, and oats. However, because vitamin K can only be absorbed when it is dissolved in fat, a deficiency can occur when there is a problem with fat absorption, as in the presence of such conditions as gallbladder disease, celiac disease, and ulcerative colitis. The long-term use of antibacterial drugs like *penicillin* and *tetracycline*, which kill the bacteria in the intestine, can also cause a deficiency. The anticoagulant drug *coumarin* and the *salicylates* prevent vitamin K from causing blood to clot, which can lead to bruising.

Strategy Try increasing your intake of foods containing vitamin K. If this does not cause an improvement within a week, see your doctor. (See page 322 for table of vitamin K–containing foods.)

Other Advice

Many serious diseases cause extensive bruising, such as severe allergies, hemophilia, and leukemia.

Strategy It is important to seek advice from your doctor if you consume a balanced diet but have bruising problems.

There are a number of *naturopathic* remedies (the type of remedies found in the health food store) that are said to cure bruises. However, there is absolutely no evidence to show that they do so. Some of the supposed remedies are the following:

VITAMIN A Daily megadoses of vitamin A (50,000 to 100,000 international units) are extremely dangerous and can cause joint pain, abnormal menstruation, breakthrough bleeding, loss of appetite, irritability, restlessness, headache, nausea, muscle weakness, stomachache, diarrhea, weight loss, dry and itching skin, rashes, dry and scaling lips, hair loss, and brittle nails.

BIOFLAVENOIDS Another "remedy" is said to be bioflavenoids (five to ten grams per day is a common dosage); while not dangerous, bioflavenoids are not required by the human body.

VITAMIN E Vitamin E in itself is harmless in most people at up to 1,000 international units, but in those deficient in vitamin K due to anticoagulant drugs, it can increase the tendency to hemorrhage.

ZINC For wounds and minor cuts, this mineral is definitely needed, but if you are getting the Recommended Dietary Allowance, a supplement will not aid the healing process. In fact, doses of 75 milligrams of zinc a day will impair the absorption of copper and iron and result in anemia. It may also significantly increase blood cholesterol levels and raise the risk of a heart attack or stroke.

If you would like further information about bruising, contact the National Heart, Lung, and Blood Institute, National Institutes of Health, Room 504, Federal Building, 7550 Wisconsin Avenue, Bethesda, Maryland 20205, phone (301) 496-6931.

10
Bulimia

Bulimia is the term used to describe the condition in which people go on uncontrolled eating binges, followed by self-induced purging by vomiting or the use of laxatives or diuretics. Obsessed with becoming thin and not gaining weight, they will also employ prolonged fasting, excessive exercise, and amphetamines to counter possible weight gains after binge-eating.

The precipitating event for binge-eating is usually emotional stress, boredom, or loneliness. The binge is used as a means of releasing tension brought on by these various stresses. It does dispel the tension, but results in feelings of guilt, shame, disgust, and fear of being found out. It also leads to a panic that weight will be gained, which draws the person to purge to undo the effect of binging. Some guilt remains, however, which eventually builds up enough tension to start the whole cycle anew.

Bulimics characteristically feel alienated and self-conscious, are overly dependent on the opinions of others, have difficulty expressing their feelings, especially anger, and have low self-esteem. Their obsession with weight loss is a way of gaining approval from society and raising their self-esteem. They are also chronically depressed and have difficulty controlling impulses toward alcohol and drug abuse and stealing.

Warning Signs

- Frequent weight fluctuations of more than ten pounds
- Chronic indigestion or constipation

- Facial puffiness
- Irregular menstrual cycles
- Sore throat
- Muscle weakness or lethargy
- Eroded tooth enamel
- Hair loss

Epidemiological Data

The average bulimic is a white, single, college-educated female of normal weight. Typically, the bulimic is in her early to mid-twenties and suffers from the condition for four to six years before seeking treatment.

About 5 percent of adolescent and young adult women are believed to suffer from bulimia.

Although about 50 percent of all patients with anorexia nervosa have bulimic episodes, only patients of average weight or above are by definition bulimics.

Ten to 13 percent of all bulimics are male.

Suicide is the most common cause of death in bulimics.

Prevention and Treatment

- Consult a psychotherapist to help deal with your emotional problems and to modify your eating habits.
- Take vitamin and mineral supplements.

CASE HISTORY: Sally Lawson

As a child, Sally was chubby. Neither her mother nor her father ever seemed to have much time to spend with her, but instead tried to keep her quiet and happy with food.

Sally got the idea early on that food was something one ate to feel better. In her early teens, for example, she would from time to time buy herself a box or two of candy at the local deli to elevate her spirits.

When dating time came around, Sally was a little too overweight for the boys to find her attractive. Her opinion of herself was already low, and her lack of appeal to members of the opposite sex only served to lower her self-esteem even further. Eventually she went on a diet and lost the weight she wanted. And, true to form, the boys noticed the "new" girl and asked her out. But her chronic lack of self-confidence and constant need for reassurance drove the boys away. They found her mood swings and impulsive behavior difficult to deal with.

She just didn't seem to be able to control herself in general, but her eating habits continued to be the least predictable part of her personality. She would go through periods of gaining weight when she was upset about something, only to take it off when she felt better.

At eighteen, she witnessed her parents giving up on their marriage. As often as not, Sally had taken their frequent fights personally, but the divorce truly upset her. The day she learned of the split, she went out and ate an entire half-gallon of ice cream at one sitting. (The only thing that prevented her from eating more was a severe stomachache.) When she realized what she had done, she became very upset at the thought that this might put back some of the pounds she had lost, and she put her fingers down her throat and vomited.

That was the first of her many binges on sweet, calorie-dense foods. In college over the next few years, she would binge when she was upset, then purge. In her senior year, she reached the stage when she would fast for a week after a binge, just to make sure she would not gain weight.

She managed to keep her bizarre eating habits a secret until she went to see her dentist after not having visited him for several years. He noticed immediately that she had several cavities and very badly eroded tooth enamel. He suspected that she was bulimic—he had seen the symptoms before—and after a little persuasion she admitted to him that she had a problem. He urged her to consult her doctor, impressing on her that not only would all her teeth fall out but her hair would, too, if she kept up the binge-purge cycle.

Sally was quickly referred to a psychotherapist by her doctor. She helped Sally cope with her emotional problems, and prescribed an antidepressant medication. After a few individual sessions, Sally agreed to participate in group sessions, which proved very helpful in enabling her to deal with her problems, as she learned that there were others out there like her. With this guidance and help, she was able to adopt normal eating habits.

Dietary and Life-style Recommendations

Consult a Psychotherapist

Psychotherapy concentrates on the reasons for the emotional problems that lead to the eating disorder. The psychotherapist tries to help the bulimic cope with the anxiety, anger, depression, and low self-esteem that trigger bingeing episodes and to substitute alternative means of releasing tension. Group therapy sessions are very effective in this respect. Many psychotherapists feel that bulimia results from an abnormality in brain biochemistry, and use antidepressants and anticonvulsants as adjuncts to psychotherapy. A dietician is brought in to help the bulimic design and follow a normal diet.

Strategy Obtain professional psychiatric and nutritional guidance in confronting your problem. If you don't know where to turn, ask your doctor to refer you to a qualified professional.

Take Vitamin and Mineral Supplements

The abuse of laxatives in particular leads to malabsorption; laxatives flush out necessary vitamins and other nutrients before they can be properly and fully absorbed, leaving the bulimic seriously deficient in vitamins A, D, E, and K, as well as other nutrients.

Likewise, abuse of diuretics causes dehydration and potassium deficiency. Vomiting has the same effect. If untreated, this can lead to urinary infections, kidney failure, and an irregular heart rate.

Strategy Bulimics are well advised to take a one-a-day vitamin containing the Recommended Dietary Allowances for vitamins.

A doctor may also find it necessary to prescribe potassium supplements (though these should not be taken without the advice of a physician). But all bulimics should be encouraged to drink plenty of fluids (eight cups or more a day) and eat foods rich in potassium every day. (See page 313 for table of potassium-rich foods.)

Other Advice

If you would like further information about bulimia and other eating disorders, contact the National Association of Anorexia Nervosa and Associated Disorders, Box 271, Highland Park, Illinois 60035, phone: (312) 831-3438.

11
Celiac Disease

Celiac disease is a congenital, hereditary disorder caused by a sensitivity to *gluten*, a protein found in wheat and other grains. When someone with celiac disease consumes gluten, it damages the lining of the intestine and reduces food digestion and absorption.

The disease first appears when cereals are introduced into a child's diet at four to six months of age. Often there is an unexplained interval of several months before symptoms appear. Gluten is found in wheat and to a lesser extent in other grains such as rye, barley, and oats. Even minute amounts of gluten are enough to cause severe symptoms. In some children the intolerance persists throughout their lives, but in others some tolerance develops to the protein.

Warning Signs

- When given a diet including gluten, patients with celiac disease may suffer from persistent pale and foamy diarrhea with a very unpleasant odor
- Irritability, vomiting, loss of appetite, fatigue, pallor, and, in severe cases, a potbellied appearance, poor growth, and wasting (the wasting is apparent in the buttocks and on the inside of the thighs, but in children it is often missed unless the child is examined naked and standing upright)
- In adults, the symptoms are the same except for the characteristic pot belly and, of course, the growth failure
- Anemia, caused by sustained loss of blood in diarrhea

- Tiredness, irritability, lethargy, and, in older children, impaired school performance may result from a deficiency of folic acid consequent to the persistent diarrhea
- Celiac disease can be easily confused with lactose intolerance, so consult your doctor to be sure of the identity of the problem

Epidemiological Data

One in every 8,000 children has celiac disease.

The disease is most common among whites.

A child whose mother, father, brother, or sister suffers from celiac disease has a one-in-five chance of having it.

Adults with celiac disease who do not adhere to a gluten-free diet have an increased risk of developing cancer.

Prevention and Treatment

- Remove the offending protein (gluten) from your diet.
- Replace the nutrients lost because of the diarrhea and malabsorption.
- Watch for lactose intolerance.
- After an outbreak of physical symptoms, reduce the fiber in your diet until the symptoms subside, and then gradually increase fiber as tolerated; fat should also be restricted while the symptoms persist, as it will be poorly absorbed at this time.
- Modify recipes to exclude gluten-containing foods.
- Read food labels in order to avoid foods containing gluten.

CASE HISTORY: Jacqueline Dubée

Baby Jackie is the much-doted-on firstborn child of a French Canadian couple living in Maine. She weighed a healthy seven and one-half pounds at birth and developed a voracious appetite that insured good weight gain. But as her mother introduced cereal into her diet at the age of four months, she almost immediately became Little Miss Finicky. She developed persistent foamy, pale-colored diarrhea, too, which did nothing for her temperament. Given its foul smell, her parents were none too thrilled with the turn of events, either.

The happy child gave way to an irritable one, almost overnight. Her mother's first guess was that the problem was the new food introduced to her baby's diet, but when the problem persisted for several weeks, she consulted her pediatrician.

He diagnosed celiac disease and put Jackie on a gluten-free diet. He also prescribed a multivitamin supplement. The symptoms disappeared almost as rapidly as they had arrived. Happy Jackie was back.

After three years of gluten-free eating, her doctor suggested that her mother try cereals again. They reintroduced the child to gluten—the process was gradual and staged—and found that Jacqueline was able to tolerate substantial amounts in her diet with no adverse effects.

Dietary and Life-style Recommendations

The following recommendations are for *older children and adults only;* babies and very young children should be fed a gluten-free diet prepared under the guidance of the child's pediatrician.

Remove Gluten from the Diet

Anyone with celiac disease should be placed on a gluten-free diet. It is very important that the diet be followed carefully, since even small mistakes can lead to a recurrence of most or all of the symptoms. For example, even a single sip of rye whiskey can start up the disease process again.

Strategy In principle, the diet is simple, as all foods rich in gluten are omitted but plenty of protein is consumed by incorporating lots of lean meat, fish, and whole milk. (See page 327 for a list of foods that must not be included and those that can be used on a gluten-free diet.)

After two years or more, a child may develop some tolerance of gluten. Your doctor will probably suggest the slow introduction of small amounts of gluten-containing foods into the diet. If they are tolerated, the child can begin to eat a regular or nearly normal diet.

This is also true of adults. However, recent evidence would suggest that if you have had celiac disease diagnosed at any time, you are best advised to consume a gluten-free diet for the rest of your life, as this may help to prevent the increased risk of cancer associated with the disease.

Replace Nutrients Lost Through Diarrhea and Malabsorption

Vitamins A, D, E, and K, and magnesium and calcium are all lost during episodes of diarrhea. In addition, owing to bleeding in the digestive tract, iron is often lost in significant amounts. Some patients are also found to have low levels of folic acid, vitamin B_{12}, and the other B-complex vitamins.

Strategy A multivitamin containing the Recommended Dietary Allowances of all the vitamins should be taken, as well as a 1,000-milligram supplement of calcium that contains some magnesium. If anemia is present, an iron supplement should be taken, but check with your doctor before doing so, as iron can be very dangerous if taken for a period extending beyond a few weeks.

Watch for Lactose Intolerance

When the lining of the small intestine is damaged by gluten, the ability to digest milk and other foods is impaired.

Strategy At this time, reduce your consumption of foods rich in lactose (see chapter 35).

Limit Fiber Intake

The intestine will be easily irritated during and immediately after an outbreak of the physical symptoms of celiac disease. Consequently, you should reduce the presence of fiber in the diet while you are suffering from the symptoms. When they subside, you may slowly reintroduce fiber into the diet.

The damaged intestine will also not digest or absorb fat very well, so fatty foods should be eliminated from the diet at this time. A low-fat diet is a good one for everybody to follow, so this might be a good time to reeducate your palate to accept low-fat foods.

Strategy Limit your intake of fiber during acute intervals of celiac disease (see table on page 303 for foods high in dietary fiber), and cut down on consumption of fats (see tables on pages 304, 305, and 306 for fatty foods).

Other Advice

Modify your recipes to exclude foods containing gluten. Rice can be used in place of macaroni and other pasta products in baked cheese or cold salad recipes. Rice cakes and tortilla chips make excellent snacks or accompaniments for soups and fish or salads, and are widely available.

When recipes incorporate an egg and two tablespoons of flour as a thickener, use one tablespoon of corn starch instead of the flour. Carob powder can be used in place of cocoa in cooking. Corn-flake crumbs can be used as breading. Nearly all pastries are not allowed on a wheat-free diet, but easy-to-make corn-flake macaroons and meringue cookies make a tasty replacement.

Substances containing gluten are sometimes added to processed foods, and you should be watchful when using such foods as cereals, starch, flour, thickening agents, emulsifiers, stabilizers, and hydrolyzed vegetable proteins. Wheat starch is generally tolerated because the gluten has been removed.

If you would like further information about celiac disease, contact the National Digestive Disease Education and Information Clearinghouse, 1555 Wilson Boulevard, Suite 600, Rosslyn, Virginia 22209, phone (301) 496-9707.

12
Colitis

Colitis is an inflammation of the colon and/or rectum that commonly causes an increased urgency to defecate, mild lower abdominal cramps, and intermittent diarrhea with mucus and blood in the stool.

Ulcerative colitis, to use its more complete medical name, is most frequently found in 15- to 40-year-olds, but can occur at any age. Its nature is still obscure, but there are several theories as to its cause. They range from the possibility that it is an autoimmune disease (in which the body's own immune system attacks its intestine) or a bacterial infection, to the theory that it is caused by an allergy to milk or some other substance.

Warning Signs

- Diarrhea with mucus and blood in the stool
- Hard stools accompanied by mucus and blood
- Diminution of appetite, weight loss, anemia, skin rash, arthritis-like pain, sore mouth, kidney- or gallstones
- In children, a failure to grow and thrive
- Severe but episodic abdominal pain and cramping
- A history of the disease in your family

Epidemiological Data

Ten percent of all patients with ulcerative colitis die after one attack; in patients over 60 years of age, the death rate rises to 25 percent after the first attack.

Ten percent of all patients make a complete recovery after one attack and are never troubled again.

For patients suffering from colitis attacks for a period of ten years or longer, the risk of colon cancer is significantly increased; in fact, sufferers who have had colitis for four decades have a seven-in-ten chance of getting colon cancer.

One out of three colitis patients needs surgery at some time during the progression of the disease.

Prevention and Treatment

- Adopt a low-fiber diet devoid of raw fruit and vegetables during flare-ups, and take a daily multivitamin supplement.
- For colitis sufferers who are sensitive to milk (one in three), avoid dairy products and take a 1,000-milligram calcium supplement daily.
- Avoid iced or carbonated beverages.
- Take frequent small, bland meals rich in protein and calories.
- If anemia is present, take iron supplements.
- If you have frequent diarrhea, include lots of foods rich in potassium in your diet and drink eight to ten glasses of fluid per day.
- Learn techniques of stress management.

CASE HISTORY: Philip Strong

Philip Strong was the general manager of a small manufacturing company. He was married, had two delightful daughters, and, at thirty-five, felt happy with his lot in life.

But Philip suffered from feelings of general malaise. He had lost his relish for food, and over a period of months he lost weight and developed arthritis-like pains in his joints. At first he attributed them to stiffness from old athletic injuries, but they became too widespread to explain that way.

For a while he tried to put all his physical troubles down to difficulties at work. There was new, foreign ownership of the company, and he worried for his own position and especially for those of the people he had brought in and trained over the years. "Just too much stress," he said to himself.

It was the bloody diarrhea that finally drove him to visit his doctor. On the basis of an X-ray and an examination of the tissue in his rectum and lower colon (an exploration, sometimes called a "procto," in which a hollow, lighted instrument called a *sigmoidoscope* is inserted into the anus), it was determined that he had ulcerative colitis.

"You have to relax more," Philip's doctor told him. The doctor also gave him some specific advice on stress management. He advised Philip to eat a normal diet, but to avoid raw fruit and vegetables during episodes. He also prescribed *diphenoxylate* to prevent his diarrhea.

Philip still has occasional bouts of colitis, especially in times of pressure, but he is relaxing more. And although he misses some of his favorite foods, his golf game has improved with the extra time he spends on the course. An even trade, he figures.

Dietary and Life-style Recommendations

Consume a Low-Fiber Diet During Flare-ups

Because fiber increases stool volume and distends the bowel, omitting or reducing it prevents irritation of the colon and permits it to rest and heal. Raw fruits and vegetables are major sources of fiber, as are grains, nuts, seeds, and legumes.

Strategy   Avoid those foods listed in the table on page 303 that are high in dietary fiber. Many of these foods, however, are among the richest sources of the B vitamins and vitamin C, so a multivitamin supplement containing the Recommended Dietary Allowances should be taken to replace these lost nutrients.

After the diarrhea has subsided, gradually introduce raw vegetables and other fiber-rich foods.

Avoid Milk If You Are Sensitive to Lactose

One-third of all patients with ulcerative colitis have milk intolerance. If they drink milk, it will further irritate the bowel.

Strategy   All dairy products should be omitted from the diet of these people. As dairy products are the best sources of dietary calcium, they should be replaced by a 1,000-milligram supplement of calcium as 2,500 milligrams of calcium carbonate. Take 500 milligrams of calcium at night and 500 at midmorning.

Avoid Iced or Carbonated Beverages

These stimulate the activity of the muscles in the intestine and will worsen the diarrhea.

Strategy   Do not consume carbonated beverages or any other fluids to which ice has been added.

Eat Frequent Small and Bland Meals

Smaller, more frequent meals are less likely to distend the bowel and will optimize the healing process. Patients will usually have lost a good deal of weight and so it is important for them to consume as many calories as possible.

Strategy As you recuperate from an attack of colitis, increase the number of meals you eat daily. A high-protein diet (three to four portions of protein-rich foods per day) is also necessary for the healing process.

A bland diet will also help you avoid foods known to cause diarrhea or to irritate the intestinal lining. (See page 326 for table of bland foods.)

Take Iron Supplements if Anemia Is Present

A sore mouth is an indicator of an iron deficiency, as are tiredness, pains in the chest on physical exertion, and brittle nails.

Strategy All colitis sufferers should take a one-a-day vitamin and mineral supplement that contains the Recommended Dietary Allowance of iron. If anemia is present, your doctor will advise an iron supplement, but do not take supplemental iron at levels above the Recommended Dietary Allowance unless your physician instructs you to do so, as too much is as bad as too little. (See chapter 4 for further discussion of iron deficiency anemia.)

If You Experience Frequent Diarrhea, Eat Plenty of Potassium-Rich Foods and Drink Lots of Fluids

Diarrhea leads to the loss of potassium and fluids from your body. Potassium deficiency can lead to heart failure, and dehydration to feelings of weakness.

Strategy Include lots of potassium-rich foods in your daily menu (see table on page 313). Be sure to drink eight to ten glasses of fluids per day.

Other Advice

Learn techniques of stress management, as stress has been linked to ulcerative colitis. (See Appendix 3 for specific suggestions.)

Certain medications taken to treat colitis may have some nutritional interactions.

While taking the antibiotic *Azulfidine (sulfasalazine* is its generic name) make sure that you drink at least two quarts of fluids a day and take a 400-microgram supplement of folic acid. Because the drug is also a gastric irritant, you should take it with meals.

Diphenoxylate (a diarrhea medication) should be taken one half hour before meals.

If your doctor prescribes a *corticosteroid* medication, limit your sodium intake to 2,000 milligrams (two grams) a day while taking the drug. See table of foods high in sodium on page 315.

If you would like further information about colitis, contact the National Foundation for Ileitis and Colitis, Inc., 295 Madison Avenue, New York, New York 10017, phone (212) 683-3440.

13
Colon and Rectal Cancer

Owing to the effects of an irritant, virus, or other metabolic product, a group of cells in the colon or rectum begin to grow abnormally. The large clump of cells that results is a tumor.

The *colorectal tumor* attaches to the lining of the intestine and destroys the healthy tissue. At some point in the development of the tumor, some of its cells may metastasize, or break away from the original area of activity and, via the bloodstream or lymph system, travel to other locations and begin secondary growths.

Warning Signs

• Persistent constipation or diarrhea
• Bright red or very darkly colored stools (due to the presence of blood)
• Stools that are consistently smaller than usual
• A feeling of bloating or fullness
• Frequent cramps or gas pains
• A feeling that the bowel doesn't empty completely
• Unexplained weight loss
• Constant tiredness

Epidemiological Data

Six percent of the U.S. population is affected by colorectal disease. Each year, 138,000 new cases of colon and rectum cancer are diagnosed and 60,000 people die of the disease.

When detected early and treated promptly, cancer of the colon and rectum is curable, and more than three-quarters of the patients treated early are able to return to normal lives.

Colorectal cancer death rates are slightly higher among women and among people with higher incomes and levels of education. The incidence of colorectal cancer is greater among white men and women than among blacks or Hispanics.

More than 90 percent of cases of colorectal cancer occur after the age of 50.

People with a close relative who had *polyps* (swollen lining of the colon) or bowel cancer have an increased risk. There is also a correlation between the incidence of colorectal cancer and obesity and inflammatory bowel disease (periods of diarrhea alternating with constipation and extreme flatulence, as in colitis).

There are more cases of colorectal cancer among both men and women in the United States than in any other country. Colorectal cancer is rare in areas of the world where a high-fiber, low-fat diet is consumed.

Prevention and Treatment

• Cut down on total fat intake.
• Eat fruits, vegetables, and whole-grain cereal products daily.
• Eat a well-balanced, varied diet.
• Prepare foods by risk-reducing methods.
• Take 30 milligrams of beta-carotene every other day.
• Do not consume large amounts of vegetable fat.
• Take a 1,000-milligram supplement of calcium daily.

CASE HISTORY: Barry Higgins

Barry Higgins weighed too much. He had long blamed his extra heft on his bad knees (he found most exercise painful) and too many business lunches.

The fact was that he just plain ate too much. Barry was often heard to say, in disparaging tones, that salad was "rabbit food." He was a meat-and-potatoes man and proud of it.

When Barry, a lifelong salesman, moved to a new job as a sales manager at the age of fifty-five, he found that his new managerial post offered a variety of benefits. Among them was a big life insurance policy, but in order to fulfill insurance company requirements, Barry had to have a thorough physical examination.

The doctor began by taking his history. She learned that his father had died at sixty-two of cancer of the colon. She gathered a good deal of other data, too, but it was only when she inserted a gloved, lubricated finger into Barry's rectum that she discovered a problem.

Probing gently to feel for lumps, she discovered a swelling in the mucus membrane of the rectum. The swelling, called a *polyp*, worried her immediately. She explored further by conducting what she colloquially referred to as a "procto," a procedure in which she inserted a hollow, lighted instrument called a *sigmoidoscope* into Barry's anus. The good news was that she found no other polyps on this second entry.

She took a stool sample, too, and the laboratory tests she had conducted on it revealed no cancerous cells, but just to be on the safe side, she sent Barry to a specialist who examined the entire length of his colon using a thin, lighted, flexible tube called a *colonoscope*. He found the colon to be clear of any signs of polyps or abnormal tissue.

Based on the results, Barry's doctor advised him to lose weight, reduce his fat intake, and increase his fiber consumption. He had a consultation with a dietician who showed him exactly how to do this.

After three months he returned to the doctor, who found a reduction in the swelling in his rectum. Over the course of the following year, the polyp completely disappeared.

Dietary and Life-style Recommendations

Limit Your Intake of Dietary Fats

The food component showing the strongest and clearest association with cancer is fat. When fat is eaten, bile is secreted from the gallbladder to aid in its absorption. Bile contains *bile salts*, which may be mild cancer-causing substances, or *carcinogens*.

A high-fat diet also seems to change the normal bacterial makeup of the large intestine in such a way as to favor the survival of bacteria that can easily transform the fat or bile salts to other products. One or more of the products of this bacterial transformation may act as a carcinogen or may promote the activity of carcinogens already present in the intestine, such as the bile salts.

If you eat an average American diet, you consume 40 percent of your calories as fat. This level should be reduced to below 30 percent, as too much fat in the diet also leads to obesity, which is another risk factor for colon cancer. You can reduce your fat intake by making a few simple changes in your diet.

An average woman consumes about 2,000 calories a day; reducing the proportion of fat from about 40 to 30 percent of total calories would require cutting about 22 grams per day or 660 grams per month. For men, the average daily intake of calories is about 2,700, so a 10-percent fat reduction from 40 to 30 grams would mean about 30 grams less fat per day or some 900 grams saved a month.

STRATEGIES

• Select lean meats and low-fat products when you shop (see also the table on page 304 for foods low in fat).
• Trim excess fat from meat.
• Change to skim milk products.
• Check labels of prepared foods for fat content.
• Add more salads, low-fat soups, and bean, fish, and vegetable dishes to your weekly menu.
• Bake, broil, or boil rather than fry foods.
• Limit the use of salad dressings, rich sauces, butter, cream, margarine, shortening, and oil in food preparation and at the table; use less cooking oil and fats than called for in recipes.
• Substitute broth for fats in cooking.
  (See also the table on page 306 for reducing dietary fat.)

Eat Fruits, Vegetables, and Whole-Grain Cereal Products Daily

These foods are especially rich in fiber, vitamin C, beta-carotene, vitamin E, and selenium, all of which protect against cancer.

Fiber is thought to protect against colon cancer by increasing the bulk of the stools, hence diluting potential cancer-causing agents produced by the bacteria in the intestine. Fiber may also bind to the bile salts, making them less available for conversion into cancer-causing substances by bacteria in the colon or to do damage to the intestinal wall. In addition, because fiber is a laxative, it can move waste material through the intestines quickly, decreasing the time that carcinogens are in contact with the intestinal wall.

Vitamin C has been shown to be beneficial in some cancer studies, possibly because it is important in the maintenance of the immune system, which acts to resist cancer invasion. But megadoses of the vitamin do not give any extra benefit over that derived from moderate doses, roughly 100 to 500 milligrams daily.

Beta-carotene has a protective role to play against all forms of cancer, including colon cancer. The mechanism by which beta-carotene works is not known, but one leading theory suggests that, like vitamin E, it prevents the formation of cell-damaging agents such as those known as *free radicals.*

Like beta-carotene, selenium destroys free radicals. The quantity of selenium present in the soil determines how much will pass through to the foods grown there. Studies have shown that cancer mortality rates are higher in areas where there is little selenium in the diet.

Vitamin E and substances called *dithiothiones,* which are found in cruciferous vegetables, are also thought to have effects similar to selenium and beta-carotene.

Strategy   Consume foods rich in the nutrients discussed above.

Dietary fiber is found in vegetables, fruits, whole grains, and baked goods containing whole-grain flour. (See page 303 for table of foods containing dietary fiber.)

Vitamin C is found in citrus fruits, berries, peaches, melons, green and leafy vegetables, tomatoes, green peppers, and sweet potatoes. (See page 321 for table of vitamin C–rich foods.)

Beta-carotene is found in dark green and deep yellow vegetables such as cabbage, spinach, carrots, broccoli, tomatoes, and Brussels sprouts. Some people advocate taking a 30-milligram supplement of beta-carotene every other day, but take care not to overdo this (or eating of foods rich in beta-carotene) as in larger doses beta-carotene is stored in the skin in sufficient amounts to give you a yellowish discoloration. (All the vegetables and fruits in the table on page 318 of foods containing vitamin A are rich in beta-carotene.)

You should not take vitamin A supplements. Unlike beta-carotene, which is converted to vitamin A in the body and is harmless, vitamin A is exceedingly dangerous at doses in excess of 10,000 international units when taken over prolonged periods (five to ten years).

A safe and adequate dose of selenium is 50 to 200 micrograms per day, which is the range normally found in our daily diet. Good food sources of selenium include wheat germ, bran, tuna fish, onions, tomatoes, and broccoli (see page 314 for table of selenium-containing foods).

Though selenium tablets are a popular supplement, they are not safe. Selenium can be toxic when more than 200 micrograms are consumed daily.

Vitamin E is found in whole-grain cereals, wheat germ, soy beans, broccoli, Brussels sprouts, leafy greens, and spinach (see page 322 for table of foods containing vitamin E). It is not toxic when less than 1,000 international units are taken daily, unless a person is deficient in vitamin K or is taking anticoagulant drugs. Vitamin E in large doses reduces absorption of vitamin K, which is needed for normal blood clotting, and can lead to hemorrhaging.

Cruciferous vegetables include members of the cabbage family such as Brussels sprouts, cabbage, broccoli, and cauliflower.

Eat a Well-Balanced, Varied Diet

A balanced diet will ensure that you get all the nutrients you need for an efficient immune system to protect you against cancer-causing agents. All nutrients have an impact on the immune system, and any excesses or deficiencies reduce its effectiveness. For instance, too much vegetable fat in your diet significantly impairs the immune system, as does a daily intake of more than 2,000 or 3,000 milligrams (two or three grams) of vitamin C. On the other hand, too little of any of the vitamins and minerals can also compromise your natural defenses.

Strategy Eat a well-balanced diet, one that contains two servings of protein, four to six of vegetables and fruit, four to six of bread and cereals, and two of milk and dairy products per day (see chart on page 326).

Do Not Eat Excessive Amounts of Vegetable Fats

After the American Heart Association advised people to reduce the animal fat (*saturated* fat) and increase the vegetable fat (*polyunsaturated* fat) in their diets to reduce blood cholesterol levels and the risk of heart attack, many people went overboard and consumed more polyunsaturated fat than saturated fat. This succeeded in reducing their blood cholesterol levels, but ironically it also increased their risk for cancer. A diet high in fat of any kind puts you in a high-risk category for cancer, but polyunsaturated fats seem to be more cancer-causing than saturated ones, possibly because they impair the immune system.

Strategy The answer is moderation in all things. Aim at equal quantities of vegetable and animal fats in the diet. (See the discussion of balancing fats in chapter 6.)

Take a One-Gram Calcium Supplement Daily

Recent evidence suggests that calcium protects you against colon cancer, possibly by combining with the cancer-causing bile salts and preventing them from doing their damage to the wall of the intestine.

Strategy Take 500 milligrams of calcium at night and 500 milligrams at midmorning. The best way is to take it as calcium carbonate. One thousand milligrams of calcium is contained in 2,500 milligrams (two and a half grams) of calcium carbonate.

Other Advice

If you would like further information about colon and rectal cancer, contact the Cancer Information Clearinghouse, National Cancer Institute, Office of Cancer Communications, 9000 Rockville Pike, Building 31, Room 10A18, Bethesda, Maryland 20205, phone (301) 496-4070.

14
Constipation and Diverticular Disease

Constipation is a general condition in which bowel movements are hard and passed with difficulty, discomfort, or pain. This means that muscles of the colon have to work harder to move the small, hard stools out of the body.

The high pressure that the muscles generate to propel the hard bowel movements push outward on the colon wall. They may, in time (usually 20 years or more), force the lining of the intestine through its muscle layer. This is rather like the ballooning out of a segment of an inner tube through a weakness in a tire.

This produces little outpouchings or pockets called *diverticula*. People with this condition have what is known as *diverticulosis*, and if fecal matter becomes trapped in the diverticula, it can lead to a serious infection called *diverticulitis*.

Warning Signs

- Constipation: hard bowel movements passed with discomfort or pain
- Diverticulosis: often symptomless, but sometimes there are telling signs such as alternating diarrhea and constipation, and troublesome bouts of gas and pain in the lower left side of the abdomen
- Diverticulitis: vomiting, fever, and rectal bleeding

Epidemiological Data

People over 65 are five times as likely as younger people to have problems with constipation.

One-half of all American adults suffer from some type of digestive disorder, with constipation as the leading complaint.

Pregnant women often suffer from constipation owing to the enlarged uterus pressing on the intestines.

One-third of all Americans over 45 and two-thirds of those over 60 (more women than men) have diverticula.

The frequency of normal bowel movements varies from three times a day to three times a week. Not everybody has a bowel movement every day, or needs to. However, any change in the frequency of bowel movements may signal an underlying medical condition.

Prevention and Treatment

- Increase the fiber in your diet to 25 to 50 grams per day.
- Increase the amount of fluids you drink to one or two quarts a day or more.
- Do at least 30 minutes of vigorous exercise each day.
- Avoid foods with small seeds or sharp particles (such as nuts) if you have diverticulosis.
- Never take laxatives for more than seven consecutive days without consulting a doctor.
- Don't be surprised that you have constipation if you take antacids, diuretics, antidepressants, or high blood pressure medication regularly.

CASE HISTORY: Eleanor James

As a child, Mrs. James had established the habit of going to the bathroom every day at lunch. When she became a busy secretary, she found that it was not always convenient to do so, and she often ignored her urge to go to the bathroom at noon.

Eventually the urge stopped, and she found herself developing constipation. She tried taking a laxative to relieve the pain that occurred when she moved her bowels, and found that when she took the laxative, she had a painless, if somewhat watery, bowel movement.

After one of these watery movements, she would not have another bowel movement for a day or two. This convinced her that constipation had returned, so she would take another dose of laxative. In time, she found that she could only have a bowel movement when she took laxatives.

After nearly a year of this cycle, she complained to her doctor that she felt weak and tired. He found that her blood was low in potassium and that she was dehydrated. After questioning her about her toilet habits, he advised her never to put off going to the bathroom when she had the urge to do so.

When the urge is not heeded, he told her, it will subside temporarily. If the urge is repeatedly ignored, it will stop. When that happens, the feces harden and accumulate in the colon and rectum, and constipation results.

He also explained that the use of laxatives can actually create a constipation problem or make an existing one worse. Laxatives speed up the movement of waste through the colon and disrupt the body's normal process of eliminating waste. The pace of the waste's movement may be speeded up, and products that would normally take twenty-four to thirty-six hours to eliminate will be rushed through.

This means that although there is no need to have a bowel movement for a day or two, the laxatives deceive you into thinking that you are constipated again, and so you take another dose of laxative. In time, your body becomes "hooked" on laxatives, and your intestinal muscles weaken, impairing your natural ability to push waste along the colon and out of the body.

Mrs. James's physician advised her to get a half hour of exercise every day, to drink a quart of fluids daily, and to have bran cereal or a bran muffin for breakfast each day.

After a week following his advice, she felt much better; after a month she was back to her normal bathroom habits.

Dietary and Life-style Recommendations

Increase the Fiber in Your Diet to 25 to 50 Grams per Day

Lack of sufficient dietary fiber may be the greatest single culprit in causing constipation. Fiber is the leftover material that remains in the large intestine after food is digested. This indigestible matter is derived from plant foods like vegetables, fruits, and whole grains. As it moves through the digestive system, fiber absorbs water like a sponge, adding bulk to the stool and easing its passage through the colon.

Bran and other cereal fibers are the best in overcoming constipation, but fruit and vegetables also have some effect. Fruit and vegetables stimulate intestinal bacteria to proliferate, which adds weight to the stool. Fiber pills containing cellulose have minimal effect as a stool softener, and are a waste of money.

Strategy The average American eats only 10 to 20 grams of fiber a day instead of the ideal 25 to 50. To boost the amount of fiber you eat, eat more of the foods rich in fiber that are listed in the table on page 303. But remember, for fiber to be effective, it must be accompanied by plenty of fluids. For example, bran that contains two to four grams of fiber per rounded teaspoon should be taken with at least six ounces of fluid per teaspoon of bran.

Patients with diverticulosis should gradually increase the fiber in their diets. At first, this treatment can cause bloating, flatulence, and sometimes heartburn. These symptoms, however, soon will pass. The high-fiber diet increases the fecal mass, which physically prevents the walls of the intestine from contacting each other and causing excessive intra-intestinal pressure, which causes diverticulosis. The fiber also helps to shrink the pockets.

Patients with diverticulitis should reduce their fiber intake because the fiber may make the inflammation worse. By eating a bland diet low in spice and fiber, you avoid the laxative effect of the fiber and allow complete rest of the bowel until it heals.

Increase Your Fluid Intake

Drinking plenty of fluids helps to soften the stool and make the work of the colon easier. Insufficient liquid leads to hard, dry stools, which can lead in turn to the discomforts of constipation.

Strategy   Consume between one and two quarts of liquid per day.

Get at Least 30 Minutes of Vigorous Exercise Daily

Another cause of constipation is a lack of physical exercise, which encourages flabby muscles in the intestine and slows the propulsive effect.

Strategy   These muscles can be improved by any activity that increases the muscle tone of the entire body, such as calisthenics or aerobics. But you don't have to embark on an extensive exercise program to improve the condition. Even making a habit of walking upstairs instead of always taking the elevator can help. A brisk, 30-minute walk each day may well provide sufficient exercise for the colon.

Avoid Foods with Small Seeds or Sharp Particles if You Have Diverticulosis

These can become lodged in the diverticula and make the condition worse.

Strategy   Avoid berries, popcorn, nuts, figs, raisins, strawberries, tomatoes, baked goods containing cracked wheat, poppy, sesame, or caraway seeds, and foods that produce intestinal gas (e.g., beans, cabbage, spinach, or carbonated drinks).

Limit Your Use of Laxatives

Laxatives are habit-forming and lead to a loss of nutrients, including vitamins A, D, E, and K, as well as sodium, potassium, and water. This loss occurs because the laxatives decrease absorption by passing food too quickly through the intestines for proper digestion. Laxatives also tend to make the muscles in the intestine flabby and out of shape, which exacerbates a constipation problem.

If you feel you need to take laxatives for longer than a seven-day period, seek the advice of your doctor, as there may be a serious medical condition, such as tumors or *irritable bowel syndrome* (characterized by bouts of constipation, diarrhea, and flatulence, and thought to be due to stress; see chapter 33) causing the problem.

Strategy The most acceptable natural laxative is prunes. Eating prunes or drinking prune juice at night will ensure defecation in the morning for most people. Constipation may sometimes also be relieved by adding fat to the diet—like a little extra salad dressing or an avocado. Coffee is also a good laxative, with or without caffeine.

Other Advice

Some medications, including antacids, diuretics, antidepressants, and *antihypertensives* (high blood pressure pills) tend to cause constipation, as do calcium and iron supplements. If you experience constipation as a side effect of these drugs, seek the advice of your physician.

Iron-fortified cereals and formulas can cause constipation in an infant. Never try to treat this yourself, but ask your pediatrician.

If you would like further information about constipation, write to the National Digestive Diseases Education and Information Clearinghouse, Suite 600, 1555 Wilson Boulevard, Rosslyn, Virginia 22209, phone (703) 522-0870.

15
Crohn's Disease

Crohn's disease is a chronic intestinal inflammation. It is also known as *regional enteritis* or *ileitis* when it attacks just the lower section of the small intestine. Its causes are unknown, but it usually strikes during adolescence or during the early twenties, virtually always before the age of 40. (See also discussion of colitis, chapter 12.)

The lower part of the small intestine is most frequently diseased, but any part of the digestive system may be attacked. The disease affects short segments of the intestine, in which the wall of the intestine thickens and the opening narrows, sometimes completely closing. The lining of the intestine becomes ulcerated and the underlying lymph glands enlarged.

Crohn's disease is usually progressive and chronic, with attacks occurring every few years to every few months throughout life. However, in some cases it may occur only once or twice and never return. This disease can be life-threatening.

Warning Signs

- Intermittent stomachache with diarrhea
- Fever
- Anemia and weight loss
- Fresh blood in the stools or black, tarry stools
- Lack of appetite
- Intermittent sharp pain in the lower right side of the abdomen resembling appendicitis, with associated constipation, vomiting, and abdominal distention

- Skin rashes
- Less common symptoms are pinkeye, arthritis-like joint pain, and kidney stones or gallstones
- In children, a general failure to grow and thrive

Epidemiological Data

Thirty-five percent of people suffering from Crohn's disease have what is called *ileitis*, which is an infection of the *ileum*, or lower section of the small intestine alone. Forty-five percent have both an infected ileum and an infected colon *(ileocolitis)*, while 20 percent have the infection only in the colon *(granulomatous colitis)*. In a number of cases, the entire small intestine is affected *(jejunoileitis)*, while some patients also have stomach and duodenum involvement.

The disease affects roughly equal numbers of men and women, but is more common in Jews than in other population groups. It also tends to run in families.

It is estimated that between one and two million Americans suffer from Crohn's disease.

Prevention and Treatment

- Take supplements of iron, folic acid, vitamin B_{12}, and calcium.
- Consume a high-fiber diet between attacks.
- Consume a low-fiber and high-protein diet during an attack, and a low-fat diet when fat malabsorption is present.
- Reduce milk intake and avoid seasonings and any other foods that are not well tolerated.
- Consume foods high in potassium during periods of diarrhea, and drink eight glasses or more of fluids per day.
- Avoid stressful situations.

CASE HISTORY: Bernard Goldberg

Bernard was a twenty-four-year-old graduate student who had lately been experiencing arthritis-like pain in his joints and intermittent stomach pain. He also had had chronic diarrhea for some time. But it was the weight loss that had worried him the most and brought him to his doctor's office.

His doctor gave him a thorough physical examination. He observed that the ends of Bernard's fingers and toes were *clubbing*, a condition in which the nails curve sideways and lengthwise, and the flesh becomes enlarged so that the fingers appear like clubs. The doctor also found that Bernard had a low-grade fever and that his lower right abdomen was tender. The doctor was fairly confident of his diagnosis, but he sent Bernard off to a gastroenterologist to be sure.

The specialist conducted a series of tests, including a barium X-ray of the intestine. He concurred with the general practitioner's diagnosis: Bernard had Crohn's disease.

The doctor prescribed *sulfasalazine*, an antibiotic, to treat the bacterial infection in the intestine. He also gave Bernard steroids to suppress his other intestinal symptoms. Nutrient supplements were also part of the plan, and Bernard was instructed to follow a special diet.

Despite the treatment program, the attacks increased in frequency over the next few years, with the pain and discomfort striking every two or three months. Ultimately, as happens in roughly three out of four cases of Crohn's disease, it became necessary to remove surgically the infected section of Bernard's small intestine.

Following surgery, the frequency of the attacks lessened. However, they still do occur. Bernard is careful of his diet and has evolved as pressure-free a life-style as possible. But he and his gastroenterologist are ever on guard for the next attack.

Dietary and Life-style Recommendations

Take Supplements of Iron, Folic Acid, Vitamin B$_{12}$, and Calcium

Strategy   To safeguard against a deficiency of iron, folic acid, vitamin B$_{12}$, and calcium, Crohn's sufferers should take daily supplements. These should include 400 micrograms of folic acid, 6 micrograms of B$_{12}$, and 1,000 milligrams (one gram) of calcium (or 2½ grams of calcium carbonate).

If an iron deficiency occurs as a result of internal bleeding (which shows up as bloody or black, sticky stools), an iron supplement will be necessary. However, such supplements should be taken only on the advice of your physician, because of the potentially serious problems attendant on taking too much iron.

Consume a Low-Fiber Diet During Attacks and a High-Fiber Diet Between Attacks

In the early stages of the disease, a high-fiber diet is advised, as it may help to slow down the rate of deterioration of the intestine. However, during a flare-up of the disease, a low-fiber diet should be followed to lessen mechanical irritation and promote rest in the intestine.

Strategy Consult the table on page 303 for foods high in dietary fiber, and add and remove them from your dietary regimen as appropriate.

Eat a Low-Fat Diet When Fat Malabsorption Occurs

Greasy, smelly diarrhea is a symptom of fat malabsorption, which means your body is not absorbing the fat you eat, but is passing it directly out of your body.

Strategy Reduce your fat consumption to try to limit the extent of the diarrhea. Cut down on the high-fat foods listed in the tables on pages 304 and 306.

Drink Less Milk and Reduce Intake of Other Poorly Tolerated Foods

Many people with Crohn's disease have difficulty in digesting milk and dairy products.

Strategy If this is true in your case, eliminate such products from the diet as they will only exacerbate the symptoms of the disease by irritating the intestine. Highly seasoned foods will also tend to cause internal irritation and should be avoided.

Follow a High-Protein Diet

Foods rich in protein speed up the healing process and should be well represented in the diet of a patient suffering from a Crohn's episode.

Strategy Include at least three to four portions a day of protein in your dietary regimen. (See table on page 313 for high-protein foods.)

During Episodes of Diarrhea, Eat Foods High in Potassium

Chronic diarrhea leads to the loss of potassium, which can lead to heart *arrhythmia* (irregular heartbeat) and result in death.

Strategy To prevent this, eat plenty of foods rich in potassium (see page 313 for table of foods containing potassium). However, do not take potassium supplements unless advised to do so by your physician, as too much potassium will have the same effect as too little.

Diarrhea can also lead to dehydration, so be sure to drink at least eight glasses of water or other fluids per day while the diarrhea persists.

Other Advice

Stress seems to be a major factor in the development and progression of Crohn's disease. Try to avoid stressful situations and to develop strategies to help you deal with such situations. See Appendix 3 for suggestions on how to limit stress.

Certain medications taken to treat Crohn's disease may interact with the foods you eat. If you are taking *Azulfidine* (*sulfasalazine* is the drug's generic name), make sure that you drink at least two quarts of fluids a day and take a 400-microgram supplement of folic acid. Because the drug is also a gastric irritant, you should take it with meals.

If your doctor prescribes corticosteroids, limit your sodium intake to 2,000 milligrams (two grams) a day (see table of foods high in sodium on page 315).

If you would like further information about Crohn's disease and other gastrointestinal problems, contact the National Digestive Disease Education and Information Clearinghouse, 1555 Wilson Boulevard, Suite 600, Rosslyn, Virginia 22209, phone (301) 496-9707. You might also contact the National Foundation for Ileitis and Colitis, Inc., 295 Madison Avenue, New York, New York 10017, phone (212) 685-3440.

16
Dental Decay

Bacteria in the mouth adhere to the teeth in a gelatinlike mat referred to by dentists as *bacterial plaque*. Plaque, which contains hundreds of millions of bacteria, uses sugar as its main source of energy. One by-product of the digestion of sugar by bacteria is the production of acid, which, over a period of time, erodes the teeth to cause cavities.

Warning Signs

- White or brown spots on the teeth that are visible underneath the plaque when your dentist cleans the teeth
- Toothache

Epidemiological Data

Fluoridating the water supply has reduced the number of cavities in American children by at least 60 percent. Over 100 million Americans drink fluoridated water.

Americans on average consume 128 pounds of sugar per year; 95 pounds are in the form of sucrose (table sugar).

Some people have a genetically determined resistance to the bacteria that cause cavities.

Prevention and Treatment

- Get plenty of calcium, phosphorus, protein, and fluoride in your diet.

- Be sure your diet also contains ample vitamin A, B-complex, C, and D vitamins.
- Cut down on sugary foods; when you do eat them, consume them with meals rather than between, and switch to fibrous foods for your between-meal snacks.
- Brush and floss your teeth after eating between-meal snacks, and use a straw when drinking sugary drinks.
- During pregnancy, be sure that you get all the nutrients needed for optimal development of your child's teeth.

CASE HISTORY: Bob Franklin, Jr.

Baby Bob liked orange juice from the first time he tasted it. When he got upset, he could always be pacified with a bottle of orange juice.

His parents found that the remedy was particularly helpful at nap time. If Bob was put to bed with a bottle of juice, he often would go to sleep quietly and quickly. And when he began to teethe, the trick seemed especially helpful.

However, before very long he began to cry every time he was given anything hot or cold to eat. A visit to the doctor revealed that the front teeth in his lower jaw had several cavities. Bob had nursing-bottle syndrome, caused when the sugar in the orange juice provided an optimal breeding ground for bacteria in his mouth.

The doctor told Bob's mother not to allow him to use a bottle of orange juice or any sweet solution (including milk and formula) as a pacifier. It was fine to feed him those foods, the doctor told her, but she should make sure he finished them before going to sleep.

Dietary and Life-style Recommendations

Eat Plenty of Calcium, Phosphorus, and Vitamin D

Calcium, phosphorus, and vitamin D work together during the formation and calcification or hardening of the teeth.

Strategy Good sources of calcium include milk, cheese, yogurt, green leafy vegetables (like spinach), and canned salmon and sardines eaten with the bones. Phosphorus is found in many foods, including meats and cereals, and is rarely deficient in the diet. Vitamin D is found in all kinds of fatty fish, fish liver oil, fortified dairy products, and liver. (See tables on pages 301, 312, and 322 for other specific foods containing these nutrients.)

Eat Plenty of Vitamins A, B-Complex, and C

Vitamin A is essential for the formation of enamel, which is the hard material covering the crown of the tooth. Vitamin C is also needed for proper function and development of enamel, as well as to keep the gums healthy. The B-complex vitamins help to maintain and form the tissues in the mouth, and seem to facilitate the repair and growth of the tissues that make up the gums.

Strategy The best sources of vitamin A are broccoli, cantaloupe, carrots, liver, peaches, potato, pumpkin, squash, and fortified margarine and milk; the B-complex vitamins are found in liver, whole grains, wheat germ, and dairy products. Good sources of vitamin C include broccoli, citrus fruits, berries, Brussels sprouts, papaya, green peppers, tomatoes, and potatoes (see pages 307–308 and 318–321).

Be Sure to Eat Ample Protein

Protein is needed for the manufacture of enamel and *dentin*, which is the softer layer beneath the enamel.

Strategy The best sources of protein are meat, poultry, fish, dairy products, soy products, and peanuts and other nuts and seeds.

Get Plenty of Fluoride in Your Diet

The most important factor that affects the resistance of a tooth to attack by the acids produced by bacterial plaque is a proper level of fluoride during tooth development. About half the population gets this in their drinking water, which contains one part per million (ppm) of fluoride. The other half, who live where there is little or no fluoride in the water, should give fluoride supplements to their children until all their teeth (except for wisdom teeth) have emerged into the mouth.

Fluoride prevents cavities by becoming incorporated into the structure of the teeth as they form. The mineral makes the teeth stronger and more resistant to decay. In addition, fluoride toothpastes and rinses strengthen the surface of teeth and may prevent the growth of bacteria that cause cavities. Weekly fluoride rinses have been shown to decrease decay by 20 to 40 percent in school children.

Strategy You can find out from your local board of health what the level of fluoride in your water supply is. If it is below .7 ppm, ask your dentist or doctor to prescribe fluoride drops or tablets, or a vitamin-fluoride combination. Fluoride supplements should be chewed or sucked before swallowing by children who are old enough to do so.

The American Dental Association suggests that children living in areas with less than a .7 ppm of fluoride in the water be given fluoride supplements from birth to age 13. Before using the over-the-counter fluoride supplements, check with your dentist.

The American Academy of Pediatrics suggests starting formula-fed infants on fluoride shortly after birth if they live in unfluoridated areas. Also, if you live in a fluoridated area but give your baby ready-to-use formula that does not require adding water, your baby may not be getting enough fluoride, because formulas do not contain fluoride.

Check with your doctor or dentist when in doubt. Breast-fed babies should get a one-quarter-milligram daily supplement of fluoride even if the community's water is fluoridated, because babies drink little or no water and breast milk contains little fluoride, no matter how much water a mother drinks.

The proper dosage of fluoride is important. With too high a dose, the teeth will develop white spots or discolorations called *fluorosis*. There need be no concern, as there are no side effects to the proper use of fluoride, and no effects other than fluorosis when levels of fluoride become elevated. It does not adversely affect the maternal milk supply, cause Down's syndrome in children (a genetic abnormality formerly called *mongolism*), or contribute to risk of heart disease or cancer as some health faddists claim.

To prevent fluorosis, a few safety precautions should be followed. Keep supplemented toothpaste, supplements, and rinses out of the reach of small children. Advise children not to swallow fluoridated toothpaste and rinses. Children under five should not use fluoride rinses. Use a small amount of toothpaste in children under six (about the size of a pea). Parents should always supervise brushing.

A combination of dietary fluoride and topical fluoride can reduce cavities to zero. Good oral hygiene will add an additional margin of safety.

Limit Consumption of Sugary Foods

Although sucrose, or white table sugar, is the biggest culprit in causing tooth decay, the other sugars, such as glucose and fructose, are not much better. Bacteria in the mouth ferment these substances (that is, they use them for energy) and form the acid that eats into the teeth. Sugars are now commonly added to so many foods that it is sometimes difficult to identify potential cavity-makers. Here are some examples of foods that contain both natural and added cavity-causing sugars:

Kind of Sugar	Natural Sources
SUCROSE	Constitutes a large percentage of the total carbohydrates in sugar cane, sugar beets, maple syrup, molasses, fruits, soft drinks, pastries, candies, chewing gums, and desserts; there is a moderate amount of sucrose in vegetables and ready-to-eat cereals.
GLUCOSE	Found in moderate amounts in honey, corn syrup, and table syrup (pancake syrup); in smaller amounts, it is to be found in fruits and vegetables and in the form of starch in grains, legumes, and tubers.
FRUCTOSE	Found in large quantities in honey and in moderate amounts in fruits, vegetables, table syrup, and candies.
LACTOSE	Found in milk.

Here is a list of substances recommended as sweeteners because they cannot be used by cavity-causing bacteria:

Sweetener	Natural Sources	Products Used In
XYLITOL	Many plants	Chewing gums
SORBITOL	Fruits and vegetables; commercially produced from sugar	Dietetic foods, chewing gums, mints, pharmaceuticals
MANNITOL	Manna ash tree, seaweed, commercially produced from sugar	Chewing gums, dietetic products
SACCHARIN	Commercially produced from coal tar	Soft drinks, toothpaste, dietetic products, pharmaceuticals
ASPARTAME	Made from aspartic acid and phenylalanine, two amino acids	Soft drinks, processed foods

With the exceptions of saccharin and aspartame, these substances are very slowly absorbed in the digestive system, and when eaten in large amounts can cause diarrhea. As a result, it is best to use them sparingly.

The cancer-causing potential of saccharin limits its use as a large-scale sugar substitute (in fact, large amounts have been shown to cause bladder cancer). The use of aspartame also has its limitations because of its behavioral effects (it is suspected of causing depression) and because it has a limited shelf life (it loses its sweet taste over time). In addition, high temperatures cause aspartame to break down, limiting its usefulness in cooking.

Sucrose (table sugar) has the most important role of all carbohydrates in the diet because of the unique way it is used by a specific strain of bacteria found in the mouth called *Streptococcus mutans*. By splitting the sucrose molecule in half, the bacteria is able to make its own energy. That energy is then used to make a new sugar that can be used for further energy later, when the sucrose is used up. This sugar is also broken down to produce acid, even when the mouth is free of cavity-causing foods. In fact, for 30 minutes after sugary food is eaten, the sugar made by the bacteria is incorporated into the plaque for that later use.

There is, however, no direct relationship between the amount of sugar in a food and the extent of cavities resulting from eating it. In other words, it does not follow that food made just from sugar will necessarily be more harmful than an item containing only half as much sugar. Not all sugar-rich foods are equally destructive. Many factors come into play.

How quickly a food leaves the mouth is a critical factor in determining the destructive potential of a given food. Sticky foods such as taffy or dried fruit will remain on the surface of the tooth longer and provide food to feed the bacteria over an extended period of time. Since honey is seen as a "natural" sugar, it is preferred by many people to refined sugar, yet the fact is that honey is as bad as, or worse than, other sugars for teeth because it coats the teeth. Liquids, on the other hand, tend to pass through the mouth quickly and cause less destruction.

Foods that contain small particles like seeds can lodge between the teeth and encourage acid production.

Luckily, some foods seem to have inherent protective properties. Rice hulls have an unidentified substance that acts as an anticavity agent. Phosphorus in foods also protects the teeth (see table of phosphorus-rich foods, page 312). Some foods in combination—such as alkaline and acidic foods—neutralize the acids in the mouth.

Strategy Limit the sugary foods eaten between meals. Brush and floss the teeth after meals.

Sugary Foods Should Be Consumed with Rather than Between Meals

When sugary foods are eaten with meals, rather than as snacks, the mechanical action of chewing meats and vegetables and so on helps to clean the teeth of sticky foodstuffs. Liquids drunk with meals also help to wash away sticky carbohydrates.

Strategy The best snack foods are fibrous foods, such as raw fruits and vegetables. These are quickly cleared from the mouth and stimulate the flow of saliva as they are chewed, which helps to rinse sugar-containing particles from the teeth. For this reason, the sugar in raw fruit is less cavity-promoting than that in other sweet foods. When salivation is suppressed, such as during sleep or when a person is on certain drugs, cavities will become more prevalent.

If You Snack on Sugary Food Between Meals, Brush and Floss Afterward

Your first line of defense is avoiding sugary foods between meals. However, if you consume such foods at other than mealtimes, you should use the following strategy.

Strategy If you cannot resist sweet snacks between meals, try to brush and floss when you have finished (it is a good idea to brush and floss after meals, too). If this is not possible, water is a useful rinse for clearing the mouth, which makes it an excellent between-meals beverage. If you're a soft-drink or fruit-juice fan, the use of a straw will reduce the contact between the sweet beverage and your teeth.

When you are awake, you swallow 1,000 to 2,000 times a day, constantly washing away oral bacteria. During sleep, however, you may swallow as few as 20 times a night. Consequently, brushing immediately before bed is important for the removal of bacteria from your teeth.

Make Sure You Get All the Nutrients Needed for Tooth Building During Pregnancy

The major impact of food and water on teeth occurs during development, well before they emerge though the gums into the mouth. For the baby teeth, this occurs by the fourth month of pregnancy. By birth, calcification of the primary teeth is well advanced, and the first permanent molar has begun to calcify.

Defects in tooth structure can be caused by deficiencies of vitamins A, C, or D, or by severe protein deficiency during pregnancy or early childhood.

Fluoride supplements are of no value to the unborn child of a pregnant woman, or to the infant child of a nursing mother. Fluoride does not cross the placenta from the mother to the fetus, nor is the fluoride level of mother's milk affected by the amount of fluoride she consumes.

Strategy An adequate intake of calcium, phosphorus, and vitamins A, C, and D and protein (see table on page 324 for Recommended Dietary Allowances) is necessary for the pregnant woman to ensure adequate calcification and tooth development in her baby.

Other Advice

Chocolate has been shown to have decay-inhibiting properties due to the fat in cocoa, which forms a coating over the tooth that protects it from the action of the bacteria. Very acidic foods and beverages will eat away at the tooth enamel and cause cavities. Examples of acidic foods are soft drinks containing phosphoric acid, and lemons.

If you would like further information about dental care, write to the American Dental Association, 211 East Chicago Avenue, Chicago, Illinois 60611, phone (312) 440-2500.

17
Depression

There are two popularly held explanations for the feelings of sadness, withdrawal, or lethargy characteristic of *depression*. Both explanations have to do with the levels of *neurotransmitters* or chemical messengers in the brain. One theory attributes depression to a low level of one such messenger, called *serotonin*, and the other to a low level of another, called *norepinephrine*. Almost all the drugs psychiatrists use to treat depression increase the levels of one or both of these chemicals.

Deficiencies of vitamins B_1, B_6, C, and A, folic acid, niacin, copper, magnesium, and iron can all cause depression by affecting serotonin and norepinephrine metabolism. Brain levels of norepinephrine can be raised by taking supplements of *tyrosine* and *phenylalanine*, since they are converted into norepinephrine in the brain. The same is true of *tryptophan*, which makes serotonin and so can raise its brain levels when you get enough of it into your body. Both tyrosine and tryptophan have been shown to be useful in the treatment of unipolar depression, a condition that causes the patient to swing from a normal, well-adjusted mood to a period of withdrawal, sadness, and lethargy. However, these substances are of no value in treating *bipolar depression*, in which mood swings range from irrational elation to total depression.

Warning Signs

• An outlook that seems always to perceive the negative
• Low self-esteem; an inability to make oneself feel better no matter what one does, and a feeling that there's nothing that will improve

the situation; decreased interest in sex, food, work, entertainment, and so on

- Difficulty in sleeping, particularly when you go to sleep easily but awaken a few hours later and find it impossible to get back to sleep
- Changes in appetite, either increased or decreased
- Lethargy and slowness of speech
- Thoughts of suicide

Epidemiological Data

Thirty percent of the population will develop depression during their lifetime; at any given moment, 15 percent of the population is depressed, making it the nation's number-one mental health problem.

Only one-fifth of depressed people consult a physician.

Depression is two to four times as common in women as in men.

Prevention and Treatment

- Make sure you have a diet that provides adequate amounts of calcium and protein.
- Watch out for low levels of vitamins B_1, B_6, B_{12}, C, and A, folic acid, niacin, copper, magnesium, and iron.
- If you crave carbohydrates, go on a high-carbohydrate diet, supplemented with 500 to 1,000 milligrams of *L-tryptophan*, taken three times a day with juice.
- If you are lethargic and depressed, and do not crave carbohydrates, take a gram of tyrosine three times a day with meals.
- If you are taking *monoamine oxidase inhibitors (MAO inhibitors)*, be sure to consume a tyramine-restricted diet.
- If you are on antidepressants, watch your weight carefully.

CASE HISTORY: Lynn Trewin

Lynn had always been a happy sort of teenager, but during the last six months she seemed to have changed completely. In fact, since her seventeenth birthday she had gradually drifted away from most of her friends. She had stopped caring about her looks, lost interest in everybody and everything, and withdrawn into herself. She had also lost her appetite and found it difficult to sleep. Her schoolwork, too, suddenly seemed unimportant to her, and her performance in school fell off precipitously. Her mother noticed that Lynn had gained a good deal of weight, and that she would binge on cakes, cookies, and chocolate at almost any time of day.

Lynn's mother had confided her concern about her daughter to a friend, and the friend had told her that she had been given a tryptophan supplement when she felt depressed and that it had worked well.

Lynn went to a psychiatrist specializing in nutritional therapies. He ruled out physical or metabolic causes for her depression, such as *hypoglycemia* (see chapter 31), and he agreed that tryptophan might help. Lynn started taking one gram of tryptophan three times a day. After four weeks, she said she began to feel much better.

Within a year, she was able to stop taking the tryptophan and is once again a sociable young woman, as well as a successful student looking forward to college.

Dietary and Life-style Recommendations

Consume Adequate Amounts of Calcium and Protein

During stressful times, body protein is broken down to provide the body with energy. Over an extended period, this can lead to a loss of muscle. Another nutrient lost from the body during stress is calcium. This can be extremely serious, as it weakens the bones and increases the risk of *osteoporosis* (see chapter 39).

Strategy To safeguard your body's supply of these nutrients without compromising its health, make sure that you get plenty of foods containing these nutrients (see tables on pages 301 and 313 for foods high in calcium and protein). Ideally, you should eat two portions of protein-rich foods and 1,000 milligrams (one gram) of calcium daily. Getting this much dietary calcium from foods is difficult, however, so an acceptable alternative is to take a calcium supplement. Five hundred milligrams of calcium should be taken twice daily in the form of 1,250 milligrams of calcium carbonate, at midmorning and just before bedtime.

Watch Out for Low Levels of Vitamins A, B_1, B_6, B_{12}, and C and Folic Acid, Niacin, Copper, Magnesium, and Iron

Deficiencies of any of these nutrients can result in depression. Consult the tables in Appendix 1 that list foods rich in these nutrients to get some idea as to whether you are likely to have a depression related to specific nutrient deficiencies.

Strategy To be on the safe side, anybody with depression should be taking a one-a-day vitamin supplement containing the Recommended Dietary Allowances of vitamins and minerals. The B vitamins are often the problem, and a one-a-day supplement will correct any B-complex deficiency.

If You Are a Carbohydrate Craver and Feel Depressed, Consume a High-Carbohydrate Diet and Take an L-Tryptophan Supplement

Tryptophan is useful in treating depression when it is taken by someone who is experiencing carbohydrate craving. It is believed that such cravings are caused by inadequate levels of serotonin in the brain. A carbohydrate-rich, low-protein meal increases brain serotonin levels because such a meal reduces the blood levels of most amino acids (the building blocks of protein), but not of tryptophan. Tryptophan competes with many of the other amino acids for a place on the transport mechanism that gives entry into the brain. After a high-carbohydrate meal, tryptophan has less competition and so brain levels rise. This serves to increase brain serotonin levels as well.

Though the increases produced by eating a high-carbohydrate meal only are small, taking a tryptophan supplement greatly increases relative brain levels. Protein-rich meals have, of course, the opposite effect, decreasing both tryptophan and serotonin levels.

Strategy If you are suffering from depression and also find yourself craving carbohydrates, try eating a diet in which no more than 10 to 15 percent of your total calories come from protein sources (see tables on pages 313 and 301 for foods rich in protein and carbohydrates). If this doesn't seem to have much of an effect, a daily supplement of 1,000 to 3,000 milligrams of tryptophan per day might be the answer. It should be taken in three equal doses (for example, three doses of 800 milligrams each) and consumed after meals. The effects of tryptophan last only a few hours, and so repeated doses are necessary. Taking the supplement after meals will prevent the nausea some people experience as a side effect. Obviously, the lower the dosage the better, and so you should experiment within the dosage range (500 to 1,000 milligrams three times a day) in order to see at which level you get concrete results. Never take more than 3,000 milligrams (three grams) of tryptophan a day without a doctor's supervision.

If You Are Lethargic and Depressed and Do Not Crave Carbohydrates, Take One Gram of Tyrosine Three Times a Day

Tyrosine (along with phenylalanine) and tryptophan share the same carrier mechanism for entry into the brain. In the case of tyrosine, a meal rich in carbohydrates will depress brain levels and reduce the amount of norepinephrine made in the brain from tyrosine. A protein-rich meal, on the other hand, will elevate these levels.

Strategy   The changes produced by a high-protein diet are small, but tyrosine supplements can have significant effects. Initial tests using tyrosine to treat depressed patients have been encouraging. A higher-protein meal plan and/or one to three grams of tyrosine taken daily at spaced intervals may be the answer for many depressed people. Taking the tyrosine with meals avoids mild stomach upset (due to tyrosine's acidity). Never take more than three grams (3,000 milligrams) without the supervision of your doctor.

Obviously, there are two very different treatments advised here regarding depression. The tryptophan route appears to work in those people with depression coupled with carbohydrate cravings. Tyrosine also works on depression in other types of people, and can be effective in the treatment of lethargy (the lack of interest in doing anything) in people over the age of 40. If there is no clear-cut way of determining which route to take, experimenting for a month with one method and then a month with the other will clearly show the way.

If You Take an MAO Inhibitor, Consume a Tyramine-Restricted Diet

Toxic reactions to cheese and other tyramine-containing foods are likely to occur in patients taking antidepressants in the monoamine oxidase (MAO) inhibitor class. Attacks are characterized by transient high blood pressure, headaches, palpitations, nausea, and vomiting.

The severity of the attacks has been shown to have a relationship to the level of tyramine in particular foods. The ingested tyramine is usually converted in the liver to an inactive form through the action of monoamine oxidase (MAO). However, drugs in the MAO inhibitor class leave tyramine in its active form. As a result, the tyramine remains in the blood and can increase blood pressure to dangerous levels. Reactions usually occur within a half hour of the ingestion of the offending food or drink.

Other foods that contain *dopa* or *dopamine* have similar effects. Both tyramine and dopamine enter the general circulation and release norepinephrine from nerve endings in the body. This increases blood norepinephrine above normal levels, but since MAO inhibitors are being taken, it cannot be degraded by the body and so stays high enough to increase blood pressure. Other antidepressant drugs, such as amphetamines, also act as MAO inhibitors and, when combined with foods containing tyramine and dopamine, can precipitate severe or even lethal side effects.

Strategy   Foods containing tyramine and related substances must be restricted while you are being treated with MAO inhibitors. (See table on page 317 for foods high in tyramine.)

Raisins and avocados should also be avoided, because they contain dopamine, which has the same effect as tyramine.

Alcohol should not be consumed by people taking MAO inhibitors, as these drugs prevent the body from detoxifying it at the normal rate and the alcohol has a more pronounced effect, making one drunk more easily.

Since these drugs upset the digestive system, they should always be taken with food or milk.

If You Take Antidepressants, Watch Your Weight

It is likely that you will find that your appetite increases while you are taking antidepressants, with a resultant weight gain. If you do gain weight, you should make a special effort to cut back on your caloric intake.

Strategy If you have already gained weight, you should cut back on the carbohydrate component of your diet, remembering that a reasonable and moderate weight-reduction program should aim at a manageable loss of one to two pounds per week. Cutting back by 500 calories per day, for a weekly total of 3,500 calories, will result in a loss of one pound per week regardless of your present weight. Two eggs and a milk shake, one and one-half cups of tuna salad, four ounces of a roast, three frankfurters, two cups of ice cream, or two pieces of cheesecake represent approximately 500 calories each (see chapter 37).

Other Advice

There are many people who feel that controlling depression through natural dietary supplements and adjustments is far preferable to the use of antidepressant drugs, like the MAO inhibitors or tricyclic antidepressants.

However, in cases of massive, continuing depression, or true emotional imbalances that severely disrupt a person's life, a doctor's care and appropriate medication are advised. The simple dietary supplements discussed here are intended for people who are usually well balanced, and who suffer only rarely or occasionally from depression and/or lethargy. The emotionally ill, on the other hand, show dramatic changes in neurotransmitter levels that cannot be corrected solely by dietary supplements.

Coffee will not cure depression. It is a brain stimulant and will temporarily improve your energy level and concentration.

Although some unconventional therapists suggest that certain foods cause depression, this has yet to be proved. There is no harm in trying this approach, though it is unlikely that the majority of patients will benefit. In those cases where there is an apparent success, it also generally takes a long time to isolate the problem food, during which time the patient gets no relief.

If you would like further information about depression, contact one of these organizations: the American Mental Health Foundation, 2 East 86th Street, New York, New York 10028, phone (212) 737-9027; the National Association for Mental Health, 1800 North Kent Street, Arlington, Virginia 20006, phone (703) 528-6408; or the National Clearinghouse for Mental Health Information, Public Inquiries Section, Room 11A-21, 5600 Fishers Lane, Rockville, Maryland 20857, phone (301) 443-4513.

18
Diabetes

Diabetes is a disease in which insufficient amounts of the hormone *insulin* are made in the body to meet its needs. This hormone, which is produced in the pancreas, is needed in order for the tissues to take up glucose from the blood and use it as fuel. A person may be diabetic because (1) the pancreas is unable to make insulin or because (2) the tissues are not able to absorb glucose even in the presence of insulin.

In the first type, called *insulin-dependent diabetes*, the *beta cells* of the pancreas, which produce insulin, are destroyed. This type of diabetes is thought to result from a genetically determined susceptibility to a virus that invades the pancreas. There is no known dietary pattern that increases your chances of developing this type of diabetes.

The second type, called *non-insulin-dependent diabetes*, usually occurs in the sixth or seventh decade of life (fifties or sixties) and is not associated with any abnormality in the pancreas. Insulin is processed in normal amounts or even increased amounts, but the tissues of the body are resistant to its effects. This type of diabetes has a genetic basis and is more common in certain families than in others. However, it has a nutritional component.

Non-insulin-dependent diabetes is much more common in obese people than in lean people. Thus, to the extent that diet is involved in obesity, overeating is a contributing cause of the disease. Overeating heightens a person's risk of contracting diabetes because fat tissue increases the body's resistance to the action of insulin. For this reason, weight reduction alone may control this kind of diabetes.

Although nutrition plays only a limited role when it comes to the causes of diabetes, it plays a major role in the management of the disease. Treatment of any patient with diabetes, regardless of the

118

type, will have two major themes: control of the level of blood glucose and prevention of the serious complications of the disease, which are heart attack, stroke, gangrene, kidney disease, and blindness. Although insulin and other drug therapy may be of primary importance in treating people with diabetes, proper nutrition will make it easier to achieve these aims.

Warning Signs

• Any change in vision
• Obesity
• Slow healing of cuts and bruises
• Anxiety, sweating, and hunger three to four hours after a heavy meal
• Thirst accompanied by frequent urination
• Weight loss
• Easy tiring, weakness, irritability, and nausea
• Vaginal irritation
• Dry, itching skin, as well as frequent skin infections
• Tingling of the hands, feet, and legs

Epidemiological Data

About two people in every hundred have diabetes. There are an estimated 12 million diabetics in America; approximately 85 percent of them have non-insulin-dependent diabetes.

The prevalence of the disease increases with age, so that in the part of the population over 65 years of age, the prevalence is over 6 percent.

Diabetes tends to run in families.

Prevention and Treatment

• More and smaller meals are best, perhaps five or six planned "snack meals."
• Caloric intake should be aimed at achieving an ideal weight (in the insulin-dependent diabetic, this generally means gaining weight, but for the non-insulin-dependent diabetic it usually involves losing weight).
• Fat should be limited to 20 to 30 percent of total caloric consumption; saturated fat should supply 10 percent of the total calories, and polyunsaturated and mono-unsaturated fats (vegetable fat) 10 percent each.

- Protein should range from 12 to 24 percent of all calories, though this is a less critical consideration.
- Simple sugars should be kept to no more than 10 to 15 percent of all calories consumed, and only a small amount of this should come from refined sugars.
- The remainder of the calories (40 percent or more) should come from complex carbohydrates, usually starch.
- Sodium intake should be limited to no more than three grams (3,000 milligrams) per day.
- An adequate intake of fiber, chromium, and potassium is important.
- Get regular exercise.
- If you are taking *sulfonylureas (Orinase, Diabinese)*, avoid alcohol.
- Do not take large doses of vitamin C within 24 hours before testing your urine for sugar.

CASE HISTORY I: Jim Handly

Until the age of five, Jim was a perfectly normal, healthy child. Then he began to complain of being very thirsty, and became a frequent bed wetter. He also lost weight.

His family doctor ran some tests and shortly discovered that his blood glucose levels were very high and that he had glucose in his urine. Jim was diagnosed as having diabetes.

The doctor prescribed intravenous doses of insulin and a dietary regimen that emphasized complex carbohydrates and severely limited simple sugars. When, after two weeks, his doctor observed that Jim's pancreas was again producing adequate quantities of insulin, he discontinued the insulin shots.

For the next six months, Jim's treatment consisted only of dietary measures. However, Jim's original symptoms returned, and when new test results showed that his blood and urine glucose levels were again elevated, Jim's doctor put him on permanent insulin therapy. He is now sixteen, and continues to use insulin daily.

CASE HISTORY II: Ted Leveritt

Ted was a healthy (though overweight) thirty-nine-year-old, happily married, successful businessman. Work seemed to consume him; he got little exercise and ate too much, in part because of the pressures of his job.

He began to suffer spells of anxiety, sweating, and acute hunger three to four hours after heavy meals. He consulted his doctor about the problem, but tests revealed nothing except that he had a drop in his blood sugar levels several hours after eating. His doctor prescribed a diet consisting of six smaller meals daily, and the symptoms improved considerably.

When Ted was forty-three, his doctor found that his blood sugar was almost twice the normal levels. He had to get up in the night several times to urinate, but except that he weighed over 220 pounds, he was otherwise healthy.

His doctor prescribed a weight-reduction diet. Ted wasn't able to follow it, so six months later his doctor prescribed an oral drug, *tolbutamide*, which stimulates the pancreas to produce more insulin. For the next nine years the drug kept his blood sugar under control.

After that time it was no longer effective, and Ted's blood sugar increased. So Ted's doctor put him on insulin. Ted also complained of dizziness and headaches and problems with his vision, and his physician found that Ted's blood pressure was elevated and that there were scattered, tiny blood clots in the blood vessels in his eyes. He also had a slight heart abnormality.

Two years later, Ted's health took another turn for the worse. He experienced chest pain whenever he performed any strenuous physical exercise, for which his doctor prescribed nitroglycerin. In addition, Ted's insulin requirements ceased to be stable and vacillated to an alarming degree.

At age fifty-three, Ted had a heart attack. A brief stay in the hospital helped Ted to stabilize his insulin needs and enabled him to find the motivation to control his diet. Now, at sixty, he watches his diet carefully (under the supervision of his cardiologist and physician, he got down to 175 pounds) and is enjoying an active life.

Dietary and Life-style Recommendations

Eat More and Smaller Meals

In addition to *what* is eaten, *how often* meals are taken is extremely important, particularly for the insulin-dependent diabetic. Even though the modern insulin preparations can release insulin slowly from the injection site, injected insulin cannot mimic the immediate response that insulin secreted from the pancreas provides. Therefore, it is important to avoid periods of feast (when blood sugar may rise too high) or famine (when blood sugar may fall too low). There is some evidence to show that avoiding these wide swings in blood glucose levels can help avoid the complications associated with the kidneys and eyes.

Strategy Any diabetic requiring relatively large quantities of insulin for control should eat five or even six small meals during the day.

Caloric Intake Should Be Aimed at Achieving Ideal Weight

Women should estimate ideal body weight by allowing 100 pounds for the first 5 feet and 5 pounds for each additional inch over 5 feet. In men, 106 pounds should be allocated for the first 5 feet and 6 pounds for each additional inch. If you have a medium or heavy frame, add 5 to 10 pounds. Hence, a man with a medium frame who is 6 feet tall will have an ideal weight of approximately 185 pounds (106 + 72 + 7).

Now calculate the amount of energy you need per day on the basis of body weight and activity.

	Sedentary (calories per lb.)	Active (calories per lb.)	Very Active (calories per lb.)
Overweight	9–11	14	16
Normal	14	16	18
Underweight	16	18	20–23

Strategy To lose weight, reduce your calculated figure by 500 calories a day. For every 3,500 calories you cut from your diet, you will lose one pound. Hence, at 500 calories a day, you will lose one pound a week. This is a safe rate of loss for a diabetic. Many insulin-dependent diabetics are underweight and need to gain rather than lose weight. They need to add 500 calories a day to their requirement to gain a pound a week.

Limit Your Fat Intake to 20 to 30 Percent of Your Total Calorie Consumption

Diabetes is often associated with high levels of fats in the blood, which increases the risk of atherosclerosis. Atherosclerosis is responsible for all the complications of diabetes listed above. High blood fat levels can often be brought down by reducing the amount of total fat, saturated fat, and cholesterol in the diet (see chapter 6). Thus, the person suffering from either form of diabetes should consume a prudent diet that is lower in saturated fat and cholesterol and higher in polyunsaturated fat than the usual American diet. Lowering the percentage of total calories derived from fat will, of necessity, increase the percentage of calories derived from carbohydrates. Therefore, the best diet for a diabetic will be one that is *relatively* high in carbohydrates.

Your Protein Consumption Should Be in the Range of 12 to 24 Percent of Your Total Caloric Consumption

Ideally, you need between .6 and .7 grams of protein per pound of ideal body weight.

Strategy Consult the table on page 313 for protein-rich foods, and incorporate them into your diet.

Simple Sugars Should Be Limited to 10 to 15 Percent of All Calories Consumed

Simple sugars are absorbed very rapidly and will therefore raise blood sugar to very high levels before the insulin (which has been administered) can bring the levels back into the normal range. Of all the simple sugars, fructose is best (fructose is the natural sugar found in fruit). Although all sugars must be converted to glucose in the body, they raise blood sugar levels to different degrees. Sucrose (table sugar), which is one-half glucose to begin with, releases its glucose directly into the bloodstream. Fructose, when taken in the form of fruit or even directly, must be converted by the liver to glucose, a process that takes considerable time. Thus, fructose will produce a more gradual increase in blood glucose than will sucrose, and this is desirable in a diabetic.

The same is true of complex carbohydrates such as starch. They take some time to be broken down in the digestive tract, which results in fairly slow absorption and a gradual increase in blood glucose.

Strategy As small a percentage as possible of your sugar intake should be from refined sugars; the remainder should come from complex carbohydrates (usually starch).

Your diet should include 50 to 60 percent complex carbohydrates. (See page 301 for table of foods rich in simple and complex carbohydrates.)

Limit Your Intake of Sodium to Three Grams per Day

As discussed in chapter 6, a high-salt (sodium) intake is a major risk factor for atherosclerosis.

Strategy Avoid salty foods and refrain from adding salt to food. (See chapter 30 for guidelines for eliminating dietary salt.)

Ensure that You Have an Adequate Intake of Fiber, Chromium, and Potassium

High-fiber diets cause a slower and more sustained release of glucose from the gastrointestinal tract into the bloodstream, which will prevent wide swings in blood sugar that may occur when simple sugars are ingested in the absence of fiber. In addition, the amount of insulin necessary to control blood sugar is also often reduced by high-fiber diets.

Strategy   From a practical standpoint, this means that for the diabetic, sugars should be eaten in a form that is as close to the natural state as possible; an apple is better than apple sauce or apple juice. In addition, there is no reason why a person with diabetes should not increase the fiber content of his regular diet and even add fiber to the diet in the form of bran or raw vegetables (see table on page 303 for a list of high-fiber foods).

Chromium is required by insulin to help cells absorb glucose. Without adequate chromium, a person develops a "pseudo-diabetic state" with high blood glucose levels. Processed foods have much lower chromium contents than unprocessed foods, and overeating them can lead to a chromium deficiency. Chromium can be obtained from brewer's yeast or in fresh foods such as whole grains, peanuts, and organ meats. However, chromium deficiency does not cause diabetes, nor will chromium cure it. Never try to replace insulin with chromium if you are a diabetic. Without insulin, chromium can do nothing to aid glucose absorption.

Potassium is essential to the formation of insulin, and helps to counteract the tendency of dietary sodium to raise blood pressure. (See table of potassium-rich foods on page 313.)

Take Regular Exercise

Twenty minutes or more of vigorous daily exercise can reduce the amount of insulin required, because exercise makes the cells more susceptible to the action of insulin. In other words, less insulin is needed to enable the cells to absorb glucose.

If you are planning to start an exercise program, check with your doctor first. When you take part in physical activity, your body uses up more glucose than normal, and it can lead to abnormally low blood glucose levels. However, by advance planning you can cater to this increased demand. The basic rule is never skip meals or snacks. If you are going to take part in an endurance event, a complex source of carbohydrates may be necessary both before and during the event.

Strategy   Thirty minutes a day, three to four days a week, of an aerobic exercise like swimming, walking, ice skating, dancing, or bicycling is ideal.

Do Not Take Large Doses of Vitamin C Within 24 Hours Before Testing Your Urine for Sugar

If you have taken a large dose of vitamin C (over 100 milligrams) within the 24-hour period preceding your test, the results will give a false positive, indicating glucose in your urine.

Other Advice

If alcohol is drunk after *sulfonylurea* drugs (*Orinase* and *Diabinese*), it will cause symptoms such as severe headaches, flushing, nausea, vomiting, low blood pressure, weakness, vertigo, blurred vision, and possibly convulsions. Such a reaction will occur within five to ten minutes of drinking.

Keep in mind that any insulin-dependent diabetic should have a bedtime meal. The insulin-dependent child also requires midmorning and afternoon snacks.

If you would like additional information about diabetes, contact the American Diabetes Association, 2 Park Avenue, New York, New York 10016, phone (212) 683-7444; or the Joslin Diabetes Foundation, 1 Joslin Place, Boston, Massachusetts 02215, phone (617) 732-2400.

19
Diarrhea

When food moves too rapidly through the intestines for fluid to be absorbed from it, or if excess water is added from the cells lining the intestines, diarrhea results and bowel movements are more liquid and frequent than normal.

A number of factors can cause diarrhea, including stress; nervous tension; overeating; certain drugs; foods and spices that irritate the gastrointestinal tract; spoiled food; and bacterial infections. Usually, an acute bout of diarrhea lasts less than 24 hours.

Chronic diarrhea for periods lasting longer than 48 hours is much more serious and may indicate the presence of some serious medical condition. In such cases, help from a physician should be sought.

Warning Signs

• Severe stomach cramps

Epidemiological Data

In parts of the world where public sanitation is minimal, diarrhea is endemic and a common killer. In Latin America alone, an estimated 150,000 people die each year of an illness that causes diarrhea.

Normal frequency of bowel movements ranges from two to three times a day to two to three times a week.

Diarrhea and vomiting are the second most common disorders affecting people, after respiratory infections.

Prevention and Treatment

- Avoid carbonated beverages.
- Avoid coffee.
- Avoid large amounts of *sorbitol* and *mannitol*, which are used as sugar substitutes in dietetic foods, candy, and chewing gum.
- Drink clear liquids to prevent dehydration.
- As you begin to feel better, introduce apple sauce and bananas, followed by toast and bland foods.
- In infants, use 50-percent strength formula (formula diluted with water). Add 5 to 10 percent apple powder, banana flakes, or pectin agar to the formula.

CASE HISTORY: Jennifer Lane

Jennie's winter vacation was approaching, and she planned a trip to the warm Caribbean. She wanted to drop the eight or ten extra pounds she'd added over the holidays, so she decided to go on a diet.

To suppress her hunger, she bought lots of diet foods with sorbitol and mannitol in them, and drank seven or eight cups of coffee a day. Within forty-eight hours, she developed severe diarrhea.

She was careful to drink plenty of fluids, in particular flat ginger ale, which helped to settle her upset stomach. After twenty-four hours, the diarrhea had abated and she was able to start eating a more varied diet. She first ate a little fruit, and gradually added bland foods such as dry toast and a soft-boiled egg. Within a week, she had worked her diet back up to normal.

When she went back to her diet a week later, she approached it a little less aggressively, and tried to eat a little less of her usual foods. She lost the weight and the diarrhea did not recur.

Dietary and Life-style Recommendations

Avoid Carbonated Beverages

Carbonated beverages speed up the contractions of the muscles in the intestines, making food pass down the gastrointestinal tract more quickly.

Strategy Limit your consumption of carbonated beverages to flat ginger ale or cola to help relieve nausea.

Avoid Coffee

Both decaffeinated and regular coffee are natural laxatives.

Strategy   Avoid all coffee while suffering from diarrhea.

Avoid Dietetic Foods

Any foods containing sorbitol and mannitol, such as dietetic foods, candy, and chewing gum, speed up the motility of the gastrointestinal tract and are slow to be absorbed. Both make diarrhea worse as the unabsorbed sorbitol and mannitol remain in the intestine and draw more water into the stool.

Strategy   Do not consume dietetic foods during or immediately following an episode of diarrhea.

Gradually Introduce Other Foods

Certain substances can help make the stool firmer, including pectin, which is the chief ingredient in Kaopectate. Bland foods, too, are a good idea as you should avoid eating foods that irritate the intestine and exacerbate the diarrhea.

Strategy   Apples and bananas contain pectin. Incorporate apple sauce and bananas into your recovery diet as you feel better. Eat bland foods (see page 326 for table of bland foods).

Reduce Infant Formula Strength

If your baby has diarrhea, cut down the concentration of the formula you feed him or her to 50 percent of normal by diluting it with water, but first check with your pediatrician.

Strategy   Five to 10 percent apple powder, banana flakes, or pectin agar added to the formula will help thicken the stool. You may also try feeding the child apple sauce or banana once the baby is ready to eat solid foods.

Other Advice

If you would like additional information about diarrhea, contact the American Digestive Disease Society, Suite 217, 7720 Wisconsin Avenue, Bethesda, Maryland 20814, phone (301) 652-5524; or the National Digestive Disease Education and Information Clearinghouse, Suite 600, 1555 Wilson Boulevard, Rosslyn, Virginia 22209, phone (703) 522-0870.

20
Epilepsy

Epilepsy is a disorder of the nervous system that causes recurrent periods of loss of consciousness, convulsions, poor control of movement, and behavioral abnormalities. The seizures result from excessive electrical activity in the brain.

There are two basic types of seizures: generalized seizures that involve the whole brain from the moment they begin, and partial seizures that begin in a small area of the brain and may or may not spread to the rest of the brain.

Generalized seizures fall into two categories. The first are called *grand mal* seizures; they occur in adults and are by far the most common. Half of the time the episode is preceded by an experience called an *aura*. Auras take different forms: a fearful sensation, an unpleasant odor or taste, or a distortion in vision. Hallucinations also occur in the form of *déjà vu* phenomena, in which the sufferer has the feeling of having seen or experienced a situation before.

Once the grand mal seizure begins, consciousness is completely lost. The epileptic falls down stiffly, his eyes staring and open. After about a half-minute of stillness, the epileptic's limbs begin to jerk rhythmically. The epileptic may bite his tongue or urinate. This more violent portion of the episode may last for about two minutes, to be followed by a more relaxed state of unconsciousness which lasts for another minute or more. When the epileptic comes out of the seizure, he or she is confused and tired, and usually sleeps for one to three hours.

Petit mal or "absence" seizures constitute the second type of generalized seizure. These last merely a few seconds, during which time

129

there is a loss of consciousness. The epileptic stares straight ahead, and sometimes the eyelids or the face twitch rhythmically. Such episodes are most common in children of two years of age and older. Petit mal seizures almost never continue to occur beyond adolescence, but may be superseded by grand mal seizures.

Partial seizures may occur as temporary disturbances of consciousness. They begin with an aura, followed by *automatism*, a condition in which the epileptic carries out purposeless movements such as chewing, moving the hands in a rhythmic way, fidgeting, or repeatedly swallowing. Afterward the person is temporarily confused and remembers little of the episode.

Partial seizures may take another form, in which they begin in part of the body, such as the thumb, and spread out to involve other parts of the body. Partial paralysis of the affected limb may last up to three days.

Warning Signs

- Partial and generalized seizures often begin with an aura or with a jerking movement in one limb or part of a limb.
- Other observed symptoms include blank staring, angry verbal outbursts, lip-smacking, chewing, sudden headaches, and abdominal pains.

Epidemiological Data

Epilepsy develops in 1 to 2 percent of the population, with 75 percent of the cases arising before the age of 18. Heredity is believed to play a minor role in epilepsy, serving mainly to enhance (or diminish) a person's susceptibility to developing seizures. Although many people with epilepsy have close relatives with epilepsy, only about 2 to 5 percent of children of epileptics develop the condition.

Seizures usually begin between the ages of 2 and 14; in fact, 75 percent of cases arise before the age of 18. Young children may have as many as *several hundred* petit mal seizures a day.

No obvious causes can be found in three out of four adults who have seizures.

Prevention and Treatment

- Attacks may be triggered by high fevers (in children), television, disco strobe lights, stress, anxiety, fatigue, PMS, alcohol, or hypoglycemia (in diabetics).
- Water intoxication (consumption of too much water at one time) may bring on a seizure.

- Stimulants such as coffee, tea, cola, and other foods containing caffeine can bring on seizures.
- A diet rich in folic acid and vitamins B_{12}, K, B_6, and D is needed by epileptics, as their medication leads to deficiencies in one or more of these nutrients.
- Consider the use of a *ketogenic diet* if medication is not effective.

CASE HISTORY: Jean Fitzgerald

Jean was dancing—as she often did—in a Manhattan discotheque when she suddenly went into a convulsive seizure.

She was taken to the emergency room at a nearby hospital. Jean's boyfriend told her doctor that the episode had occurred when they began to dance under a strobe light.

The doctor took a full medical history. He also did a clinical examination to exclude possible causes of her loss of consciousness such as cardiovascular disease, hypoglycemia (low blood sugar), hypocalcemia (abnormally low blood calcium levels), kidney or liver disease, or drug poisoning. The next day, Jean was given a chest X-ray, a skull X-ray, and an EEG or electroencephalogram, which measures the electrical activity in the brain.

Everything seemed normal except her EEG. Jean remained under the doctor's care, consulting him at regular intervals. Six months later she had another fainting fit. Her doctor then did further tests to rule out brain tumors and other disorders. She had a CAT scan, an NMR brain scan, and her cerebrospinal fluid was also examined. All the tests were negative.

Several months afterward she had a third fainting fit. At that point Jean was given Dilantin, a prescription antiepileptic medication, to take daily. Now, three years later, she continues to take the drug, and has had no more episodes.

Dietary and Life-style Recommendations

Avoid Stimuli that May Trigger Attacks

Attacks may be triggered by high fevers (in children), or by television, disco strobe lights, stress, anxiety, fatigue, PMS, alcohol, or hypoglycemia (in diabetics).

Strategy If you are epileptic, you should sit at least ten feet back from the television and avoid frequenting places where there are flashing lights.

You should also be careful to manage the stress in your life. (See Appendix 3 for some strategies for stress management.) If you suffer from PMS, consult chapter 44 for suggestions on dealing with it.

Also, you may choose to consult your doctor about the possibility of taking hormone therapy (usually progesterone).

Avoid getting overtired. Avoid alcohol, as alcohol tends to lower blood sugar levels and to stimulate electrical activity in the brain, either of which can bring on a seizure. Diabetics have to be especially careful of a drop in blood sugar (as can occur when too much insulin is given), which can also trigger an attack. Reactive hypoglycemics, or people who produce too much insulin when they eat a meal very high in sugar, who suffer seizures, should also be especially careful (see chapter 31).

Avoid Excessive Consumption of Water

Excessive consumption of water was one of the first behaviors observed to bring on seizures. Many weight-loss diets call for the consumption of two or more quarts of water per day. This can induce seizures even in people whose epilepsy is well controlled with medication.

Strategy If you are epileptic, do not follow diets that demand a high consumption of fluids. Water consumption won't help you lose weight in any case.

Avoid Stimulants

Foods containing caffeine or *theobromides*, if consumed in excess, can cause seizures.

Strategy Try to cut down on coffee, tea, colas, chocolate, and other foods rich in these substances (see tables on pages 300 and 317 listing foods to avoid).

Supplement Your Diet with Foods Rich in the Vitamins Depleted by Your Medication

Phenobarbital causes possible deficiencies of folic acid and vitamins B_{12}, D, K, and B_6; *phenytoin* (its brand name is *Dilantin)* can cause deficiencies of vitamins D and K, and folic acid. *Primidone (Mysoline)* may cause deficiencies of vitamins K and D and folic acid.

Strategy Be sure you consume plenty of foods rich in these vitamins. (See tables on pages 320, 321, 322, and 307 for foods high in vitamins B_6, B_{12}, D, K, and folic acid.)

You should also take supplements of 400 international units of vitamin D and 400 micrograms of folic acid daily.

Consider a Ketogenic Diet for Infants

If drug therapy does not work for an infant, a *ketogenic* (high-fat) diet may prove to be the answer. This means gradually reversing the usual ratio of fat in the diet, so the diet has a three-to-one ratio of fats to carbohydrates and protein.

Strategy Such a diet is not very palatable, and is difficult to get a child to eat. Consult your doctor before using this approach, because you will need expert advice to put together a balanced diet.

Other Advice

If you would like additional information about epilepsy, contact either the Epilepsy Institute, Suite 308, 225 Park Avenue South, New York, New York 10003, phone (212) 667-8550; or the Epilepsy Foundation of America, Suite 406, 4351 Garden City Drive, Landover, Maryland 20785, phone (301) 459-3700.

21
Extended
Immobilization

Patients recuperating from orthopedic injuries may lose 15 to 20 pounds from stress, immobilization, trauma, and bed rest. They may also suffer from bedsores, muscle wasting, anemia, and other medical complications.

Prevention and Treatment

- Eat at least one to two grams of protein per kilogram of body weight.
- Eat at least one gram (1,000 milligrams) of phosphorus and one gram of calcium daily, and eat generous amounts of foods rich in potassium.
- Take or eat 200 milligrams of vitamin C daily.
- Incorporate 25 to 50 grams of fiber into the daily diet.
- Drink at least eight glasses of liquid daily.
- Get as much exercise as your condition allows during convalescence.
- When you are back on your feet, regain any weight lost during convalescence.

CASE HISTORY: John Winthrop

Downhill skiing was John's passion. A banker in his early thirties, he led a conservative, disciplined life. He found the familiar routine quite agreeable, not least because once a year he was off to Colorado for two weeks to ski like a mad demon. It was his one chance to blow off a little steam.

But last year his long-anticipated ski holiday was abruptly terminated by a very bad fall in which he broke his hip. His brief annual sojourn in the mountains became a ten-week stay in a hospital.

Normally a very active person (his usual schedule included regular games of tennis or squash), he found his hospital stay extremely stressful, not to mention painful. His treatment involved three separate operations to repair his hip, and lots of time immobilized in bed.

He lost eighteen pounds during his stay in the hospital; for a man as fit as he, the loss was more than noticeable. By the sixth week he developed bedsores where his elbows and buttocks came in contact with the mattress. When he returned home after his extended "vacation," he hobbled and was almost emaciated and very depressed.

His doctor immediately put him on a special dietary regimen, much like the one below. Over a period of months he made an almost total recovery, thanks in part to his physical therapist, but most of all to a healthy diet and a disciplined attitude. The following year he went back to Colorado—his abandon tempered and his hip still a bit stiff—to watch his family ski.

Dietary and Life-style Recommendations

Consume Ample Protein

After an injury, the body tends to lose protein as the muscles break down. This has several effects.

If and when bedsores develop owing to friction between the body and the bed, there is too little protein available to ensure rapid healing of the skin. If the sores become infected, they may take a long time to heal because the body's immune system is seriously compromised by that protein deficiency.

In times of protein shortage, a blood protein known as *albumin* is lower than normal. Albumin usually binds to calcium in the blood and reduces the level of calcium that reaches the kidneys. When albumin levels are low, however, more calcium is left free in the blood. When this flows through the kidneys, it may be deposited in the kidney as stones.

Protein is also required for production of *hemoglobin* (which carries oxygen to all the body's tissues) and red blood cells. In times of shortage, the body frees protein from red blood cells for other uses, and anemia results.

In addition, extended immobilization makes it more difficult than normal to urinate properly, which means some urine remains in the bladder at all times, rendering the bladder very susceptible to infection. A diet high in protein will lead to the production of acidic urine, which will protect against such infections. Other foods making the urine acidic are listed in the table on page 300.

Strategy   For all the above mentioned reasons, the diet should contain 1.2 to 1.5 grams of protein per kilogram of body weight (a kilogram is 2.2 pounds). This translates in general to eating 60 to 100 grams of protein per day, or three 3-ounce portions of good-quality protein like meat, poultry, or fish. (See table on page 313 for foods rich in protein.) If you are a vegetarian, you must learn to combine foods to improve their protein quality. (See chart on page 7, which shows how to complement proteins for this purpose.)

Get Plenty of Phosphorus, Calcium, and Potassium

When bones are immobile for an extended time, calcium is lost. Low blood phosphorus levels tend to raise blood calcium levels to high levels, which can result in kidney stones. By including plenty of phosphorus in the diet, however, this can be controlled to a degree, because the phosphorus combines with the calcium to form calcium phosphate, which is redeposited in the bones. This not only reduces the blood calcium levels and the risk of kidney stones, but helps to restore lost calcium to the bones.

Any form of stress tends to deplete the body not only of calcium and protein, but of potassium as well. Potassium is essential to the normal functioning of the muscles, nerves, brain, and heart. To complicate matters further, diuretics are often prescribed for im-mobilized patients who have trouble urinating. Many of these "water pills" will further deplete the body of potassium.

Strategy   Consume one gram of phosphorus daily. (See table on page 312 for foods rich in phosphorus.)

One thousand milligrams (one gram) is a good estimate of the amount of calcium needed when following the treatment plan outlined in this chapter. Be sure to get this much by including calcium-rich foods in your diet. If these foods are not well represented in your diet, take a 1,000-milligram calcium supplement. Calcium carbonate is best; two and one-half grams of it contain 1,000 milligrams of calcium. (See table on page 301 for foods rich in calcium.)

Be sure to get ample potassium by including in your daily diet quantities of the foods listed on page 313 that are rich in potassium.

Ensure an Ample Daily Intake of Vitamin C

Vitamin C is very important for the production of *collagen*, an important protein in the skin. Without adequate vitamin C, you are not able to replace skin lost due to friction with the bed, and ulcers or bedsores are more likely to occur.

Strategy Be sure to get plenty of vitamin C in your diet by including foods rich in the vitamin (see table on page 321 for foods rich in vitamin C); 100 milligrams is the recommended dose. A vitamin C supplement may also be taken.

Consume Plenty of Fiber in Your Diet

Immobilization in bed means that all the muscles in the body are rested more than normal, including those in the digestive system. When the muscles are not exercised, they become weak, and those lining the digestive tract are not able to push food and waste products through the intestines as forcefully as necessary for regular bowel movements. Constipation can result.

Strategy To reduce the chances of constipation occurring, get plenty of fiber—25 to 50 grams per day is recommended—by including those fiber-rich foods listed in the table on page 303.

Drink Plenty of Fluids

Fluids help to flush out of the body any excess calcium in the blood, and also prevent calcium from depositing in the kidneys as stones. A good fluid intake also helps to prevent constipation.

Strategy Drink eight or more glasses of fluid a day.

Other Advice

If you lose weight during your recuperation, follow the guidelines in chapter 50 to gain back the lost pounds.

The earlier you exercise the injured limb, the sooner it will be healed and the stronger it will become. When your doctor and physiotherapist give you the okay, do your assigned exercises as diligently as possible. It may be painful to begin with, but the quick recovery will more than make up for it.

Clean, unwrinkled sheets and a thick, soft mattress cover (such as sheepskin) may help to reduce the risk of bedsores.

22
Food Allergies

If a significant amount of a protein from a food substance gets into the bloodstream without being properly digested, it will sensitize the body to produce antibodies to attack that protein whenever it is introduced into the body. Though this can happen to anyone, it occurs to a greater extent in those with a genetic predisposition.

The body identifies the food protein in the same way as it does a bacterial protein, and attempts to neutralize the invading substance. When the food protein is eaten again, it triggers the whole immune system, including the white blood cells, lymph tissues, thymus gland, and bone marrow, which overreact and produce vast numbers of antibodies.

The antibodies in turn trigger the release of *histamine*, which irritates the body tissues, causing the gastrointestinal, respiratory, and skin problems we all associate with food allergies. These reactions may occur within a few minutes or after as much time as five days.

Warning Signs

- Sudden burning or itching in the mouth after consuming even tiny amounts of an offending food
- Any of the following symptoms, occurring at any time up to five days after eating the offending food:

  a. gastrointestinal symptoms including vomiting, stomachache, or diarrhea

  b. respiratory symptoms including runny nose, asthma, coughing and wheezing

c. skin reactions such as rashes and eczema

d. *anaphylaxis*, or shock characterized by narrowing of the airways and dilation of blood vessels, resulting in breathing difficulties, a rapid pulse, or a fall in blood pressure

Epidemiological Data

If one parent has allergies, a child has a 40-percent chance of developing allergies before the age of 12. If both parents have allergies, the chances are three in four that their children will develop one or more allergies by the age of six.

The younger a child is when he or she is exposed to an *allergen* (an allergy-causing substance), the more likely it is that the child will develop an allergy to that substance.

Two out of five Americans believe that they are allergic or at least sensitive to certain foods. In reality, only one-half to one-third of this number actually have such problems. Fewer than 1 percent of Americans have true food allergies.

Approximately 70 percent of those who develop allergies do so before age 30. After that, the incidence of new cases is about 5 percent per decade. People's allergies tend to improve as they get older. Some people experience an allergy for as short a period as six months, and never suffer from it again. People who have hay fever are more likely to develop food allergies or other kinds of allergies.

Ninety percent of food allergies are caused by the protein in cow's milk, egg whites, peanuts, soybeans, and wheat. Yet milk allergies occur in 1 to 3 percent of infants, and are rarely encountered in children over three years of age.

Several hundred Americans die from the most extreme symptom of food allergy, namely *anaphylactic shock*, each year.

Prevention and Treatment

• Breast-feed your baby exclusively until he or she is six months of age.

• If you think that you have a food allergy, write down everything you eat and determine whether the time interval between your consumption of that food or foods and the appearance of your symptoms is consistent; if so, remove the offending food from your diet.

• If your symptoms do not clear up after removing the offending food, consult a physician certified by the American Board of Allergy and Immunology.

• Do not believe doctors or other so-called allergy experts who tell you that food allergies account for symptoms other than those described above.

- Avoid doctors who use such tests as the *cytotoxic* test, *provocation and neutralization*, and *yeast hypersensitivity* treatment.
- Learn to distinguish between a food allergy and a food sensitivity.
- Make up for any nutritional deficiencies that may arise from leaving out certain foods from the diet.

CASE HISTORY: Jeremy Phillips

John Phillips and his wife, Samantha, recently had their first child, Jeremy. Because both John and Samantha suffer from allergies and have since they were children, they were determined to safeguard their child as much as possible.

One strategy they employed was that Samantha breast-fed the infant, knowing that would help protect him from some substances to which he might be allergic. They were careful to protect him from dusty places and animal fur, which provoked their own allergic reactions.

Jeremy was a big baby, and after four months Samantha was unable to produce enough milk to sustain his normal rate of growth. On the pediatrician's advice, they began feeding him infant formula to complement her breast milk. The first two days, Jeremy took the formula and seemed unperturbed, but on the morning of the third day, a full fifty hours or so after his first encounter with the infant formula, he began to develop allergic symptoms. He became very cranky and developed a runny nose and colic. Recognizing these common signs of an allergy from personal experience, they immediately took their baby to the pediatrician.

The pediatrician explained to them that the reaction could be a stomach bug that Jeremy had coincidentally picked up at about the same time as they began to feed him formula. If that were the case, it might not be an allergic reaction to that particular formula. However, he advised them to switch to another formula if the symptoms did not improve over the next couple of days.

No improvement occurred, so John and Samantha switched Jeremy to another leading brand of cow's-milk-based formula. The child's symptoms did not change, so after a week on the second formula, they once again visited the doctor. He suggested switching the baby to a soy-based formula. They did so, and within a few days Jeremy once again became the healthy, good-natured child he had always been.

Jeremy's problem was an allergy to milk. When Samantha weaned Jeremy at seven months, she tried feeding him a little cheese, and he reacted in exactly the same way as he had to milk. Hence, Jeremy was given no dairy products throughout his first two years of life.

At a cousin's birthday party, six months after his second birthday, all the other children were given ice cream. While his mother's back was turned,

Jeremy, not wanting to be left out, grabbed a spoonful of ice cream from his cousin's plate. Samantha was upset, but this time around no symptoms of an allergic reaction appeared in the following days. When she consulted Jeremy's pediatrician, he advised her to reintroduce milk into the child's diet, though in small amounts at first. No symptoms of an allergic reaction occurred again. Luckily, like many other children, Jeremy had grown out of his allergy.

Dietary and Life-style Recommendations

Breast-feed Your Baby Until Six Months of Age

Infants suffer from food allergies much more frequently than do adults. However, in two out of every three cases in which parents report that their children are allergic to foods, no allergy can be confirmed when the children are tested.

The explanation for the frequency of allergies in infants is that the digestive and immune systems in the very young are immature. Proteins get through the wall of the digestive tract in an incompletely digested form and cause an allergy. As soon as the digestive system is more completely developed during the second half of the first year of life, the proteins will no longer be able to travel where they should not, and the chances of a child's becoming sensitized to certain foods are much lower. Five to 10 percent of non-breast-fed youngsters are allergic to cow's milk.

Strategy By feeding a child only breast milk until the seventh month, you can prevent any allergy from developing, because you are only giving the child proteins similar to its own, and no foreign protein is introduced into the body. At six months, you may add one grain cereal (rice is perhaps the best), served with water in the ratio of one part cereal to six parts water. Next you can add strained vegetables and fruits, one at a time. Each time a new food is introduced into the diet, you must watch for signs of an allergy. After a week has passed since the introduction of a new food, you may introduce another.

On the other hand, if allergic reactions manifest themselves (indigestion, runny nose, wheezing, mood changes, skin reactions, or diarrhea and other gastrointestinal symptoms), remove the offending food from the diet. Wait until all the symptoms disappear, then reintroduce it. If the symptoms appear again, it is reasonable to assume the child is allergic to that particular food.

Children certainly do grow out of allergies. The earlier the offending food is found and eliminated from the diet, the sooner the child will grow out of the allergy. Several months after your first attempts, you may find that the child will tolerate the food, though you may also discover that the food causes a different symptom. Diarrhea, for example, may be replaced by eczema.

There are 20 different proteins in cow's milk that can cause allergies in a baby. Such an allergy usually appears 12 to 48 hours after the introduction of formula in the diet. If milk is introduced into the diet before six or seven months of age, this can also cause an allergy. The chief culprits are pasteurized or evaporated milk, or milk processed at ultra-high temperatures. These can lead to blood loss in the stools, anemia, mild diarrhea, edema, and general failure to thrive. You should not introduce milk into the diet until the seventh month, and then only as directed by your pediatrician. Such allergies to milk often subside after a few months, or are usually greatly reduced in severity after two or three years.

If a person is allergic to cow's milk, he or she is usually allergic to goat's milk as well. Goat's milk also has certain disadvantages in that it is lower in vitamin D and folic acid than cow's milk, and supplements may be needed. Soy formulas are not the right solution for everyone, as they also can set up allergies.

If there is a family history of allergies, you can help protect your infant from developing allergies by keeping him or her from being exposed to dust, mold, and animals as well as potentially allergenic foods. Remember that 43 percent of allergic reactions in adults and children are due to nuts, 21 percent to eggs (never give an infant egg white before 12 months of age), 18 percent to milk, and 9 percent to soy.

If You Have Food Allergies, Keep a Food Diary

Record everything you eat and when you eat it, and keep an accounting of any symptoms that you show.

Strategy If you observe that consumption of a particular food leads to the development of the same adverse symptoms each time you eat it, eliminate the food from your diet for a few days. If the symptoms disappear, add back the suspect foods and see whether the symptoms reappear. If they do, you can be sure that you have found the culprit. Keep in mind that a reaction to a food may take a few minutes or as much as five days to show itself. An immediate response is more common with raw foods. In fact, just cooking an offending food may alleviate some of its allergenic properties.

If You Are Unable to Isolate Allergenic Foods, Consult a Specialist

Often it is not as easy as it may seem to identify the specific food or foods causing your problem, particularly if there is a lapse of many hours or days between consumption and the appearance of the symptoms. Often, patients require a visit to a physician certified by the American Board of Allergy and Immunology to help them isolate their problem.

This qualified allergist will take a detailed history of your medical problems, and your family's, as well, and give you a physical examination. He will take special note of the symptoms you have and when they occur in relation to eating foods. He will then make you keep the diet diary described above.

Strategy If the physician is unable to determine the source of your problem by means of the diet-diary method, he may ask you to follow a *restrictive elimination* diet, in which all but well-tolerated foods are eliminated. This includes very small amounts used in prepared or processed foods, so be sure to check all food labels.

Once your allergenic reactions have ceased, foods will be gradually added back to ascertain which of them you develop a reaction to. This is also a good way to detect food intolerances. (See the discussion below of food intolerances vis-à-vis food allergies.)

Another way to detect food allergies in people over three years of age is to place liquid extracts of single foods on the skin of the arm or back, and prick or scratch them into the skin with a needle. If an itchy swelling results within 20 minutes, the person may have an allergy to that food. But this is not foolproof, so the doctor will try to confirm the positive result with the elimination diet described above.

The only definitive way to test a food is by the *double-blind challenge test*. In this test, capsules of dried food extracts and capsules of nonreactive substances are made to look exactly the same. The doctor is not aware of which he is giving the patient, but a third party is. If the patient reacts positively to a capsule containing a food extract, this usually means an allergy is present. The double-blinding is necessary to remove the possibility that emotional factors will affect the patient's response; the doctor, consciously or otherwise, might offer the patient a clue as to which capsule is being taken.

A doctor may test you for blood levels of histamine when you are suffering from an allergic reaction. A false positive test can be obtained if you eat foods rich in histamine, including Chianti or Burgundy wine, blue and Parmesan cheeses, spinach, and eggplant; so be sure your doctor is aware of the nature of your diet in recent days.

Leaving a food substance found to cause an allergic reaction out of the diet for an extended period of time sometimes desensitizes a person to that food. Patients become desensitized to milk, eggs, and soy in a shorter time, no matter what their age, than to peanuts, fish, shrimp, or walnuts. It may require years of abstinence before a person can eat them without reaction—or desensitization may never occur.

Beware of Health Professionals Who Make Exaggerated Claims

Apart from the adverse reactions caused by the foods described above, there is no evidence that food allergies cause any other disorders, including hyperactivity, chronic headaches, arthritis, weight fluctuations, or serious mental illness.

Strategy The following tests have absolutely no validity, and neither prove nor disprove the presence of an allergy:

CYTOTOXIC TESTING Extracts of foods are placed in a tube with some of the patient's white blood cells. If the cells become distorted or change shape in any way, the patient is said to be allergic to the food. This is totally invalid, as there is no correlation between this reaction and the presence of an allergic reaction. Although not approved by the Food and Drug Administration, this testing is quite common.

PROVOCATION AND NEUTRALIZATION TESTING A small amount of a food is given to a person to provoke an allergic reaction. When such a reaction occurs, a larger quantity of the food is given, which is said to neutralize the first dose. In reality, the more of a food given to a person who is allergic to it, the worse the symptoms will become.

YEAST HYPERSENSITIVITY TREATMENT The theory behind this treatment is that a yeastlike fungus called *Candida* is the cause of all allergies. Removing all yeast- and mold-containing foods as well as fruits, milk, refined carbohydrates, and processed foods for a period of time is supposed to correct the allergic condition. However, there is absolutely no evidence that Candida has anything to do with food allergies.

RADIOALLERGOSORBENT TESTING (RAST) This is a valid testing methodology for pollen allergies, but not for food allergies. It is an expensive blood test and less sensitive than skin tests.

Learn to Distinguish Between Food Allergies and Sensitivities

A food allergy results from an immunological reaction caused by a food, generally a protein of some kind. Food intolerances, on the other hand, are adverse reactions to specific foods that arise from non-immunologic mechanisms such as enzyme deficiencies, toxins, metabolic diseases, and psychological disorders. An enzyme deficiency, for example, causes lactose intolerance (see chapter 35). Toxins and *aflatoxins*, which are found in molds and bacteria, can cause food poisoning (see chapter 23). Metabolic diseases that cause food intolerances include liver disease and diabetes (see chapter 18). The psychological disorders include such things as colitis (see chapter 12).

In addition to the previously described food intolerances, some people show adverse reactions, though not allergic reactions, to various food additives. A few people get asthma attacks when they eat foods colored with the yellow dye *tartrazine* (FD and C yellow dye number 5). Perhaps as many as 90 thousand asthmatics in the United States are sensitive to *sulfites*, which are preservatives added to processed foods and dried fruits.

Many people are sensitive to some degree to *monosodium glutamate (MSG)*. Symptoms of this sensitivity may include burning sensations in the neck and forearms, headache (pain that feels like a band is being pulled tightly around the head), facial pressure, and chest tightness that can mimic the pain of a heart attack. The more MSG is consumed, the worse are the symptoms. This phenomenon is a pharmacologic or chemical effect and is not an allergic phenomenon. It is called "Chinese restaurant syndrome," because of the large amounts of MSG used in cooking by many of these establishments, and the range of susceptibility to it varies greatly from one person to another.

Other Advice

If you would like additional information about food allergies, contact the Asthma and Allergy Foundation of America, Suite T900, 1835 K Street, N.W., Washington, D.C. 20006, phone (202) 293-2950.

23
Food Poisoning

Food poisoning is a gastrointestinal infection caused by eating contaminated food, which leads to a combination of symptoms, including one or more of the following: loss of appetite, nausea, vomiting, diarrhea, and stomachache.

Warning Signs of Bacterial Poisoning

STAPHYLOCOCCAL POISONING   An attack of staphylococcal food poisoning occurs suddenly two to eight hours after eating the contaminated food. Generally, it lasts three to six hours, and is characterized by severe nausea and vomiting, abdominal cramps, diarrhea, sometimes headache and fever, and occasionally the appearance of blood and mucus in the stools.

BOTULISM POISONING   Some 18 to 36 hours after ingesting the toxic food, dry mouth, double vision, nausea, vomiting, abdominal cramps, diarrhea, dizziness, and headache occur. Difficulty in speaking, breathing, and swallowing will follow, and finally, if the victim is left untreated, his muscles will become very weak and the respiratory and heart muscles will eventually stop.

CLOSTRIDIUM PERFRINGENS POISONING   Mild *gastroenteritis* (inflammation of the stomach or intestinal tract) consisting of one or a combination of the following symptoms will occur: anorexia, nausea, vomiting, diarrhea, and stomachache. Occasionally, severe diarrhea and stomach pain, abdominal distension and gas, or bodily collapse may also occur.

146

SALMONELLA POISONING   Twelve to 48 hours after eating food contaminated with salmonella, the victim usually suffers a mild stomachache or discomfort with minimal diarrhea lasting less than a day (the stools are usually loose and paste-like). Fever may accompany the other discomforts for a day.

Warning Signs of Nonbacterial Poisoning

MUSHROOM POISONING   The two most common offenders among mushrooms are those producing the poisons *muscarine* and *phalloidin*. The symptoms of poisoning due to the muscarine-producing mushrooms (Amanita muscaria) begin two hours after ingestion, with tearing of the eyes, salivation, sweating, *miosis* (abnormal contraction of the pupils), vomiting, stomach cramps, diarrhea, vertigo, confusion, and eventually coma and sometimes convulsions. Without treatment, patients die in a few hours, while with treatment recovery is usually within 24 hours.

Symptoms of poisoning by the phalloidin-producing mushroom (Amanita phalloides) occur within 6 to 24 hours of consumption. The symptoms are the same as those of muscarine poisoning except that the victim either urinates frequently or cannot urinate at all. Jaundice may develop in two to three days, owing to liver damage. Death occurs in half of all cases within five to eight days.

FISH POISONING   *Ciguatera* poisoning occurs as a result of eating fish such as snapper, sea bass, barracuda, and amberjack head caught off Florida or the West Indies, or from the Pacific, that have consumed certain unicellular organisms. The poisoning first reveals itself in such symptoms as stomach cramps, nausea, vomiting, and diarrhea that last 6 to 17 hours. A rash, numbness in the hands and feet, headache, muscle ache, tingling of the lips and tongue, and face pain may also occur. The poisoning may render the sufferer unable to work for months.

Tetradotoxin poisoning manifests symptoms similar to ciguatera poisoning; it results from eating the puffer fish of the Pacific Ocean.

Scombrid poisoning results from eating tuna, mackerel, bonito, mahi-mahi, bluefish, or albacore, and occurs as a result of bacterial decomposition after the fish is caught. It causes an immediate reaction of facial flushing and can also produce nausea, vomiting, pain around the abdomen, and a rash within a few minutes of eating it. Symptoms last less than 24 hours.

SHELLFISH POISONING   From June to October (especially on the Pacific and New England coasts), mussels, clams, oysters, and scallops may ingest a poisonous unicellular organism that produces a substance toxic to the human nervous system that is not destroyed by cooking. Five to 30 minutes after ingestion, the area around the mouth becomes numb. Nausea, vomiting, and stomach cramps develop, followed by muscle weakness and paralysis of the arms and legs. Death from paralysis of the respiratory muscles may ultimately occur.

CONTAMINANT POISONING   Chemical poisoning may occur from eating unwashed fruit and vegetables sprayed with insecticides. Vomiting, nausea, and diarrhea are common symptoms.

Epidemiological Data

STAPHYLOCOCCAL FOOD POISONING   The risk is high where food handlers have skin infections and work with food left at room temperature. Custards, cream-filled pastry, milk, and processed meat and fish all provide an environment for the growth of this bacteria.

BOTULISM   Foods need to be heated to 120 degrees Celsius or 248 degrees Fahrenheit for 30 minutes to prevent botulism. Home-canned foods are the most common source of botulism, and account for one out of ten reported cases. Vegetables, fish, fruits, and condiments are most commonly infected, but beef, milk products, pork, and poultry are often involved as well.

CLOSTRIDIUM PERFRINGENS   This organism is found widely in soil, air, water, and feces. Contaminated canned meat is the most frequent source of the poisoning in humans.

SALMONELLA   This type of poisoning is most commonly contracted from contaminated poultry products, including eggs, and from foodstuffs containing dried eggs and milk. It can also result from eating contaminated meat. Salmonella is responsible for three out of four cases of bacterial food poisoning in the United States.

Prevention and Treatment

- Take clear liquids for 24 hours.
- Gradually introduce bland foods into the diet and progress to a normal diet.
- If your symptoms are severe, consult a doctor; if your symptoms appeared after eating mushrooms or canned foods, or if you have difficulty in speaking, swallowing, or breathing, or if you experience changes in vision or paralysis, go to the emergency room.
- Do not eat moldy or bruised fruit.
- Store all meat in the refrigerator. Promptly refrigerate all leftovers as well.
- Don't store ground meat for longer than two days in the refrigerator before eating.

- Cook all ground meat until at least brownish pink.
- Don't eat green potatoes.
- Don't eat moldy or shriveled peanuts.
- Don't eat foods that have been exposed to uncooked poultry juices unless they are washed thoroughly or well cooked.

CASE HISTORY: Sylvia Allen

Sylvia went to dinner at her fiancé's grandmother's house. Though the old woman had lived in this country for almost sixty years, she still spoke with a strong Italian accent—and she still remembered all the cooking tricks she had learned in Genoa as a child.

Unfortunately, her culinary expertise was lost on Sylvia. She didn't like tomatoes and took to any new food either very slowly or not at all. While those around her, including her fiancé, Ted, enjoyed a sumptuous Italian repast, Sylvia ate a hastily prepared sandwich made from a jar of bottled meat that Grandma found on her kitchen shelf.

The next evening, Sylvia and her husband-to-be went to the movies. Partway through the show, she began having difficulty focusing her eyes on the screen. She suddenly developed a severe headache and stomach cramps. She excused herself and went to the ladies' room, where she experienced a violent attack of diarrhea.

She left the theater, assuring Ted that she would be fine and that it was just her nervous stomach acting up. Over the next hour or so, Sylvia vomited and had diarrhea almost continuously. Her mouth became extremely dry, and she found it difficult to swallow. Ted decided to take her to the emergency room at a local hospital.

On Sylvia's arrival, the resident who examined her found her to be severely dehydrated. She was given intravenous fluids and a shot of *Compazine*, which prevented further nausea and diarrhea. After twenty-four hours in the hospital, she felt much better. A day later she was able to eat dry toast and a soft-boiled egg, and was allowed to go home.

Dietary and Life-style Changes

After Food Poisoning, Resume Drinking and Eating Gradually

Eat or drink no foods or medicines while vomiting is going on. Once it abates, nothing but clear liquids should be eaten for the first 24 hours, and only bland foods for the next 24 hours.

Strategy Fluids such as sweetened tea, soda pop, strained broth, or bouillon with added salt, when tolerated, should be eaten once vomiting stops.

Once fluids are tolerated comfortably, gradually introduce cooked cereals, gelatin, simple puddings, soft-cooked eggs, and other bland foods (see Appendix 2 for outline of bland food diet).

If Your Symptoms Are Severe, Consult a Doctor

If vomiting or diarrhea is severe, check for dehydration by pinching the skin on the back of the hand. If it stays pinched, that is a strong indication that you may be dehydrated.

Strategy   Go to your doctor or an emergency room as quickly as possible. The doctor may give you intravenous fluids and a medication to prevent diarrhea or vomiting. If fever, persistent localized abdominal pain, blood in the vomitus or stool, or abdominal distension is present, you may be in a life-threatening situation.

Beware of Spoiled Foods

Some fruit molds are believed to produce some very toxic substances. Unrefrigerated meat, including smoked and salted ham, can be a breeding ground for harmful bacteria. Ground meat is handled a great deal before it gets to you, which increases its chances of bacterial infection.

Other leftovers, too, should be refrigerated, as sometimes the most unlikely sources of food poisoning can prove deadly. For example, people have died from botulism after eating foil-wrapped baked potatoes left at room temperature for a day or two—even after they had been reheated.

Avoid green potatoes, as they contain a chemical called *solanine*, which can cause an upset stomach. Grains and peanuts are subject to molds that can cause cancer, especially cancer of the liver.

Foods that have been contaminated with uncooked poultry juices may contain salmonella, which could cause food poisoning.

Some low-acid foods most commonly involved in botulism outbreaks are beans, corn, spinach, peppers, asparagus, and mushrooms.

Strategy   Always cut off moldy sections of fruit. Also remove any greenish sections on potatoes before eating. Don't eat moldy peanuts or grains.

Refrigerate all meats, and promptly refrigerate all leftovers. Never use ground meat if it does not smell right, has been left in the refrigerator for more than two days, or has been left unrefrigerated for any length of time. If foods have been contaminated by poultry juices, wash or peel thoroughly. If the food was soaked, you are better off throwing it away.

Try to thaw all meats and poultry in the refrigerator. If you are in a hurry, you can place them in a plastic bag and hold under cold running water. But don't place them in hot or warm water, or let them stand all day to thaw. If the temperature is not low enough, it will encourage bacterial growth on the surface. And after cooking, don't let food stand on the stove. Place it in the refrigerator. If this is inappropriate, place it in a cool area briefly (meats) or wash it lightly in cold water (vegetables) and then refrigerate.

After cutting raw meat, be sure to wash the knife and cutting surface before using them again.

Other Advice

Free information on food poisoning may be obtained by writing to the United States Department of Agriculture, Public Awareness Branch, Room 1163, South Building, Washington, D.C., 20250, and requesting a copy of *The Safe Food Book: Your Kitchen Guide*. For answers to specific questions, you may also call the USDA's Meat and Poultry Hotline at (202) 472-4485.

24
Gallbladder Disease

The liver manufactures bile from another of the liver's products, cholesterol. Bile is then passed to the gallbladder, an organ attached to the liver, where it is stored and concentrated. When you eat foods that contain fat, bile is passed into the intestine from the gallbladder to aid in its digestion.

When bile in the gallbladder becomes too concentrated, gallstones can form. More than four out of five cases of gallstones are thought to result from the production of too much cholesterol.

The presence of gallstones, bacterial infections, or digestive enzymes in the gallbladder may irritate the gallbladder wall and cause an inflammation; the resulting medical problem is called *chronic cholecystitis*. If this inflammation becomes very severe (as will happen when a gallstone blocks the outlet to the intestine), *acute cholecystitis* may occur, which can be so severe as to cause death of the tissue of the gallbladder and eventual gangrene and can be a life-threatening condition.

Warning Signs

GALLSTONES The presence of gallstones is indicated by such symptoms as indigestion, abdominal discomfort, bloating, belching, and food intolerance. One episode of sharp pain or several attacks of severe but not continuous pain in the abdomen can be due to a stone blocking the outlet duct from the gallbladder.

CHRONIC CHOLECYSTITIS This condition is also accompanied by flatulence, occasional nausea, loss of appetite, and gassiness. More than one episode of abdominal pain occurs in chronic cholecystitis, and the pain extends into the upper part of the right side of the abdomen and radiates to the back, below the tip of the right shoulder blade. The pain may range from mild to excruciating, but it is steady and not abrupt as is the case with gallstones, and usually occurs after eating a fatty meal.

ACUTE CHOLECYSTITIS This problem usually occurs at night or in the early morning. It is localized to the upper abdomen on the right side, but generalized abdominal discomfort and pain radiating through the tip of the right shoulder blade are quite common (as distinct from the pain of appendicitis, which is well localized in the lower right side of the abdomen). The pain of cholecystitis may come on suddenly or gradually, but it will reach a severe level and will maintain it with little fluctuation. Nausea, vomiting, and flatulence often accompany acute cholecystitis.

Epidemiological Data

One-half million people are hospitalized in the United States each year because of gallbladder disease, although more than 60 percent of people with gallstones will experience only one painful attack.

Approximately 10 percent of the total population and 20 percent of those over 40 years of age have gallstones.

Many people who develop gallbladder disease have other diseases associated with the gastrointestinal system, such as diabetes, diseases of the small intestine, and cirrhosis of the liver.

Gallbladder disease is twice as common in women as in men, and is also more common in Asian, Latin American, and Indian peoples. It seems to run in families as well.

Acute cholecystitis is most common in women over 50.

Being overweight and having a high blood cholesterol count seem to predispose people to gallstones. An often accurate cliché has it that gallbladder disease sufferers are "fair, fat, and forty."

Ninety percent of patients with acute cholecystitis have gallstones.

Prevention and Treatment

• If you are overweight, lose weight.
• If you have painful attacks after eating fatty foods, go on a low-fat diet.
• Increase the amount of fiber you eat.

CASE HISTORY: Agatha Frampton

At seventy, Mrs. Frampton was overweight and she knew it. She also had severe angina, and a cholesterol level of 380 milligrams per 100 milliliters of blood, as opposed to a normal level of close to 150 milligrams per 100 milliliters.

For years she had complained of mild symptoms of indigestion, but one morning she experienced a severe pain in the upper right-hand corner of her abdomen, unlike anything she'd felt before. Fearing a heart attack, she asked her husband to call an ambulance.

When she arrived at the hospital, an electrocardiogram revealed that she had not, in fact, experienced a heart attack, but the examining physician immediately suspected a gallbladder problem. Indeed, on being X-rayed, Agatha was found to have several small gallstones in her gallbladder.

Because of her history of severe angina, the attending physician decided to try conservative therapy to dissolve the stones (most younger people would have the stones surgically removed). She was given a bile acid called *chenodeoxycholic acid* with breakfast and dinner. In addition, she was counseled by the dietitian on how to lose weight and increase the fiber content of her diet.

It worked. After three years of continuous therapy, Agatha (like 50 to 75 percent of patients who take this drug) was told that her gallstones had completely dissolved.

Dietary and Life-style Recommendations

If You Are Overweight, Lose Weight

Since overweight people seem to be more susceptible to gallbladder disease, you should try to get down to your ideal body weight.

Strategy   See chapter 37 for some suggestions on weight loss.

Should You Limit Your Consumption of Fatty Foods?

It used to be a matter of routine to tell all patients with gallbladder disease to cut down on fatty foods.

The reasoning behind this treatment approach was that since fats need bile in order to be absorbed, the gallbladder would have to contract to push the bile into the intestine, whereupon pain would be caused by the blocked outlet.

However, clinical experience shows that only some people with gallbladder disease are susceptible to fatty foods. Interestingly, there is also a psychological factor at work, in which patients who *think* they are eating fatty foods will have an attack.

Strategy   If you have an adverse reaction to fatty foods, be mindful of them when selecting a menu. (See tables on pages 304 and 306 for listings of fat-rich foods.)

Patients with acute cholecystitis are usually told to rest and take antibiotics and painkillers prescribed for them until the inflammation goes down, after which the gallbladder is removed. During this waiting period, a fat-free, bland diet is advised in order to avoid gallbladder distension, irritation, and increased contraction. All of these will tend to make the pain worse.

Patients with chronic cholecystitis are also usually operated on to remove the gallbladder. While they are waiting for the operation, a low-fat diet (40 to 50 grams per day) may help some people.

After removal of the gallbladder (*cholecystectomy*), you should limit your fat intake for a few months to give the liver a chance to compensate for the absence of the gallbladder. Fats should gradually be added to the diet, and you should not eat large amounts of fat at one meal. And stick to small meals for a few months.

Increase Your Fiber Intake

Fiber will help prevent constipation and diverticulosis, and it also seems to help prevent the formation of gallstones.

Strategy   Consume at least 25 grams of fiber in your diet each day for maximum protection. (See table on page 303 for foods high in dietary fiber.)

Other Advice

If you are interested in obtaining additional information about gallbladder disease, contact either the American Digestive Disease Society, Suite 217, 7720 Wisconsin Avenue, Bethesda, Maryland 20014, phone (301) 652-5524; or the National Health Information Clearinghouse, P.O. Box 1133, Washington, D.C. 20013-1133, phone (703) 522-2590 (Virginia only), or (800) 336-4797.

25
Gastroenteritis or Gastritis

Inflammation *(itis)* of the lining of the stomach *(gastro)* and/or intestine *(enteron)* can be caused by alcohol, food allergies or poisoning, intestinal viruses, and certain drugs. Usually, symptoms subside within 48 hours and the problem is said to be *acute*. When the symptoms persist for a long period of time, the condition is termed *chronic*.

Chronic gastritis can lead to the loss of cells lining the stomach, with a consequent reduction in the secretion of gastric digestive juices. No one is sure of the cause of chronic gastritis, although several have been suggested, including overeating, eating too quickly, eating when emotionally upset, eating certain foods, drinking alcohol or coffee, smoking, having gastrointestinal infections, and suffering from nutrient deficiencies.

Warning Signs

• Indigestion that may take the form of a lack of appetite, nausea, vomiting, belching, a feeling of fullness or stomachache, malaise, diarrhea, and occasionally fever and prostration.

Epidemiological Data

People with a history of food allergies or intolerances are susceptible, as are people who overindulge in alcohol, are under stress, or eat too much and/or too quickly.

Prevention and Treatment

- Avoid food entirely for a day or two in acute attacks, after which time, gradually advance from liquids to a bland diet.
- In both chronic and acute cases, avoid alcohol, foods and beverages containing caffeine, and drugs that irritate the stomach and intestines, such as aspirin.
- In chronic cases, eat small frequent meals of bland food.
- Also in chronic cases, eat lots of foods rich in vitamin B_{12}.

CASE HISTORY: Janice Smith

Jan was going through a particularly bad spell in her life. She was a writer, but had not been able to sell anything for a long time. The last book she wrote had been severely criticized by her editor, and was going through the third rewrite. She had not only lost confidence in her writing, but she had even begun to think she wasn't an attractive person.

All of this had a devastating effect on her financial situation, and she found she had to cut back on expenses. When she stopped going to her aerobics classes (they were an expendable item in her budget), she gained several pounds. She felt tired all the time, and felt full and bloated whenever and whatever she ate. She also had begun to have diarrhea almost all the time.

Although this went on for three years, she was reluctant to go to a doctor, since she was without health insurance and had no extra money to spend on medical bills. But when the tiredness seemed to get worse and when she felt a tightness in her chest after exercise, she wisely went immediately to her doctor.

Her doctor diagnosed chronic gastritis and anemia resulting from a vitamin B_{12} deficiency. He explained to her that the lining of the stomach produces a substance called *intrinsic factor*, which must be present if vitamin B_{12} is to be absorbed; a person who has chronic gastritis loses part of the lining of the stomach, and with it the ability to make intrinsic factor. He advised her to avoid the coffee she habitually drank in large quantities, and to eat a number of small, snacklike meals of bland foods rather than the two large ones she customarily ate.

Within six months, her luck changed. She found a publisher for her next book, and her health improved dramatically. Her symptoms disappeared and she was soon eating all her favorite foods again.

Dietary and Life-style Changes

Withhold Food at First; Gradually Work Up to a Bland Diet

Eating a bland diet eliminates all foods that could conceivably irritate the lining of the stomach, as it is low in fiber, contains little or no salt, pepper, or spices, and has no highly acidic or high-fat foods to slow the rate at which food passes through the digestive system.

Strategy If you cannot eat owing to nausea or vomiting, or have chronic diarrhea, don't eat for a 24- to 48-hour period to rest the stomach and allow it to heal. Sip crushed ice to relieve thirst.

After the fasting period, gradually introduce liquids into your diet, such as sweetened tea, soda pop, strained broth, or bouillon. When these are tolerated, gradually include bland cooked cereals, gelatin, soft-boiled eggs, and other bland foods. (See the table on page 326 for a list of bland foods.)

Avoid Substances that Irritate the Digestive System

Overindulgence in alcohol, food allergies, food poisoning, stress, overeating, eating too quickly, smoking, drinking beverages or eating foods containing caffeine, or nutritional deficiencies can be the cause of acute or chronic gastritis, as can certain drugs like aspirin or laxatives.

Strategy In cases where the gastritis is traceable to a particular food or behavior, the solution is simply to eliminate the source, whether it means removing a food or drug from the diet, changing one's eating habits, or finding tension-relieving activities. (See Appendix 3 for stress-reduction techniques; see also page 300 for table of foods and beverages high in caffeine.)

In Chronic Cases, Consume Foods High in Vitamin B_{12}

In some people with chronic gastritis, the loss of the cells in the stomach lining and the intrinsic factor they produce impair B_{12} absorption and cause a deficiency.

Strategy People with chronic gastritis should be sure to include foods rich in vitamin B_{12} in their diets, such as seafood, meat, dairy products, and enriched vegetable products. (See table on page 320 for B_{12}-rich foods.)

Other Advice

If you are interested in additional information about gastroenteritis or gastritis, contact either the American Digestive Disease Society, Suite 217, 7720 Wisconsin Avenue, Bethesda, Maryland 20014, phone (301) 652-5524; or the National Health Information Clearinghouse, P.O. Box 1133, Washington, D.C. 20013-1133, phone (703) 522-2590 (Virginia only), or (800) 336-4797.

26
Gout

Gout results from the deposit of crystals of *sodium urate* in and around the joints and tendons. These crystals cause inflammation resulting in severe pain and, if untreated, can lead to the erosion of the joints as in arthritis (in fact, gout is also known as *acute gouty arthritis*).

Gout is caused by abnormally high uric acid levels in the blood. These may be caused by an inherited tendency to make too much uric acid, or can result from a number of other diseases as well as certain therapeutic drugs. High blood pressure, obesity, diabetes, coronary artery disease, psoriasis, *hypothyroidism* (too little thyroid hormone), and too little or too much parathyroid hormone can all lead to raised uric acid levels or can impair the kidney's ability to excrete uric acid in the urine. *Thiazide diuretics* (e.g., *Diuril*, *Hydrodiuril*, *Esidrix*, and *Enduron*) and low levels of *salicylates* such as aspirin also reduce the ability of the kidneys to eliminate uric acid and may predispose you to gout.

The first symptom of gout is usually an excruciating pain in the big toe of one foot. Initial attacks are just in one joint, but later attacks may affect more than one; first attacks tend to last only a few days, but later attacks may persist for weeks in an untreated patient. Without taking preventive measures, the patient may experience several attacks per year. Between attacks, the joints slowly return to normal, but may eventually become severely damaged and require surgery if, over time, the attacks become frequent or numerous.

These days, patients with gout are successfully treated with drugs, which permits them to lead a normal life free from dietary restrictions. However, some patients may control their problem with di-

etary adjustments, as anti-gout drugs are very toxic to the gastrointestinal tract and not ideal for patients with stomach or intestinal problems.

For acute attacks, the drug of choice is *colchicine*, a potent anti-
inflammatory drug. This will begin to reduce the pain and swelling
immediately, and within a 36- to 48-hour period all symptoms should
subside. However, colchicine cannot reduce blood uric acid levels and
hence cannot prevent the joint from being exposed to very high acid
levels and becoming eroded. For that, a patient needs to take *allopurinol*, a drug that prevents the body from producing uric acid in
larger-than-normal quantities, or *probenecid* or *sulfinpyrazone*, which
permit the kidneys to excrete uric acid in larger than normal doses.
With the help of these drugs, the level of blood uric acid is kept in the
normal range and further damage to the joints is prevented.

Diets high in uric acid can exacerbate the problem, and, in some
cases, *are* the problem. Most patients do not want to stay on these
drugs all the time, and by controlling diet some can reduce the
number of attacks and the need to take the drugs.

Warning Signs

- A sudden, excruciating pain in the last joint of the big toe. It usually
  starts at night and gets progressively worse by the hour.
- The affected joint tends to be dusky red or purplish, hot, very
  tender, and the skin stretched over it tense and shiny.
- The condition is usually precipitated by trauma (including surgery),
  exercise, dietary excess, alcohol consumption, or a fast. It can also be
  caused by fatigue, emotional stress, infection, and the administration of drugs that raise blood uric acid levels, such as penicillin,
  insulin, and certain water pills.

Epidemiological Data

The first attack occurs in the big toe in three out of four cases. In
some cases the ankle, knee, or more than one joint are involved.
Occasionally, the wrist and elbow are involved.

Approximately 1 million Americans currently have gout.

Only 5 percent of all gout cases occur in women, and most of them
are postmenopausal.

Six people in every thousand are born with the abnormality that
makes them produce too much uric acid in their bodies.

Thirty percent of all gout cases have a family history of the disorder.

Ten to 20 percent of gouty people develop kidney stones.

Gout is more severe in people whose symptoms first appeared before age 30.

Prevention and Treatment

- Be prudent with your consumption of alcohol, and avoid it entirely until your medication has had time to work.
- If you are overweight, lose the extra pounds gradually.
- Drink at least three quarts of fluids each day.
- Cut down on the uric acid–rich foods in your diet if you are not on medication for gout. (If you are on medication, this is not necessary.)
- Avoid stressful situations.
- Increase the amount of carbohydrates you eat, and reduce fat consumption.
- Be aware of the food and drug interactions of your medication.

CASE HISTORY: Gordon Miller

Sixty-seven-year-old Gordon Miller had suffered several heart attacks in the last few years. But his blood pressure was now controlled with thiazide diuretics, and he led a fairly normal life and felt optimistic about his future.

Then one day he wore a new pair of shoes during his daily walk through the park. They felt a little uncomfortable, and he was glad to get them off on his return home.

In the middle of the night, he woke up in great pain. Although it was different from his heart attacks, it was excruciating; it came from the last joint in his big toe on the right foot. On examining the toe, he found it to be extremely swollen and tender and purplish in color. The pain got worse as the night wore on, and though he didn't feel it was life-threatening, he caught a taxi to his doctor's office and was the first patient to arrive there the next morning.

On initial examination of the toe, Gordon's doctor suspected gout. He took a blood sample and found that Gordon's uric acid level was extremely high. The doctor then gave him a prescription for colchicine. Gordon promptly purchased the drug, took it as instructed, and to his relief the pain began to subside within twelve hours. After thirty-six hours it had gone completely.

Further tests confirmed the doctor's diagnosis. Gordon was given another prescription for allopurinol, which he was to take on a daily, maintenance basis.

Unfortunately, every time Gordon took the medication, he had pains in his stomach. So instead of taking the drug he followed a diet low in uric acid that his doctor outlined for him. Now, over the last two years, he has had only two bouts of gout, each of which lasted less than a few days. On both occasions he had let his diet lapse, had eaten too much of what he knew were the wrong foods, and had consumed alcohol, too, against the recommendations of his doctor. But once he took colchicine, the problem cleared up in short order.

Dietary and Life-style Recommendations

Consume Alcohol Prudently

Alcoholic beverages, especially wine and spirits, impair the kidneys' ability to eliminate uric acid from the blood, which may cause an attack.

Strategy When you have an attack, cut out alcohol altogether and only reintroduce it in moderation when your symptoms have subsided and the medication you are taking has had a chance to work.

If You Are Overweight, Gradually Lose the Extra Weight

Obese people have a greater propensity for gout. Hence, if you are a chronic gout sufferer and are 10 to 20 percent or more overweight, you would be well advised to drop the extra pounds.

Strategy Do it gradually. No more than one to two pounds should be lost per week, as rapid weight loss tends to increase blood uric acid levels and could precipitate an attack. Consult chapter 37 for guidance in developing a weight-loss program.

Cut Down on the Uric Acid–Rich Foods in Your Diet

Overindulgence in the finer things in life was once thought to be the cause of gout, but today it is believed that the basic cause of gout is not dietary excess.

Although uric acid–rich foods (see page 317 for table of such foods) may contribute to a high level of uric acid in the blood, it is not necessary to eliminate or restrict your consumption of these foods if you are taking medication to prevent flare-ups of your gouty condition. The drugs will clear the blood of any excesses in the diet by causing you to excrete more in your urine.

Strategy However, if you are not taking a gout-preventive medication and have a tendency to gout, you should avoid excesses of uric acid–rich foods such as shellfish, anchovies, smoked meat, sardines, meat extracts, and dried peas.

Fruits and vegetables will tend to reduce the acidity of the urine, and decrease the likelihood of a uric acid buildup, so these foods should be emphasized in the diet as well.

Other Advice

Drinking plenty of liquids will keep your urine dilute and prevent the formation of kidney stones from uric acid crystals. Be sure to consume at least three quarts of water per day.

A high-carbohydrate diet increases the excretion of uric acid, as does a low-fat diet. Increase the carbohydrate content of your diet and decrease its fat. (See pages 301 and 306 for tables of foods high in carbohydrates and fat, respectively.)

As stress often precipitates gout attacks, avoid stressful situations. (See page 334 for hints on how to manage stress.)

Be aware of the food and drug interactions of your medication. The following are the most likely of these to occur:

INDOMETHACIN   This anti-inflammatory drug may upset your stomach, so it should be taken with milk or meals. Because it may also cause some bleeding in the gastrointestinal tract, you should also increase your intake of iron. (See table on page 309 for iron-rich foods.)

NAPROXEN   Another anti-inflammatory drug, it should be taken with meals or milk to prevent stomach upset.

HYDROCORTISONE   If taken with meals or milk, this anti-inflammatory is less likely to cause stomach upset. While taking hydrocortisone, reduce your intake of sodium to prevent edema (water bloating), and increase dietary calcium, potassium, vitamin B_6, vitamin C, and zinc. (See tables on pages 301, 313, 320, 321, 315, and 323.)

COLCHICINE   Take this drug immediately after meals to reduce stomach upset. Since it causes malabsorption of nutrients, you are advised to take a daily vitamin supplement, and drink plenty of fluids.

ALLOPURINOL   This drug reduces the body's production of uric acid, and should be taken immediately after meals to prevent stomach upset. Increase your consumption of foods rich in iron, and drink plenty of fluids as well.

PROBENECID   This drug increases the kidney's excretion of uric acid. Take it immediately after meals to reduce the chances of stomach upset, and drink plenty of fluids.

IBUPROFEN   This analgesic (pain-reducing) drug is best taken with meals or milk to prevent possible stomach upset.

PHENYLBUTAZONE   An anti-inflammatory drug, this drug should be taken with meals or milk to prevent stomach upset. Increase your intake of foods rich in iodine. Reduce your salt intake to reduce the risk of edema or hypertension.

SULFINPYRAZONE   Sulfinpyrazone helps the body excrete uric acid. Drink plenty of fluids while using it, and take sulfinpyrazone directly after meals to avoid stomach upset.

If you would like additional information about gout, contact the Arthritis Foundation, 3400 Peachtree Road N.E., Atlanta, Georgia 30326, phone (404) 266-0795.

27
Heartburn and Hiatal Hernia

A *hiatal hernia* is a protrusion of a portion of the stomach through the diaphragm muscle that separates the chest from the abdomen. The diaphragm opening *(hiatus)* around the *esophagus* (the tube leading from the mouth to the stomach) becomes enlarged. In some cases there are no symptoms, but in others *heartburn* (acid indigestion) occurs, swallowing is difficult, and the vomiting of blood results.

Heartburn is a burning pain that occurs when the contents of the stomach are pushed up into the esophagus. The pain usually begins behind the breastbone, comes in waves, and spreads to the neck and back of the throat. Heartburn is most likely to happen when the pressure in the stomach exceeds that in the esophagus, which occurs for the most part when a person lies down or bends over. If this happens frequently, the acid in the stomach's contents will irritate and inflame the lining of the esophagus.

Warning Signs

- Heartburn, or a burning behind the breastbone or in the neck and throat
- Food gets "stuck" and is difficult to swallow; this may be accompanied by an acidic taste in the throat
- Vomiting of blood

Epidemiological Data

Hiatal hernia is probably present in some 40 percent of the American population at any one time, though it rarely exhibits any symptoms in most people. There are indications that it runs in families. It tends to occur in midlife, and in the fat and flabby.

Hiatal hernia is quite common in the later months of pregnancy, owing to the fact that the high progesterone levels in a woman's body at this time cause the *cardiac sphincter* (the band of muscle around the base of the esophagus) to relax.

Prevention and Treatment

- Take a swallow of milk or suck a candy to relieve an acute attack of heartburn.
- Avoid stooping, bending over, or lying down after eating, and sleep with your head elevated.
- Avoid excessive swallowing of air at mealtimes.
- Forgo foods and drinks that trigger attacks, such as high-fat foods, those containing caffeine, and acidic foods such as fruit juices, citrus fruits, and tomatoes.
- Increase your consumption of foods high in protein, and eat frequent, small meals instead of two or three large ones.
- Lose weight if you are above your ideal body weight.
- Make sure that you have adequate iron intake.
- Stop smoking.
- Avoid tight belts or other restrictive clothing; avoid heavy lifting as it may contribute to the problem by damaging the diaphragm muscle; similarly, poor abdominal muscle tone will weaken the diaphragm and make a hernia more likely.
- Take antacids one hour after eating.
- Consult your physician if you suffer from heartburn regularly.

CASE HISTORY: Sandy Turner

At sixty-five, Sandy was an overweight psychiatric nurse who had worked night duty for more than thirty years and was accustomed to sleeping during the day.

She had recently retired, but still found that she woke up hungry in the middle of the night, so much so that she would make sandwiches and leave them by the bed at night for her nighttime snack. Lately she had experienced terrible heartburn in the early hours of the morning, which woke her up.

This grew worse over the course of a year, and when she began to vomit blood, she sought help from her doctor.

He performed a number of tests on her, including a *barium X-ray*, and discovered that she had a hernia. The blood was coming from an ulcer in the esophagus caused by the recurrent floods of acid flowing up from the stomach.

He advised her to stop eating in the middle of the night, and to lose some weight. He also forbade her to eat within two hours of bedtime, and prescribed a medication to treat the ulcer. He referred her to a dietitian to help her design a weight-loss diet.

Sandy's discomfort ceased almost immediately. Within a month the doctor told her the ulcer was cleared up. She managed to make the dietary adjustments asked of her and, in the next few months, lost thirty pounds. Then she truly began to enjoy her retirement.

Recommended Dietary and Life-style Changes

Avoid Stooping, Bending, or Sleeping After Eating

Try to remain upright for two to three hours after eating. This tends to discourage the movement of food from the stomach back into the esophagus, as gravity pulls it downward.

Strategy Don't eat within two hours of bedtime, and elevate the head of your bed so that your chest is higher than your stomach to help prevent reflux during sleep.

Avoid Excessive Air Swallowing at Mealtimes

Whenever the stomach becomes overly distended, the pressure in the stomach exceeds the pressure in the esophagus and increases the chance of the contents of the stomach returning (called *reflux*) to the esophagus.

Strategy Don't chew with your mouth open, talk while chewing, or gulp down your food too quickly. Foods causing gas, such as peas and cabbage and carbonated beverages, are also best avoided for the same reason. (See table on page 308 for a list of foods that tend to cause gas.)

Forgo Foods that Trigger Attacks

Certain foods that lower esophageal sphincter pressure will trigger attacks. These include foods high in fat, caffeine-rich foods and beverages, and peppermint, spearmint, after-dinner liqueurs, and other alcohol.

Strategy   Avoid those foods mentioned above. (For a more complete list of fatty foods, see the table on page 306; for foods and beverages containing caffeine, see page 300.)

In addition, you should avoid foods that increase acid secretion, which includes regular as well as decaffeinated coffee and tea. Acidic foods like citrus fruit, fruit juices, tomatoes, and tomato sauce are best avoided, as they will irritate an already inflamed esophagus. (See table of acidic foods, page 300.) Spicy foods have the same effect in some people and should also be avoided.

Keep a food diary, too, as it may help you to rule out offending foods.

Consume a bland diet during acute episodes (see page 326 for advice on bland diet).

Eat Frequent and Smaller Meals

It is advisable to eat smaller, more frequent meals. This will reduce the danger of the stomach becoming distended.

Strategy   Rather than eating two or three large meals, try eating smaller portions at mealtime and add planned snacks between breakfast and lunch and lunch and dinner. Don't, however, eat within two to three hours of bedtime, for the reasons discussed above.

Also, avoid drinking liquids during the hour immediately before and after meals, as they can have the same distending effect.

Lose Weight if You Are Overweight

Although the mechanism is not well understood, heartburn occurs quite frequently in obese people, and improves when they lose weight.

Strategy   If you are overweight and suffer from hiatal hernia, put yourself on a reducing diet (see chapter 37 for details).

Increase Your Protein Intake and Make Sure You Consume Adequate Iron

Foods high in protein stimulate the secretion by the stomach of a substance called *gastrin*, which tends to increase tension in the sphincter muscle and reduces the likelihood of reflux.

Iron can be lost through bleeding that results from ulcers in the esophagus.

Strategy Be sure your diet contains iron- and protein-rich foods, and that you consume at least two portions per day of such foods. (See tables on pages 309 and 313 for iron-rich and protein-rich foods.) If you are a vegetarian, see the chart on page 7 for advice on how to combine foods to improve the quality of vegetable protein.

Other Advice

Tight-fitting clothing increases the pressure in the stomach and can cause food in the stomach to reflux, so avoid tight belts and other restrictive clothing.

Avoid stress at mealtimes, as emotional upset affects the nerves that control the cardiac sphincter muscle and weakens the tension within it, which can allow the stomach contents to reflux. (See page 334 for strategies for handling stress.)

Smoking lowers the tension in the sphincter around the lower esophagus, which tends to lead to reflux. Stop smoking if you suffer from hiatal hernia.

Antacids must not be taken immediately after eating, because the acid is needed to digest your food. When you take them at other times, they neutralize the acid in your stomach, and won't interfere with digestion.

Take a swallow of milk or suck a hard candy for heartburn relief. This technique is often enough to wash down the acidic material in the esophagus, relieve the burning feeling, and get rid of the acid taste.

Because of the danger of a serious ulcer condition developing in the esophagus, you should seek help from a doctor if you frequently suffer from heartburn. He may want to prescribe a drug to reduce acid secretion.

If hiatal hernia is the cause of your heartburn, surgery is sometimes required to correct the problem.

If you would like additional information about hiatal hernias, contact the American Digestive Disease Society, Suite 217, 7720 Wisconsin Avenue, Bethesda, Maryland 20014, phone (301) 652-5524; or the National Health Information Clearinghouse, P.O. Box 1133, Washington, D.C. 20013-1133, phone (703) 522-2590 (Virginia only) or (800) 336-4797.

28
Hemorrhoids

Hemorrhoids are saclike protrusions into the rectal passage of a part of one or more of the many veins in that area of the body. Like varicose veins, these rectal veins become irritated and inflamed.

Hemorrhoids are sometimes *external* and sometimes *internal*. The external type are commonly called *piles* and lie outside the rectum. These are covered with skin. When the hemorrhoidal vein swells or is blocked by a blood clot, the covering skin becomes stretched, causing painful itching and swelling. When the swelling goes down or the clot is absorbed by the body, the skin remains stretched.

Internal hemorrhoids are not covered with skin and so have no nerve endings to cause pain. These may also swell to such a degree that they protrude outside the rectum. The protuberance may break and bleed, and is generally responsible for bright red blood in the toilet bowl or on the toilet tissue.

Warning Signs

- Rectal pain caused by the passage of a hard stool that presses against a clot in the walls of an external hemorrhoidal vein
- Itching in the rectal area
- Lumps around the anus
- Blood in the stools (if this occurs, check with your doctor to rule out more serious conditions)

170

Epidemiological Data

Hemorrhoids occur most often in pregnant women, women who have had children, overweight people, those who stand or sit for long periods, and those who do a lot of lifting. Each of these activities increases the pressure on the walls of the rectum.

Hemorrhoids affect more than 75 percent of American adults, though in most cases they cause little or no discomfort most of the time.

Hemorrhoids tend to occur in people in whose families other sufferers are to be found.

Fifty percent of all hemorrhoids can be successfully eliminated, though some shrinkage and scarring or "stretched skin" remains.

Prevention and Treatment

During a flare-up:
- The hemorrhoid sufferer should avoid foods that may cause irritation or diarrhea such as fruits and vegetables and spicy foods.
- Drink eight to ten glasses of fluids per day.
- Drink a glass of prune juice first thing in the morning and at bedtime.

To prevent hemorrhoids:
- Drink eight to ten glasses of fluid per day.
- Increase your fiber intake to 25 to 50 grams.
- Avoid heavy lifting and prolonged bouts of sitting or standing.
- Develop a regular exercise routine.
- Never spend more than five minutes sitting on the toilet.
- Use laxatives rarely, if at all.

CASE HISTORY: Grace Bartholomew

Grace was never happier than when she was pregnant. She was healthy, happy, and never got morning sickness.

She was thirty-five and in her fifth month of pregnancy when she noticed bright red blood on the toilet tissue after going to the bathroom. Her mother had suffered from hemorrhoids all her life, and Grace immediately suspected that she was following in her mother's footsteps. Her obstetrician confirmed the diagnosis that she had internal hemorrhoids. He told her that her unborn baby increased the pressure in the rectal area and was causing the veins in that area to project into the rectum.

He told her to avoid sitting or standing for more than thirty minutes at a time. Since her job as a secretary meant sitting for long periods, her doctor advised her to break up the day with brief rest periods in which she raised her legs. She was told not to wear tight belts or panty hose that might increase rectal pressure. For the same reason, she no longer sat with her legs crossed. Each night she came home and spent half an hour lying in bed on her side (which gave her a good opportunity to read a couple of the baby books she had been collecting). She also made sure to drink at least eight glasses of liquids a day.

As soon as the bleeding stopped, she increased her dietary fiber and got plenty of exercise. All this helped but did not totally solve the problem. However, as soon as her baby was born the hemorrhoids began to retract and eventually disappeared.

Dietary and Life-style Recommendations

Drink Lots of Fluids Every Day

This will help keep the stools soft and will prevent the necessity to strain on the toilet. Straining can bring hemorrhoids on.

Strategy Drink eight to ten glasses of fluids every day.

Limit Foods that Cause Irritation or Diarrhea

During a flare-up, cut back on foods that cause irritation or diarrhea.

Strategy Foods high in fiber are rough and can further irritate a sore hemorrhoid, so they should be limited during a flare-up (see page 303 for table of foods rich in dietary fiber).

Very spicy foods and relishes also tend to irritate hemorrhoids, so all of these foods should be restricted during a flare-up to reduce pain and discomfort.

Drink Prune Juice During a Flare-up

Prune juice is a very mild laxative and natural stool softener that will help prevent constipation and keep the stool soft to prevent friction between the hemorrhoids and the solid matter passing over it.

Strategy Drink a four-to-six-ounce glass of prune juice in the morning and another at bedtime.

Between Flare-ups, Increase Your Fiber Intake
Fiber from vegetables, fruits, and grains softens the stools and increases their bulk, which reduces the need to strain on the toilet. It also prevents constipation, which tends to worsen hemorrhoids.

Strategy Consume 25 to 50 grams of fiber per day. (See table on page 303 for foods high in fiber.)

Do Not Use Laxatives
Constipation sufferers often resort to chronic use of laxatives. This slowly weakens the muscles in the rectum and around the anus that support the hemorrhoidal veins. Without this support, they tend to rupture and bleed.

Other Advice
Develop a regular exercise routine. Any kind of regular exercise strengthens and tones up all the muscles in the body, including those in the rectum and around the anus. These support the veins in this area and prevent them from rupturing or bleeding. The stronger the muscles in the rectum and in the lining of the rest of the intestines, the better able they are to propel fecal matter down through the digestive system and to prevent constipation. This precludes the necessity to strain excessively on the toilet.

Never spend more than five minutes sitting on the toilet. In fact, if you are troubled by hemorrhoids, you should spend as little time as possible straining on the toilet, as that only worsens hemorrhoids. Although some people like to read while going to the toilet, sitting for long periods with the muscles around the anus (the anal sphincter) relaxed puts extra pressure on the hemorrhoids, tending to worsen the condition by increasing the size of the saclike protrusions. Give yourself a time limit of five minutes, even though you may feel as if you haven't "finished"; people with internal hemorrhoids often feel this way.

You should avoid heavy lifting and prolonged bouts of sitting or standing, as these practices tend to increase the pressure on the rectum and make hemorrhoids worse. Try to limit periods of sitting or standing to no more than 30 minutes at a time. If you must work in a seated position, break up the day with brief walks or rest periods when you have your legs raised.

For further information about hemorrhoids, contact the American Digestive Disease Society, Suite 217, 7720 Wisconsin Avenue, Bethesda, Maryland 20014, phone (301) 652-5524.

29
Hyperactivity

Hyperactivity is most frequently found in children who have a very limited ability to concentrate and are restless, unusually clumsy, irritable, and often aggressive.

Warning Signs

• Inability to sit still
• Tendency to touch everything and everyone in the vicinity
• Inability to concentrate: short attention span, tendency to jump from one activity to another, easily distracted
• Unpredictable behavior, quick temper, easily panicked, cries easily; aggressiveness may lead to difficulties with peers and adults
• Poor school performance: has difficulty in organizing work, needs constant supervision, calls out in class, has trouble awaiting turn in games
• Sleep disturbances
• Depression and low self-esteem

Epidemiological Data

Six hundred thousand children in the United States take medication for hyperactivity. The disorder is ten times more prevalent in boys than in girls. Three percent of preadolescent children may have the disorder. Symptoms usually begin before age three.

• Avoid foods containing red dye number 3.

• All meals should be balanced, and snacks or meals that consist mainly of carbohydrates should be avoided.

• Remove foods from the diet for a trial period that are believed to exacerbate the abnormal behavior; some parents have found the Feingold diet a useful guide to this process.

• As much time as possible should be spent with the child encouraging him and building up his self-confidence.

• If your child gets more hyperactive after eating foods rich in caffeine, try to reduce the level of caffeine in his diet.

CASE HISTORY: John Philipson, Jr.

Little John, as his mother calls him, is eight years old. His grandmother likes to call him "fidgety," because he won't sit still for her kindly ministrations, whether it is time for reading a storybook or getting his hair cut or even eating a sandwich.

Unlike his siblings, Little John does not excel in school. His teachers call him "uncooperative" and "moody," and he himself is the first to admit he doesn't like to play with "those other kids." Part of the reason, his mother thinks, is that they pick on him; his father thinks that Little John probably brings it on himself because he cries easily when provoked. He also has poor motor coordination, so games and sports are frustrating for him.

John has sleeping difficulties, too. He often awakens during the night, sometimes with nightmares. In the morning, however, he is difficult to awaken.

John's parents consulted their pediatrician. He determined from questioning John and his parents that the boy ate large quantities of chocolate and cola drinks, both of which are high in caffeine. He advised that they be eliminated from the child's diet.

Though John objected strenuously, his consumption of cola and candy bars was cut down. His mother offered him other treats, including as much fruit as he wanted and other occasional (but noncaffeine) treats.

His father, previously a traveling salesman, fortuitously changed jobs at the time Little John was in the throes of his dietary change. He had more time to spend with the boy, and the evening meal was shared by the whole family for the first time in Little John's life.

After a year of the new regime, John's report card included a note from one of his teachers: "I don't think Johnny will ever win the award for 'shyest boy in class,' but his gains this year in cooperation and concentration have been substantial."

Dietary and Life-style Recommendations

Avoid Foods Containing Red Dye Number 3

Erythrosine (red dye number 3) has been shown to increase hyperactivity in children under three years of age.

Strategy Avoid feeding your children foods with red dye number 3. Carefully read all food labels to determine where it has been used. Those foods include some, though not all, soft drinks and candies. Older children, however, do not seem to be affected.

Meals Should Be Balanced, Snacks Rich in Carbohydrates Avoided

There is no doubt that children are born with a sweet tooth. Many parents and teachers accustomed to dealing with hyperactive children maintain that when their children satisfy this craving with lots of very sweet foods, their hyperactivity becomes more exaggerated. Under clinical conditions, however, hyperactivity in only a few children has been observed to worsen when sugar is eaten, while in others the consumption of sugars produces a degree of calm. Therefore, there is little proof that sugar is a major cause of hyperactivity.

Strategy This means that you do not have to keep sweets and desserts away from hyperactive children. Rather, make sure that they are eaten within two hours of a balanced meal.

Remove for Trial Periods Foods that Seem to Exacerbate the Hyperactivity

There is little doubt that individual children are allergic to specific food substances that cause hyperactive-like symptoms. However, whether or not food additives are any more likely to cause hyperactivity than other food substances is highly debatable.

The *Feingold diet* is an additive-free diet designed by Dr. Benjamin Feingold, a pediatric allergist who in 1973 found that children diagnosed as hyperactive dramatically improved when placed on a diet free of all food additives. Since that time, however, many studies have been carried out comparing the additive-free Feingold diet with an equally restricted diet containing food additives. In one study, neither parents nor children were told which diet they were eating. This study showed that, indeed, 50 percent of the children improved, but not because of the removal of food additives, as both groups of children improved to the same degree. Hence, it is clear that there is little evidence to support the use of the Feingold diet, or that removing additives from the diets of hyperactive children is the key to improvement.

Strategy On the other hand, a change in the dietary pattern may be of some benefit. And in cases where ingestion of certain foods results in an observable behavior change, those foods should be removed from the diet for a trial period.

One food substance that can cause a noticeable degree of hyperactivity in some children is caffeine. You should try to avoid giving such children foods high in caffeine. (See page 300 for foods high in caffeine.)

Other Advice

If you would like further information about hyperactivity, contact the Association for Children with Learning Disabilities, 4156 Library Road, Pittsburgh, Pennsylvania 15234, phone (412) 341-1515; the Foundations for Children with Learning Disabilities, 99 Park Avenue, New York, New York 10016, phone (212) 687-7211; or the Federation for Children with Special Needs, 312 Stuart Street, Boston, Massachusetts 02116, phone (617) 482-2915.

30
Hypertension

Blood pressure is the force exerted by the bloodstream against the walls of the arteries; *hypertension* is the term used for abnormally high blood pressure.

The heart pumps blood through the arteries to the organs and muscles, and the blood returns to the heart via the veins. The veins and arteries are joined by small arteries called *arterioles*, which control the blood pressure. When they open, blood pressure goes down, and when they close, blood pressure goes up.

Blood pressure varies with age, emotional state, activity level, and time of day. It is expressed as two figures, the normal range being 110/80 to 140/90. The first, higher figure in each pair is the *systolic* pressure, which is the peak pressure reached when the heart contracts and forces blood into the arteries. The low figure is the *diastolic* pressure, the lower pressure when the heart rests between beats.

Diastolic pressure is usually used to measure the severity of high blood pressure, as this is the pressure the arteries are under even when at rest. A high-normal reading is 85 to 89; mild hypertension is 90 to 104; moderately severe hypertension is 105 to 114; and severe hypertension is 115 and higher. Two high readings on consecutive visits to the doctor are required before a diagnosis of hypertension is made, because even the stress and worry of the visit can be enough to cause blood pressure to rise above normal.

One in ten hypertensives have the condition as a result of diabetes, kidney disease, tumors in the adrenal glands, pregnancy, birth-control pills, or congenital narrowing of the aorta, the largest artery in

178

the body. The other 90 percent of people with hypertension can be successfully treated (but not cured) with medication, accompanied by a low-salt diet and life-style changes.

Blood pressure elevations are a serious health hazard, as they are a leading cause of the half-million strokes suffered each year that are responsible for as many as 170,000 deaths. In addition, high blood pressure left untreated for 10 to 15 years can cause serious damage to the arteries in the brain, eyes, kidneys, and heart. People with high blood pressure are twice as likely to die from heart disease as those with normal blood pressure.

If the high blood pressure is caught early and treated, then a person has a normal life expectancy. In fact, early detection and treatment of hypertension has made a significant contribution to the 45-percent reduction in death from strokes over the last 13 years and the 31-percent reduction in cases of heart disease during the same period.

Warning Signs

- The vast majority of people with high blood pressure do not experience any symptoms, which is the major problem for diagnosis. When the problem becomes a matter of very serious concern, however, the patient may experience headaches, changes in vision, and difficulty in breathing.

Epidemiological Data

An estimated 60 million Americans have hypertension, and at least 50 percent of those with the disease are not aware of it.

Seventy percent of those affected have only mild hypertension (diastolic pressure in the range of 90 to 104).

Hypertension definitely runs in families. Children with one hypertensive parent have a higher risk than those with no high blood pressure in the family. Having two parents with hypertension increases the odds even more.

Blacks have twice the risk of developing high blood pressure as whites. Nobody knows why, but socioeconomic considerations and diet are probably major factors.

Birth-control pills cause a slight blood pressure rise in many women. In women over 35, a combination of the pill and smoking can raise blood pressure to dangerous levels.

A combination strategy of sodium restriction, exercise, and weight loss is enough to reduce blood pressure to normal in 20 to 25 percent of all hypertensives.

Some blood pressure increase is to be expected with age. It usually develops in people in their thirties and forties.

Prevention and Treatment

• Stop smoking.
• Cut down on salt in your diet.
• Lose weight if you are overweight.
• Get more exercise if you are sedentary.
• Increase the potassium in your diet.
• Increase the amount of calcium you eat.
• Reduce your stress level.
• Reduce the saturated fat and cholesterol in your diet, and raise your polyunsaturated fat intake.
• Limit the caffeine in your diet.
• Omit black licorice from your diet.
• Limit alcohol.
• After the age of 40, monitor blood pressure on a regular basis.

CASE HISTORY: Anne Milner

Anne Milner had worked hard all her life. Married to a dairy farmer, she had learned to accept the long days and savor the independence and special pleasures of life on a farm.

But at seventy she didn't have the energy she had had for so many years. She had always been a worrying sort, and after her husband had a major stroke, she became extremely anxious.

She had always been a big, hearty woman, but she seemed a little less able to carry her bulk. These days her sons were running the farm, and she rarely got any form of exercise to help deal with the twenty extra pounds she had gained. She still smoked a pack of cigarettes a day.

Although for years her ankles had swelled sometimes, recently she had found that the swelling was greater and quite uncomfortable. So she went to the doctor to see what he had to say.

He told her it was edema, caused by the retention of fluids in her body that settled in her feet and ankles. He promptly took her blood pressure. Her reading was a moderately high 200/100. To be sure it was an accurate reading and not due to her anxiety at being in the doctor's office, the doctor told her to come back a week later. At that time, he found it to be holding at a consistent level of 200/100.

The doctor advised Anne to stop smoking, lose the extra pounds she was carrying, and get as much exercise as possible. He also prescribed a mild diuretic.

Six weeks later she reported back to him with no side effects from her water pills. The edema had virtually disappeared. Six months later she had dropped the weight, stopped smoking, and gotten into the habit of taking a daily constitutional walk for fifteen to twenty minutes, even when she felt tired. Her doctor took her off the medication. Six weeks later he again saw his patient and found that she had a normal blood pressure of 135/87.

Dietary and Life-style Recommendations

Stop Smoking

Smoking a cigarette temporarily increases blood pressure, and also makes the heart work harder. Smoking and high blood pressure are independent risk factors for heart disease. In fact, if you have high blood pressure, high blood cholesterol levels (above 200 milligrams per 100 milliliters blood), and smoke 20 or more cigarettes per day, you run five times as great a risk of having a heart attack as does a nonsmoker with normal cholesterol and blood pressure.

Strategy   You may have tried before, but try again. Ask your physician for advice about stopping. But do stop smoking. A new successful method involves acupuncture treatments and may be worth pursuing if other, more traditional means have not worked for you.

Cut Down the Salt in Your Diet

Roughly one in five Americans is sensitive to the blood-pressure-elevating effects of sodium. An increased dietary consumption of salt (sodium chloride) increases the absorption of salt into the blood, which attracts fluid into the bloodstream and increases the amount of circulating fluid in the blood vessels. This increases the demand on the kidneys to excrete both the excess salt and the excess fluid. Should the kidneys fail to excrete all excess salt and water, the heart must work harder to pump this extra fluid. This may eventually lead to the development of hypertension and its complications.

Sodium is one of the many mineral nutrients that is found in almost all plants and animals we consume as food. The average level of consumption in the U.S. diet is estimated to be 6 to 8 grams a day. That amount is equivalent to three to four teaspoons of table salt. Even people who do not usually add salt to food take in a great deal of sodium from commercially processed foods (1.6 to 2.3 grams), moderate amounts from what is present naturally in plant and animal foodstuffs (1.2 grams), and small amounts from drinking water (.05 to .25 grams per quart).

From our present knowledge of the function of sodium in the body, it appears that an adult requires approximately .5 grams of sodium, or less than one-quarter of a teaspoon of salt, per day. Adding table salt may actually reflect a higher taste threshold: for habitual salt-users, more salt is needed to register the same level of "saltiness" on the palate over a period of time. Those who have become accustomed to unsalted food find their "old favorites" unbearably salty.

Strategy   If diuretics are used, a restriction of 2 to 3 grams of sodium per day is probably sufficient. This means simply reducing the amount of table salt used. No salt should be added at the table, but up to one-half teaspoon can be added per day during cooking. In addition, pickled foods (such as sauerkraut) and extremely salty foods (such as luncheon meat, snack chips, and processed cheeses) should be eliminated. (See table on page 315 for foods high in sodium and page 328 for a low-salt diet plan.)

Lose Weight if You Are Overweight

Being overweight puts extra demands on the heart to pump blood around the body. (There is an increase in blood pressure of 6.6 milliliters for every 10 percent of weight gain over ideal weight.) Any loss of weight in an overweight person will reduce blood pressure to some degree, though this is also partly explained by the fact that salt intake is higher in heavy people, since they tend to eat more.

Strategy   Sometimes simple weight loss can enable the hypertensive patient to avoid medication. Consult chapter 37 for hints on how to lose weight.

Get More Exercise if You Are Sedentary

Exercise improves the working of the heart and makes it work more smoothly with less strain. Weight loss is also easier when combined with a regular exercise program.

Strategy   Fifteen to twenty minutes of walking four times a week, even when you are feeling tired, will have a significant beneficial effect. Other, more vigorous forms of exercise, such as tennis, running, and swimming, are also very good, but do not start any new exercise without first consulting your doctor. It could be harmful.

Increase the Potassium in Your Diet
Potassium helps the body excrete sodium and water.

Strategy Increase the potassium in your diet by including foods high in potassium, including bananas and orange juice. (See table on page 313 for other foods rich in potassium.)

Increase the Calcium in Your Diet
People who have a lot of calcium in their diets tend to have less risk of high blood pressure than people with a low calcium intake. Calcium is involved in blood vessel constriction and relaxation, and it is quite likely that it is beneficial in some as yet undiscovered way.

Strategy Adding calcium to your diet cannot hurt you (unless you have a tendency to get kidney stones) and may help to keep your blood pressure down. Include foods rich in calcium in your diet, such as skim milk, low-fat cheeses, broccoli, and fish. (See table on page 301 for a more complete list of foods with a high calcium content.) Take a daily 1,000-milligram (1 gram) calcium supplement as a 2.5-gram calcium carbonate supplement.

Reduce the Saturated Fat and Cholesterol in Your Diet
Saturated fats, found in milk, meat, and butter, tend to increase blood pressure; on the other hand, polyunsaturated fats may decrease blood pressure. High blood pressure also tends to increase the deposits of cholesterol on the inside of the arteries, which doubles the risk for heart disease as compared to people with normal blood pressure.

Strategy If you have high blood cholesterol levels and high blood pressure, your risk for heart disease is three times that of people with normal blood pressure and normal cholesterol levels. You should therefore limit your cholesterol intake to no more than 300 milligrams daily. (See chapter 6 for a more detailed discussion of cholesterol and its control and how to design a diet that will reduce your blood cholesterol levels, and Appendix 1 for lists of foods containing high levels of saturated fat, cholesterol, and polyunsaturated fat.) Certain medications taken for blood pressure, specifically diuretics, and *beta blockers* (see "Other Advice," below) tend to raise cholesterol levels, making a careful regulation of cholesterol intake even more important.

A low-fat, low-cholesterol diet should contain approximately 15 percent protein. One of protein's component molecules (amino acids) called *tyrosine* is an active ingredient in lowering blood pressure.

Limit the Caffeine in Your Diet

Caffeine is a stimulant and raises blood pressure when taken in excess.

Strategy Limit beverages and foods containing caffeine to no more than two to three per day. (See table on page 300 for a list of caffeine-containing beverages and foods.)

Limit Alcohol Consumption

Heavy drinking can raise blood pressure.

Strategy People with hypertension should have no more than one or two drinks a day. In addition, some hypertensive drugs can combine dangerously with alcohol by further lowering blood pressure.

Other Advice

There is absolutely no doubt that stress is a big factor in the development of high blood pressure. Stress increases heart rate and causes a temporary rise in blood pressure as long as it lasts. (See Appendix 3 for some hints on how to reduce your stress level.)

You should omit black licorice from your diet. Licorice tends to raise blood pressure because of one of its ingredients, called *glycyrrhizin*, makes the body retain sodium and lose potassium, at the same time causing fluid retention.

People who are taking water pills that cause potassium loss, such as *Diuril, Hydrodiuril, Lasix,* and *Hygroton*, should also avoid black licorice. They should also not chew tobacco, as most of the licorice brought into this country goes into tobacco products. If you like the taste of licorice, check labels to make sure your licorice candy gets its taste from anise oil, a licorice-like flavoring agent that has none of the harmful effects of natural licorice. Stay away from natural licorice.

Below are listed some of the drugs commonly used to treat hypertension:

DIURETICS This family of drugs acts on the kidneys to wash out fluid and salt that build up and lead to an increase in blood volume. Fifty percent of all diagnosed hypertensives respond to a once-a-day diuretic such as *thiazide*. These are prescribed as generic drugs or as brand names. Among them are *hydrochlorothiazide* (Esidrix, Hydrodiuril) or *chlorthalidone* (Hygroton).

BETA BLOCKERS These reduce the rate of beating of the heart and the amount of blood pumped around the body, and also reduce the constriction of the vessels. These include *propranolol (Inderal), metoprolol (Lopressor), timolol (Blocadren), nadolol (Corgard), atenolol (Tenormin).*

COMBINATION PILLS   These contain both a diuretic and a beta blocker.

VASODILATORS   These relax the small arteries and ease the flow of blood. They include *hydralazine (Apresoline)* and *minoxidil (Loniten)*.

ANGIOTENSIN CONVERTING ENZYME INHIBITORS   These prevent the production of the hormone *angiotensin* by the kidneys, thereby preventing angiotensin from constricting the blood vessels and causing the body to retain sodium and water. They include *captopril (Capoten)* and *enalapril (Vasotec)*.

CALCIUM ENTRY BLOCKERS   These prevent calcium from entering muscle cells and prevent arteries from constricting. They include *verapamil (Calan* and *Isoptin), nifedipine (Procardia), diltiazem (Cardizem)*.

Other drugs work on the brain and nervous system. These tend to decrease the heart rate. They include *clonidine (Catapres), guanabenz (Wytensin), methyldopa (Aldomet), prazosin (Minipress)*, and *reserpine (Regroton, Diupres, Serpasil*, and *Salutensin)*.

Finding the drug, or combination of drugs, and the dosage that best suits you can take some time and patience. Do not stop taking the drug without consulting your doctor if you have an unpleasant side effect. You can suffer a *rebound effect* where the blood pressure shoots up to a very high level if you stop taking these drugs abruptly. Stopping beta blockers can even lead to a heart attack if it is done suddenly. There are side effects associated with just about all of these drugs, but chances are you will not suffer from any of them. Be alert, however, for such side effects as gout, weakness, and muscle cramps in the legs (while taking diuretics); fatigue, insomnia, nightmares, and depression (while taking drugs affecting the brain and nervous system); and asthma (while taking beta blockers).

Many of these drugs cause impotence and loss of sex drive in males and females, dizziness on standing, and fatigue.

If you would like additional information about hypertension, contact the American Heart Association, 7320 Greenville Avenue, Dallas, Texas 75231, phone (214) 750-5300; the National Stroke Association, 1565 Clarkson Street, Denver, Colorado 80218, phone (303) 839-1992; or The Sister Kenny Institute, 800 East 28th Street, Minneapolis, Minnesota 55407.

31
Hypoglycemia

Hypoglycemia is a condition in which the level of sugar in the blood (*glucose*) is too low as a result of a defect in the way the body processes carbohydrates.

Low blood sugar can occur as a result of eating a meal rich in carbohydrates. This is called *reactive hypoglycemia.* This occurs two to four hours after a meal as a result of an excessive outpouring of insulin from the pancreas. (When a blood test is conducted, a reading of anywhere from 35 to 50 milligrams of glucose per 100 milliliters of blood is regarded as low blood sugar.)

Hypoglycemia can sometimes occur spontaneously during pregnancy or vigorous exercise, and can also result from severe emotional stress.

Warning Signs

• Hunger, trembling, headache, dizziness, weakness, and agitation two to four hours after a high-carbohydrate meal. Fatigue, depression, anxiety, an inability to concentrate, cold sweating, and mid-morning or late-afternoon tiredness may also be accompanying symptoms.

Epidemiological Data

Hypoglycemia has become a very fashionable disease in recent years, but in reality very few people suffer from this disorder.

Genuine hypoglycemia is a relatively rare problem; in fact, experts on sugar metabolism estimate that it is substantially less commonplace than diabetes.

Prevention and Treatment

- Reduce simple carbohydrate intake and replace it with complex carbohydrates.
- Reduce alcohol and caffeine consumption.
- Drink only two cups or less of milk daily.
- Increase protein intake.
- Eat three meals and three snacks daily.

CASE HISTORY: Sara Johnson

At twenty-three, Sara Johnson finished college and finally got the job she wanted, working as a secretary in an advertising firm.

She thought her life was perfect, even though she was required to invest a great many hours on her job. She found work exhilarating, but occasionally she felt simply exhausted.

At first she thought it was the number of hours she was working, but then she observed that her feelings of exhaustion and weakness often did not coincide with her busiest or longest days. She realized that she experienced these symptoms when she ate dessert or candy.

She went to her doctor, and when she outlined her symptoms, he told her that he suspected she had hypoglycemia. Sara fasted overnight, and when she returned, ravenously hungry, to his office in the morning, the doctor gave her a sugar solution to drink. Over a period of two hours or so after she drank the glucose, he took a number of blood samples.

Sara's doctor found that her blood glucose level dropped down to 35 milligrams per 100 milliliters of blood after drinking the sugary solution. This was reactive hypoglycemia. When she ate a very sweet food, her pancreas produced more insulin than necessary to absorb the sugar in her blood; as a result, so much sugar was absorbed from the blood that its glucose levels dropped below normal, causing her exhaustion. He told her that if she cut out concentrated sugar sources like candy, cake, cookies, and chocolate, the problem would not arise. Things like starchy vegetables, such as potatoes, are broken down more slowly, so that blood sugar levels don't go up high enough and fast enough to cause the pancreas to overreact.

She followed his advice carefully, and had no more attacks until one day she experimented and ate what had been a favorite chocolate bar. Sure enough, she felt the same symptoms return, and thereafter avoided even her favorites.

Dietary and Life-style Recommendations

Limit Consumption of Simple Carbohydrates, Increase Intake of Complex Carbohydrates

Foods rich in simple sugars such as candy, cakes, and sweet sodas (see page 301 for a list of simple carbohydrates) are absorbed very quickly. Blood sugar levels go up quickly, and in response insulin is released by the pancreas to enable the sugar to be absorbed into the body's cells. In people with reactive hypoglycemia, too much insulin is produced. As a result, blood glucose levels drop below normal.

Strategy By increasing complex carbohydrates, this problem can be prevented. Complex carbohydrates such as pasta, bread, and vegetables take longer to be digested and absorbed. (See table on page 301 for a listing of such foods.) This means that blood glucose levels do not go up quickly, and only moderate amounts of insulin are produced. This tends to prevent hypoglycemia.

Other Advice

You should drink only two cups or less of milk daily, as lactose (milk sugar) triggers the secretion of insulin in exactly the same way as sucrose (white table sugar).

Alcohol prevents the liver from producing glucose when blood glucose levels go down below normal. Hence, drinking alcohol tends to exacerbate any hypoglycemic condition. Caffeine also has a hypoglycemic effect, so foods and beverages containing caffeine should be avoided. (See page 300 for a listing of foods rich in caffeine.)

On the other hand, protein tends to produce much less of an insulin response than do carbohydrates. As a result, protein should be made a larger part of the daily diet. Three to four portions of protein should be consumed each day. (See page 313 for table of protein-rich foods.)

You may also find that spacing meals evenly throughout the day helps to maintain blood glucose levels at a relatively constant level. Alternating three small snacks with three balanced meals can further enhance the leveling of the blood glucose.

Since hypoglycemia often precedes the development of adult-onset diabetes, if you suffer from the symptoms of this disorder you should check with your doctor. (See chapter 18.)

Fasting can cause some people to experience a drop in blood sugar, but not usually below the level of 50 milligrams per 100 milliliters of blood that is generally regarded as the upper limit of hypoglycemia.

If you would like further information about hypoglycemia, contact the American Diabetes Association, Inc., 2 Park Avenue, New York, NY 10016, phone (212) 683-7444; or the National Health Information Clearinghouse, P.O. Box 1133, Washington, D.C. 20013-1133, phone (703) 522-2590 (in Virginia) or (800) 336-4797.

32
Insomnia

Insomnia is the inability to fall asleep, or awakening prematurely and being unable to return to sleep.

Warning Signs

- Failure to fall asleep within 30 minutes
- Prematurely interrupted sleep, followed by extended periods of wakefulness

Epidemiological Data

Twenty-five million Americans are afflicted by insomnia all the time, and millions more some of the time.

Approximately 8.5 million Americans take prescription sleeping pills regularly.

Fifteen percent of all patients seeking help from their doctors complain of some form of insomnia.

Thirty percent of all psychiatric patients complain of insomnia.

Thirty percent of older people suffering from sleeplessness benefit from taking the amino acid *tryptophan*.

Prevention and Treatment

- Take 1,000 milligrams (one gram) of tryptophan with a carbohydrate-rich snack 30 to 45 minutes before bedtime.

- Cut out all foods and beverages containing caffeine in the evening hours.
- Omit alcohol as much as possible, and do not smoke.
- Do not eat your evening meal too early, and avoid exercise just before bedtime.
- Relax for an hour before bedtime, keep your bedroom at 60 to 65 degrees Fahrenheit, and if you can't sleep, leave the bedroom and return only when you feel sleepy.

CASE HISTORY: Theresa Dudley

Theresa suffered from mild insomnia. She wasn't worried about anything in particular. In fact, at seventy, having outlived two husbands, she had finally mastered the art of taking life as it comes. Even so, she often required an hour or more to get to sleep.

On the recommendation of a friend, she tried taking a gram of tryptophan half an hour before she went to bed, along with an oatmeal cookie. She found that she fell asleep in about half the usual time, and usually felt well rested in the morning. In fact, she confided in her friend, she felt a lot better than when she had taken sleeping tablets. They had worked only intermittently, and had left her feeling dragged out in the morning.

Dietary and Life-style Recommendations

Take Tryptophan 30 to 45 Minutes Before Retiring

A great number of studies done over the past 20 years have shown that tryptophan helps many people get to sleep. Those who appear to benefit most have mild insomnia, or take a longer time than average to fall asleep (more than 10 to 30 minutes). Tryptophan does not help people who sleep normally, or who suffer from severe or anxiety-related insomnia. Nonetheless, a recent report showed that 30 percent of older people suffering from sleeplessness benefited from the administration of tryptophan.

Strategy One gram (1,000 milligrams) of tryptophan should be taken with a carbohydrate-rich snack containing less than 10 percent of the calories as protein (such as cookies, cake, a muffin, or a granola bar). Take it one-half to three-quarters of an hour before bed. Actually, it is the cookies in the old milk-and-cookies-before-bed combination that the body needs to sleep easily and soundly, and not the protein-rich milk. Milk is a source of tryptophan, but not a good enough source to compensate for the other amino acids contained in it that compete with it for entry into the brain and make it less effective.

On this program, it will take 45 to 90 minutes before you begin to feel sleepy. If it works for you, you will get to sleep more easily and quickly, wake up fewer times during the night, and sleep longer.

People with anxiety-induced insomnia are usually treated with antidepressant drugs like those belonging to the *benzodiazepine* family, *Valium* and *Librium*. Some people with severe insomnia are given barbiturates, but they increase your need for vitamin C, so check with the list of foods rich in vitamin C (page 321) to be sure you are getting enough. To be on the safe side, it is a good idea to take a daily supplement of 100 milligrams.

Do not drink alcohol if you are taking barbiturates, as the combined depressant effect on the brain of the two drugs could put you in a coma.

Eliminate Foods and Beverages Containing Caffeine in the Evening Hours

Caffeine is a stimulant, and results in lighter sleep and more frequent periods of awakening during the night.

Strategy Take into account that it takes six to eight hours for your body to detoxify the caffeine contained in a single cup of coffee or a can of cola, and adjust your consumption appropriately. (See page 300 for a list of foods and beverages containing caffeine.)

Omit Alcohol as Much as Possible from Your Diet

Although it may help you to fall asleep initially, alcohol will not keep you asleep. Once the alcohol wears off (it takes just two hours for the body to metabolize a drink), you may wake up and not be able to get back to sleep. The type of sleep that alcohol induces is also not a natural one, and does not thoroughly rest the body and mind.

Strategy Limit your consumption of alcohol at all times, but if you do drink, do not do so within three hours of retiring, and do not have more than two drinks.

Do Not Eat Your Evening Meal Too Early

If you eat your dinner so early in the evening that you are hungry immediately before bedtime, your hunger may keep you awake.

Strategy Eat dinner three to five hours before going to bed, or adjust your dinnertime so you don't experience hunger before bed.

Other Advice

Most medications are only effective in inducing sleep for short periods of time. As a result, many medical professionals believe that sleeping pills should only be prescribed in very limited numbers for only a few nights—if at all. In fact, prescription and over-the-counter preparations can do more harm than good by altering sleep patterns and making the sleeper dependent on them.

Don't smoke; nicotine is a stimulant.

Set regular times for going to bed. If you get up and go to bed at the same time each day, you will soon find yourself falling asleep at a set time, too. You may also find that by relaxing and unwinding an hour before you go to bed, you will fall asleep more easily. Taking a warm bath, listening to music, or taking a few minutes to read are good techniques.

If you don't fall asleep within 15 minutes of retiring, get up and leave the bedroom. Return when you are sleepy. If you cannot sleep on your return, repeat the cycle until you can. Do not use the bedroom for watching TV, reading, or listening to music, but associate it only with sleeping.

Keep your bedroom between 60 and 65 degrees. Excessive hot or cold only interferes with sleep.

If you would like additional information about sleeping problems, contact the Association of Sleep Disorders Centers, P.O. Box 2604, Del Mar, California 92014, phone (619) 755-6556.

33
Irritable Bowel Syndrome

This abnormality (commonly known as *spastic colon*) is characterized by irregular contractions of the muscles in the digestive tract, which prevent food from passing along its length in a normal fashion. The rhythms of the muscles are confused so that sometimes the muscles contract too much, causing diarrhea, while at others the contractions are too few or too slight, which leads to constipation.

The reason for this problem is not well understood, but it seems to be related in many cases to stress. Type A personalities—people who are aggressive, competitive, and overly preoccupied with time—often suffer from irritable bowel syndrome, as do people who tend to be anxiety-ridden or experience intense feelings of guilt or resentment. Irritable bowel syndrome is not associated with any underlying organic disease of the colon, and the colon is usually not damaged.

Chronic users of laxatives suffer from this syndrome as well.

Warning Signs

- Irregular bowel habits characterized by fluctuating periods of diarrhea and constipation; sufferers of irritable bowel syndrome often experience diarrhea immediately upon rising in the morning, immediately after meals, or even during a meal.
- Heartburn and indigestion.
- Fatigue, depression, anxiety, difficulty in concentrating, headache, lassitude, reduced tolerance of pain.
- Nausea, increased intestinal gas, and bloating.

- Abdominal discomfort, either a sharp pain or a continuous dull ache, on the lower left side of the abdomen, which is relieved by a bowel movement.
- Attacks characteristically come during periods of stress. Patients report attacks triggered by marital discord, by anxiety related to children, by the loss of loved ones, by excessive worrying over trivial, everyday problems, by overwork, or by a new job. Attacks may also be triggered by food and drink; coffee, alcohol, spices, milk, very hot or very cold foods, salads, and raw fruits and vegetables are among those mentioned frequently.

Epidemiological Data

Up to 15 percent of all Americans get periodic attacks of irritable bowel syndrome.

Three times as many women as men suffer from the disorder.

One-half of all gastrointestinal referrals are for this problem.

Prevention and Treatment

- For those with constipation, eat wheat bran and other fibrous foods and increase exercise.
- For those with diarrhea, eat a bland diet low in fiber.
- Eat regularly and try to evacuate your bowels at the same time each day.
- Learn ways to handle stress better.
- Avoid foods that do not agree with you.

CASE HISTORY: Jim Cole

Jim Cole, a young advertising executive, was proud of his new job. His promotion to the vice-presidency had its price, however. He was now working fifteen-hour days, and this caused considerable tension in his marriage. He had no time for recreation, got little exercise, and, apart from business luncheons, he virtually always ate on the run.

Jim could remember that in his childhood his father would often complain of an upset stomach. Jim had similar complaints: severe heartburn after meals, and extremely irregular bowel movements, with alternating bouts of violent diarrhea and terrible constipation. In the midst of one particularly unpleasant episode, he went to see his doctor.

He told his doctor about these symptoms, as well as the recurring, sharp pain he had on the lower left side of his stomach. The doctor knew his patient was a driven, hardworking man, and he had treated his father as well. His immediate diagnosis was irritable bowel syndrome.

However, in order to rule out more serious conditions, such as Crohn's disease, colitis, and colon cancer, he examined a stool sample for blood. He also conducted a rectal exam, took an X-ray, and ran a blood test. All proved negative.

His advice to Jim was to take steps toward managing his stress. He also encouraged him to take one to two tablespoons of wheat bran every day at breakfast at all times except when he had diarrhea. He discussed with Jim how exercise and regular meals help control irritable syndrome.

Jim took the advice seriously. The changes he made helped, but he still found he had the problem whenever he was under a great deal of stress. After a recent, prolonged bout with the problem he went back to his doctor, who prescribed a medication for his anxiety as well as one to decrease the contractions of his intestine.

Dietary and Life-style Recommendations

Eat Wheat Bran and Other Fibrous Foods to Reduce Constipation

One to two tablespoons of wheat bran daily, taken with at least a cup of fluid; eating other foods rich in dietary fiber (see table on page 303 for a list of such foods); and regular exercise will increase bowel function if you are constipated.

Strategy Begin with small amounts of bran, about one to two teaspoons, and gradually increase the amount over several weeks until you are consuming a half-cup a day.

Laxatives containing *psyllium* (check the ingredients list) may be used occasionally if other strategies do not relieve the constipation.

For Diarrhea, Consume a Bland Diet that Is Low in Fiber

A bland diet will tend to slow down the activity of the bowel.

Strategy Such a diet is low in fiber, contains few or no condiments and spices (except salt in small amounts), and avoids very acidic foods. (See page 326 for table of foods to eat and to avoid to maintain a bland diet.)

Eat Regularly and Try to Evacuate Your Bowels at the Same Time Each Day

When you eat large meals at irregular intervals, you tend to exacerbate the irregular contractions of your intestine. If you tend to eat on the run, the likelihood is that you also eat fast foods, which, as a general rule, are low in fiber.

Strategy Adopt regular habits. This will mean that you will have a constant flow of nutrients in your digestive tract, which will help to keep the muscles contracting in a regular, rhythmic way.

Learn How to Handle Stress

Since stress is a major cause of irritable bowel syndrome, you should seek help in dealing with the problem.

Strategy This may require consultation with a psychiatrist, or may simply be corrected by taking medication. (See also Appendix 3 for some hints in dealing with stress.)

Avoid Foods that Do Not Agree with You

Dairy products often precipitate an attack in patients with irritable bowel syndrome.

Strategy If your attacks are caused in this way, avoid dairy products and compensate for the calcium loss by taking a calcium supplement. A total of 1,000 milligrams should be taken daily, in 250- to 500-milligram doses, two to four times each day.

If you have a lot of gas, you should also avoid foods like baked beans and cabbage, which tend to cause this problem. (See page 308 for table of foods that tend to cause gas.)

Other Advice

If you would like additional information about irritable bowel syndrome, contact the American Digestive Disease Society, Suite 217, 7720 Wisconsin Avenue, Bethesda, Maryland 20014, phone (301) 652-5524; or the National Digestive Disease Education and Information Clearinghouse, Suite 600, 1555 Wilson Boulevard, Rosslyn, Virginia 22209, phone (703) 522-0870.

34
Kidney Stones

Kidney stones are formed from deposits of a variety of substances as small as a grain of sand, or as much as an inch in diameter, in the kidneys.

Most stones contain calcium in the form of calcium phosphate, calcium oxalate, or a combination of the two. Less often, kidney stones are composed of food substances like uric acid, *cystine* (an amino acid or building block of protein) or *struvite* (magnesium ammonium phosphate). These compounds do not dissolve very well in urine, and when their concentrations get high enough, they precipitate as little crystals that eventually grow into stones. They sometimes form around a nucleus of organic matter, bacteria, or the remains of a previous stone that has been incompletely removed by the surgeon or only partially passed.

Between 10 and 20 percent of calcium kidney stones result from metabolic disorders. For example, the hormone *parathormone* is produced by the parathyroid gland. It is responsible for elevating blood calcium levels when they fall below normal by causing calcium to be liberated from the bones. Sometimes a tumor grows on the parathyroid gland, and such large amounts of parathormone are produced that blood and urine calcium levels go very high. Other causes include diseases of the intestine and conditions that cause malabsorption of fat, such as Crohn's disease (chapter 15), pancreatic disease, extended immobilization (chapter 21), vitamin D overdosage, excessive calcium consumption, and antacid abuse.

Over 80 percent of calcium stones in all age groups occur as a result of an unknown factor that increases calcium levels in the urine. Most people with the problem have normal diets and blood levels, but abnormally high urine levels of calcium. The best treatment for this is the diuretic *hydrochlorothiazide*, which increases the volume of urine excreted and reduces its calcium concentration.

Another, rarer kind of kidney stone is made of uric acid. People either excrete high levels because they consume too much uric acid in their diets (10 percent of cases) or because they produce too much in their bodies (90 percent of cases). Many people develop gout with the latter problem. The treatment of choice for overproducers of uric acid is to take the drug *allopurinol*, which prevents the body from producing uric acid.

Magnesium ammonium phosphate stones are caused when the urine becomes very alkaline. This is usually brought about when organisms that release ammonia infect the urinary tract.

Cystine stones are caused by a very rare genetic defect that prevents the reabsorption of this amino acid in the kidney. A buildup occurs and a stone is formed.

Anything that increases the urinary concentration of any of these compounds will increase the risk of stone formation. This is one good reason why you should drink plenty of fluids. Anything that impedes the flow of urine, such as cysts, scar tissue, or a defect in the structure of the urinary tract, will also increase the risk.

A person with kidney stones is blithely unaware of his or her condition until he is stricken with an excruciating pain caused by the stone trying to pass through the tubes transporting the urine within the kidney, or through the tubes that connect the bladder to the kidney. If the stones block the flow of urine, there is a high risk of infection (although the other kidney can usually cope with the removal of waste products from the blood) that can cause fever and chills and can further damage the kidneys.

If no infection is apparent, it is often advisable to wait weeks or even months to allow a stone to pass. If the stones must be removed, a tube is passed from the exterior to a stone in the lower reaches of the urinary tract or into the kidney directly for stones in the upper reaches. This alleviates the pain but can damage the urinary tract. Only stones of less than one centimeter in diameter may be removed in this way. If they are larger, they must be removed surgically or treated with underwater shock-wave treatments. Once removed, the stones are analyzed so as to ensure the development of a proper treatment plan to prevent the problem from developing again, and to deal with it if it does.

A person may have only one stone in a lifetime, but they usually recur, sometimes as frequently as every three or four years, sometimes as infrequently as every twenty years. Between stones, no symptoms are usually experienced. Very often the stone is broken up in transit down the urinary tract and is passed in sandlike granules.

Warning Signs

- Kidney stones give absolutely no indication that they are present until the pain of passage is felt.
- Intermittent, excruciating pain in the area of the kidneys occurs when the stones begin their passage; the pain may radiate around to the front of the body and across the abdomen, and frequently reaches into the region of the genitals and the insides of the thigh; the pain is such that it is agonizing to move, and even worse when remaining still.
- A significant number of people experience gastrointestinal symptoms such as nausea, vomiting, and abdominal distension.
- If an infection is present in the kidneys or bladder, chills and fever may occur.
- Rarely, blood in the urine may occur as a result of the stones irritating the lining of the kidney.
- Frequent urination will occur when the stones reach the bladder.

Epidemiological Data

One in a thousand adults is hospitalized annually in the United States because of kidney stones, but in the course of one in 100 autopsies, kidney stones are discovered.

Twelve to 14 percent of all males and 5 percent of all females in the United States will develop kidney stones by age 70. Once formed, stones usually recur within a five-to-ten-year period.

Eighty percent of all kidney stones contain calcium; roughly 60 percent are of calcium oxalate; less than 10 percent are of calcium phosphate; slightly more than 10 percent are of both calcium oxalate and calcium phosphate.

About 10 percent of all kidney stones are made up of uric acid, while less than 1 percent are made up of the amino acid cystine. Slightly less than 10 percent of all kidney stones are made of magnesium ammonium phosphate.

Kidney stones tend to run in families.

Ten to 25 percent of all patients with gout have uric acid stones. This is more common in men.

Calcium and uric acid stones usually appear initially in the third or fourth decade of life.

Prevention and Treatment

- Drink at least three to four quarts of fluid each day.
- People with calcium oxalate stones should restrict their vitamin C intake to no more than three grams (3,000 milligrams) per day.
- People who produce too much oxalate in their bodies should take a 100- to 200-milligram B_6 supplement each day.
- Make sure that you have 5,000 international units of vitamin A in your daily diet.
- People with stones containing calcium oxalate should limit the fat in their diets.
- If you have uric acid stones, restrict your protein intake to no more than one gram per kilogram of body weight, or 0.035 ounces per 2.2 pounds.
- If you have magnesium ammonium phosphate stones, cut down on fruit and vegetables and eat more grains and protein-rich foods.
- Do not get more than two grams (2,000 milligrams) daily of calcium in your diet if you have calcium stones.
- Decrease your sodium intake to two to three grams per day if you have calcium stones.
- If you have calcium stones and a tendency to reactive hypoglycemia, reduce your refined sugar intake.
- Be aware of the food and drug interactions associated with the drugs used to treat kidney stones.

CASE HISTORY: James Biddles

Jim Biddles had never really worried about having kidney stones. Sure, he knew all too well his father's history with them, having heard him complain of the pain and once having visited him in the hospital after surgery. But somehow he didn't really think it would happen to him.

It did. He awoke very early one morning with a groan that woke his wife. She asked him what was the matter, and suddenly he knew the answer. The pain, though excruciating, was intermittent, and in the area of his left kidney.

That morning he went to see his doctor. Urine and blood tests were conducted. The blood sample proved to be perfectly normal, but the urine showed an abnormally high level of calcium. The doctor sent him for X-rays, which revealed that Jim had a small kidney stone lodged in his left kidney.

Jim, on consultation with his doctor, decided to wait for the stone to pass. It took six months, during which, from time to time, he experienced episodes of severe pain. The pain moved to his abdomen and slowly down to his groin and genitals. He then noticed that he was urinating a great deal. He called his doctor, who analyzed the urine and found small fragments of a calcium oxalate stone. Jim had passed the stone.

Jim was put on hydrochlorothiazide and advised to restrict his intake of foods rich in oxalates. So much for his beloved baked beans, and too bad about the strawberries (and the beets and kale and grapes and the rest). But to avoid the pain, it didn't seem like too much of a sacrifice.

It is now five years since the attack, and Jim has had no trouble since that time.

Dietary and Life-style Recommendations

People with All Kinds of Kidney Stones Should Drink as Much Fluid as Possible

Fluids can dilute the urine and help prevent substances such as calcium oxalate from achieving high enough concentrations to form crystals in the urine.

Strategy   Drink at least three to four quarts per day of fluids. It is especially important to drink plenty of fluids before bedtime and during the night, since that is when urine becomes concentrated.

Restrict Vitamin C

If you have calcium oxalate kidney stones, you should restrict your consumption of vitamin C. The vitamin is involved in the production of oxalate in the body, as it is required for the conversion of glyoxalate to oxalate, and 90 percent of the oxalate in the urine is made in the body.

Strategy   As much as three to four grams (3,000–4,000 milligrams) of vitamin C seems to be safe, but more than that can increase oxalate production and increase the risk of calcium oxalate stones. As it is unlikely that you will consume more than this amount of vitamin C from dietary sources, your concern should be with limiting your use of vitamin C from supplements.

Restrict Oxalate-Rich Foods

Approximately 10 percent of the oxalate in the urine is derived from the diet. Usually this dietary oxalate combines with calcium in the digestive tract and is excreted in the feces as calcium oxalate. However, if you have a fat malabsorption disorder, the fat you eat will combine with the calcium in foods and both will be excreted in the stool. As a result, the oxalate in your diet will be left free of calcium and will be absorbed into your system. Since the oxalate cannot be broken down in the body, it will then be dispatched to the kidneys to be excreted in the urine, where it can combine with calcium to form calcium oxalate stones.

Strategy The production of oxalate stones can be reduced by restricting oxalate-rich foods. (See table of oxalate-rich foods on page 306.) Also, consume a low-fat diet. (See chapter 6 for guidance on limiting your dietary fats.)

Take Vitamin B₆ Supplements

To avoid further oxalate-based kidney stones, you should take vitamin B_6 supplements. About 90 percent of the oxalate present in the urine is made in the body, and if it is allowed to enter the kidneys, it can lead to the formation of stones. Vitamin B_6 will reduce the body's production of oxalate by as much as 50 percent.

Strategy Take a 100- to 200-milligram daily supplement of vitamin B_6. This supplement will reduce the amount of oxalate excreted into the urine and thereby reduce the risk of calcium oxalate stones.

Consume Vitamin A Daily

A vitamin A deficiency leads to changes in the lining of the urinary tract that favor the deposition of calcium and the production of kidney stones.

Strategy Be sure you get 5,000 international units of vitamin A daily. (See table on page 318 for foods rich in vitamin A.)

Restrict Your Protein Intake

Stones are rare in Eskimos, who eat a lot of fat, and in Amazon Indians, who are complete vegetarians and eat very little fat. Clearly, it is not simply fat that is to be blamed for kidney stones.

But there is a direct correlation between the incidence of kidney stone disease and the amount of protein eaten. Protein has been demonstrated to increase the acidity of the urine, and also to increase the presence of uric acid, calcium, and phosphorus in the urine. The result of an increase in concentration of these substances is, in some people, the formation of stones.

Strategy Limit protein to no more than six ounces of protein-rich foods per day. See page 313 for table of protein-rich foods.

If Your Urine Calcium Level Is High, Limit the Calcium in Your Daily Diet

In normal people, the calcium level in their urine does not increase until their calcium intake exceeds two grams. However, people who have abnormally high urine calcium levels may benefit from decreasing their calcium intake.

Strategy If your urine has unusually high levels of calcium, limit your calcium intake to 800 milligrams per day. As this may increase your risk of developing osteoporosis (see chapter 39), you should only restrict your calcium consumption on the advice of your doctor.

Calcium intake is the least important factor in the development of kidney stones. Oxalate excretion is a bigger factor in calcium oxalate stone production.

Other Advice

The more salt (sodium chloride) is eaten, the more sodium needs to be excreted and the more calcium is excreted. Consequently, you should reduce your salt intake to two to three grams per day. Consult chapter 30 ("Hypertension") for advice on sodium restriction.

Some people overproduce insulin, which is essential to normal glucose absorption, when they eat a lot of sweet foods. Insulin tends to increase calcium excretion, which increases the risk of calcium-containing kidney stones. People who have reactive hypoglycemia (see chapter 31) would fit into this category, and should limit their intake of sweet foods.

If you have magnesium ammonium phosphate stones, you should cut down on fruits and vegetables. By doing so, and by eating more protein (meat and fish and grains), you will increase the acidity of your urine. This will prevent the formation of magnesium ammonium phosphate stones, which can only be precipitated when the urine is alkaline.

FOOD AND DRUG INTERACTIONS

THIAZIDE DIURETICS These drugs can cause magnesium, potassium, and zinc deficiencies. Foods rich in these nutrients should be well represented in the diet. (See tables on pages 311, 313, and 323.) Your physician may also recommend that you take a daily potassium supplement (but do not self-medicate yourself with potassium supplements). Take these diuretics with meals or milk.

MAGNESIUM HYDROXIDE This medication tends to cause the loss of body phosphorus, which can cause brittle bones. Be sure to get plenty of phosphorus-rich foods in the diet.

CELLULOSE PHOSPHATE This drug works by reducing calcium absorption. Over an extended period it could lead to brittle bones resulting from calcium deficiency. Discuss the risk of osteoporosis with your doctor. (See also chapter 39.)

ORTHOPHOSPHATE-SODIUM This drug causes diarrhea, so you should take a daily vitamin supplement containing the Recommended Dietary Allowances to be sure you get enough of the essential vitamins.

MORPHINE This painkiller causes constipation. Increase the fiber in your diet while taking it. (See chapter 14.)

ALLOPURINOL If your doctor prescribes this drug, take it after meals in order to prevent gastrointestinal disturbances. Be sure you get plenty of iron from the foods in your diet. (See table on page 309 for foods rich in iron.)

CHOLESTYRAMINE This medication may cause deficiencies of vitamins D, A, K, E, and B_{12} and folic acid. Take a one-a-day vitamin to avoid such deficiencies.

If you would like additional information about kidney stones, contact the National Kidney Foundation, Inc., 2 Park Avenue, New York, New York 10016, phone (212) 889-2210.

35
Lactose Intolerance

The carbohydrate in all milk is called *lactose,* and is composed of two sugars, *glucose* and *galactose.* Almost all babies have an enzyme in their digestive system called *lactase* that separates the two sugars and releases them so they can be digested.

The enzyme usually remains active throughout life, but sometimes its activity slowly diminishes so that by eight or nine years of age, a child is no longer able to digest lactose efficiently.

When the undigested lactose passes down the intestines to the lower intestine, it is broken down by bacteria; this process produces gas and causes bloating and abdominal pain. Lactic acid is also produced, which irritates the intestine and causes diarrhea. The inability to digest lactose and the resulting symptoms are called *lactose intolerance.*

Warning Signs

• Symptoms varying from slight abdominal discomfort to flatulence, bloating, abdominal pain, and explosive diarrhea within minutes after eating foods rich in lactose.

Epidemiological Data

About 70 percent of the world's people become lactose intolerant in the course of their lives. Only Europeans, particularly western Europeans and their descendants, maintain high levels of lactase into adult life.

In Asians, Africans, and Polynesians and their descendants, the activity of the enzyme slowly diminishes from about six years of age onward. In 70 percent of the world's population, lactase activity is reduced to 5 to 10 percent of its pre-weaning level by the age of six.

About 12 percent of all whites and 70 percent of all blacks in the United States have some degree of lactose intolerance. Fifty percent of adult Jews and 80 percent of adult blacks have lactose intolerance.

Lactose constitutes 10 percent of the carbohydrates found in the American diet.

Prevention and Treatment

• Adjust the amount of milk and other lactose-containing foods to your individual tolerance level.

• Drink whatever milk you consume with solid foods whenever possible.

• Try adding lactase to milk before drinking it.

• Make sure that you compensate with other food sources for the loss of calcium in your diet resulting from a low intake of milk.

• Do not force a child who cannot tolerate large quantities of milk to consume more than is comfortable for him.

CASE HISTORY: Allen Schwartz

Bernard and Rose Schwartz were of Russian Jewish descent. They lived in a comfortable suburb outside Houston, and both worked in white-collar jobs in the city.

Neither of them had ever known anything but a largely American diet, and neither had ever had any trouble digesting it. Consequently, it was a considerable surprise when their youngest son, Allen, became very uncomfortable when he drank just a glass of milk.

The problem had not manifested itself until Allen was a teenager. He found that the glass of milk his mother served him at each meal gave him gas. When his condition worsened and uncontrollable flatulence resulted, Rose took her son to the doctor.

The doctor immediately diagnosed lactose intolerance, and did his best to assure the worried mother that there was nothing strange about the problem. He advised that Allen's milk be treated with powdered lactase before he drank it. He also suggested that the boy make a point of avoiding the after-school milk he was in the habit of drinking.

The strategy worked. Allen has continued to drink one to two glasses of lactase-treated milk a day, with only minor gastrointestinal discomfort. The doctor suggested that once he reached his adult height he would probably do well to drink milk only in coffee and tea.

Dietary and Life-style Recommendations

Eat Foods Containing Lactose According to Your Individual Tolerance

Different people have widely varying tolerances to foods containing lactose. About 90 percent of all lactose-intolerant people can consume up to one cup of milk at a sitting without having a problem. Hence, total elimination of foods rich in lactose is unnecessary and could compromise the nutritional status of a person. Dairy products (with the exception of butter) contribute only 10 percent of our calories while providing 75 percent of our calcium, 37 percent of our riboflavin (vitamin B_2), one-third of our phosphorus, 20 percent of our magnesium, and 20 percent of our vitamin B_{12}. Milk is also an excellent source of quality protein.

Strategy Determine how much lactose can be tolerated by trial and error and be mindful of which foods besides milk are rich in lactose. (See table on page 310 of lactose-rich foods.)

Another strategy is to drink milk with solid foods whenever possible. By consuming smaller amounts at each sitting, more milk can often be tolerated. When it is taken with solid food, the rate at which the milk passes down the digestive tract and is presented to the intestine for absorption is reduced. Thus, the lactase present has a better chance of digesting it. For example, milk eaten along with a bowl of corn flakes, a boiled egg, and toast at breakfast improves lactose absorption by 50 percent.

Whole milk contains fat, which slows down the rate at which the digestive system works, so it is better absorbed than skim milk. The same is true of chocolate milk. On the other hand, fermented dairy products are very little different from regular dairy products; the lactose content of yogurt, cultured buttermilk, and sweet acidophilus milk is much the same as that of whole milk. Yogurt is better tolerated, however, because it contains some lactase. Any advantage is lost, however, when yogurt is pasteurized.

Be sure, too, to check food labels, looking for the presence of milk, whey solids, and milk solids.

Add Lactase to Milk Before Drinking

Lactase-hydrolyzed milk and other dairy products are available. These are made by incubating milk or other milk products with lactase for 24 hours, which reduces the lactose content by between 40 and 90 percent, and lessens the symptoms of lactose intolerance.

Strategy Lactase-treated milk is quite palatable, though it has a sweeter taste than regular milk products and is more expensive. You can also add powdered or liquid lactase to milk yourself.

Compensate for the Loss of Calcium from Your Diet

If your milk consumption is reduced by your intolerance of lactose, be sure that you compensate with other foods for the resulting loss of calcium from your diet.

Strategy Since milk provides about 74.5 percent of the average American's daily calcium, careful selection of foods is needed to make up for the losses. (See page 301 for table of other sources of calcium to incorporate into your diet.)

Milk is the only dietary source of calcium that is readily absorbed by the body. Therefore, anyone with lactose intolerance should take a 1,000-milligram supplement of calcium as calcium carbonate (2.5 grams calcium carbonate). Half should be taken at midmorning and half at bedtime for maximum absorption. A daily vitamin supplement containing the Recommended Dietary Allowances is also a good idea, to compensate for the riboflavin and B_{12} normally supplied by milk in the diet.

If Your Child Cannot Tolerate Quantities of Milk, Do Not Force Him or Her to Consume More than Is Comfortable

Milk plays a special role in our society in feeding young children, but care must be taken not to force children who cannot tolerate milk to consume it in quantity. If your child has a lactose intolerance problem, don't force the child to consume milk simply because it is the societal norm.

Strategy Usually, small amounts of milk in cereal or added to a dessert are no problem; often as much as half a glass or even a glass can be tolerated. Observe your child carefully to determine his or her tolerance.

Although lactose intolerance is not an allergy, it can lead to serious problems if a child suffers from persistent diarrhea and hence to excessive nutrient losses. Infants who are born with the problem should be given formulas like *Nutramigen, Prosobee,* and *Isomil,* which contain corn syrup and/or sucrose in place of lactose. Foods containing milk or lactose should be introduced gradually and cautiously after 12 months of age. If a severe reaction is experienced, milk products should be discontinued and advice sought from a pediatrician.

If you would like additional information about lactose intolerance, you can write to the American Digestive Disease Society, Suite 217, 7720 Wisconsin Avenue, Bethesda, Maryland 20014, phone (301) 652-5524.

36
Migraine Headaches

A *migraine headache* is caused by the dilation of blood vessels in the scalp, beginning as a throbbing pain and then settling down to a dull ache. The headache is usually accompanied by other symptoms of illness such as nausea, abdominal pain, a distinct queasy feeling, loss of appetite, vomiting, or diarrhea. The sufferer may become pale and feel chilled. His or her behavior may also be altered, and irritability and fatigue may result. Visual disturbances may be present, such as blurred vision, or pain on exposure to light. Some victims become disoriented and confused.

Warning Signs

• Flashing lights or zigzag strokes, much like lightning, that seem to rise behind the eyes
• Feelings of depression, unusual anxiety, and nervousness
• Muscle weakness and extreme fatigue

Epidemiological Data

Eight to 12 percent of Americans suffer from migraines, of which 60 to 90 percent inherit the tendency.

Most sufferers get migraines one to three times per month; most sufferers begin to experience migraines between the ages of 10 and 30, and remission after 50 years of age is common; female sufferers outnumber male.

Seventy percent of migraine sufferers have pain only on one side of the head.

Prevention and Treatment

- Avoid foods containing *tyramine*, such as cheddar cheese, pickled herring, chicken livers, cured meats such as hot dogs and salami, red wine, dark beers, and alcohol in general.
- Do not eat foods containing monosodium glutamate.
- Be cautious when eating foods that have been implicated as major causal agents of headaches, such as eggs, legumes (including peanuts), garlic, wheat, milk, cinnamon, fish, pork, corn, and chocolate.
- Establish a regular schedule of getting up each morning at the same time and eating meals at regular intervals.
- Avoid emotional tension.

CASE HISTORY: Mildred Rousseau

At thirteen, Mildred Rousseau had her first migraine. Her mother consoled her as best she could, but her help was minimal; she herself had suffered from migraine headaches for thirty years, and knew the discomforts and the frustrations.

At twenty-five, Mildred now knows the telltale signs of an oncoming migraine. A feeling of emotional depression arrives some hours before the pain, followed by flashing lights that seem to rise behind her eyes. They, in turn, give way to the headache itself.

Usually the pain lasts for several hours, and Mildred employs a strategy she has worked out in consultation with her doctor. She takes a tablet of the codeine he has prescribed for her, retires to her bedroom, closes the blinds, and lies down. Three to four hours later, the pain has usually lifted. She has also found that some foods (eggs, peanuts, and corn, in particular) bring on the bouts, so she avoids them.

Dietary and Life-style Recommendations

Avoid Foods Containing Tyramine

Tyramine is a food substance that has been shown to be a potent *vasodilator*. By causing the blood vessels to dilate, it increases the flow of blood through the vessels in the scalp, which causes the pounding feeling experienced by migraine sufferers.

Strategy It is advisable to avoid the consumption of foods containing tyramine. Tyramine is contained in many foods, but it is found in the greatest amounts in high-protein foods that have undergone some decomposition, such as aged cheese. Tyramine is also found in chicken and beef livers, bananas, eggplant, sour cream, salami, meat tenderizers, chocolate, yeast, and soy sauce. (See table of tyramine-containing foods on page 317.)

Alcoholic beverages should also be avoided, in particular sherry, beer, and Chianti, Reisling, and sauterne wines.

Do Not Eat Foods Containing Monosodium Glutamate

People who are sensitive to *monosodium glutamate (MSG)* develop "Chinese restaurant syndrome," which results in a temporary burning sensation in the neck and forearms, chest tightness, and migraine-like headache.

Strategy Read the labels on processed foods to determine whether they contain MSG. All commercially prepared products except mayonnaise, salad dressing, or French dressing must list MSG on their labels. When dining in Chinese restaurants you can ask them to leave out the MSG, but since there is no assurance that they will do so, it is better to avoid Chinese restaurants if one is MSG sensitive. (See also chapter 22.)

Avoid Other Foods that Cause Headaches

A number of other foods have been implicated as major causal agents of headaches. Many of these foods contain vasodilators.

Strategy Avoid eggs, legumes (including peanuts), garlic, wheat, milk, cinnamon, pork, and corn. Coffee, tea, and cola drinks, which can trigger caffeine withdrawal headaches, should also be avoided.

Establish a Regular Daily Schedule

A consistent daily pattern of activity has been shown in some cases to be helpful to migraine sufferers to reduce the frequency of the headaches.

Strategy Migraine sufferers should rise each morning at the same time. Meals should be eaten at regular intervals. Fasting and overeating should be avoided, as either one can precipitate a headache.

Other Advice

Both mental and physical factors have a decided role in migraine headaches. Often, migraines are triggered by particularly stressful times.

Try to avoid stressful situations by anticipating events and planning ahead. Be sure your doctor is aware of your migraine headaches, so he can avoid prescribing drugs that are known to have a relationship to migraines.

Many women also get attacks just before their periods, owing to changing hormone levels, or during pregnancy and at menopause. Changes in weather, loss of sleep, and fatigue can all provoke an attack. Gastrointestinal infections or other illnesses and certain drugs, including birth-control pills, are factors commonly implicated as causal agents of migraines.

For further information on migraines, contact the Asthma and Allergy Foundation of America, 1707 North Street, N. W., Washington, D.C. 20036, phone (202) 293-1260.

37
Obesity
and Overweight

Obesity is defined as being 20 percent over the ideal weight for a person's height and bone structure. The only exceptions are people who have an enormous amount of muscle, as is the case with some body-builders and football players.

There are 34 million obese Americans. Countless more wage a continuous battle to keep their weight within the ideal range. The problem of obesity is on the rise because increasing numbers of children and adolescents are overweight, and there is substantial evidence to suggest that obesity in childhood is linked with over-weight in adulthood.

Being overweight is more serious than it may seem. It is not just a question of aesthetics. Obese people are often discriminated against, and being even 5 percent over normal weight increases the risk of cancer, heart attacks, diabetes, high blood pressure, lung disorders, gout, and osteoarthritis. If you have a family history of high blood pressure (hypertension), diabetes, or heart disease, you are especially at risk for these disorders should you be or become overweight.

There are many myths about obesity. Obese people are certainly not psychologically unstable, as many people think. All obese people do not overeat constantly; this is especially true of the mildly obese. Other myths are that people with weight problems eat their meals very quickly and in large bites. Overweight people also, on the whole, do not lack self-discipline and are not lazy.

The development of obesity is an incredibly complex phenomenon, a combination of a number of factors, including genetic predisposi-

215

tion, psychological factors, and metabolic disorders. There is no pat solution to the problem. Undoubtedly, many obese people do eat too much or exercise too little, but the solution to an obesity problem is usually more complex than that. For instance, many people with a weight problem use their food so efficiently that the only way they can maintain their ideal weight is to stay on a very restricted diet for the rest of their lives. People with this kind of problem have usually been heavy since childhood. Those who find a permanent solution to their problems in diet and exercise have usually developed a weight problem during adulthood.

Warning Signs

• A steady increase in weight from year to year.
• If your waist is bigger than your hips, you are obese.

Epidemiological Data

In the last two decades, the prevalence of obesity has increased by 54 percent among 6- to 11-year-old children, and by 39 percent among 12- to 17-year-olds.

Forty percent of children who are obese at seven years of age become obese adults; 70 percent of obese adolescents become obese adults. In fact, most children can become obese by eating as little as 50 extra calories per day. This leads to an excess weight gain of five pounds per year.

In obese people, the incidence of high blood pressure is three times that in the normal population; in those who are 50 percent or more overweight, high blood pressure is five times more likely than normal.

Ninety-five percent of people who lose weight regain it within the first year. In fact, 40 million Americans are on a weight-loss diet at any given time, and there are 30,000 methods of weight control in use in America today.

When body weight is 10 percent above the average for weight and frame size, life expectancy decreases by 11 percent in men and 7 percent in women.

Pregnant women often gain extra weight during pregnancy because their bodies work more efficiently then than at other times. By breast-feeding after giving birth, they use up this extra fat tissue. However, if a mother chooses to bottle-feed, this weight is kept and may be the beginning of a weight problem. Mothers who elect not to breast-feed should go on a diet after pregnancy to lose the extra pounds. However, a lot of the weight a mother is left with following birth is water weight, which will gradually diminish over the following month or two. If a woman is still overweight eight weeks after the birth, that is the time to diet.

When body weight is 20 percent above the average for weight and frame size, life expectancy decreases by 20 percent in men and 10 percent in women.

Heredity is also a risk factor for obesity.

People who gain weight around the waist are at greater risk of obesity-related diseases than those who tend to gain around the hips. Even if your overall weight is not excessive, a pot belly may signify a problem.

Most Americans gain 15 to 20 pounds between the ages of 25 and 50 because activity decreases and the metabolism slows down.

Prevention and Treatment

- Calculate what you should weigh by measuring your frame size and referring to the table below.
- Calculate the number of calories needed to maintain your present body weight and follow a balanced diet containing 500 calories per day less than this number to lose a pound a week, or 1,000 calories less to lose two pounds a week.
- Adopt a balanced weight-loss diet.
- Keep a food diary.
- After consulting a doctor, start an exercise program of 20- to 30-minute workouts, three times a week.
- Avoid all fad diets, drugs, and surgical means to lose weight.

CASE HISTORY: Susan Applebaum

As a child, Sue Applebaum had been chubby, and had gotten in the habit of using food as a comforter. Whenever she met with disappointment—a lost boyfriend or a bad grade—it meant a visit to the doughnut store.

When she went to college and tried to slim down to her ideal weight, she found it extremely difficult. She tried the latest crash diets, and would lose some weight. But almost as soon as she began to eat normally again, she would gain back the weight. Also, each time she dieted, she found it necessary to reduce the amount she ate even further than on the previous diet.

Upon graduating, she got a job as a laboratory technician. Sick of dieting, she began to eat normally, and gained some weight. She found it difficult to find boyfriends, and she spent many nights at home in front of the TV. By the age of twenty-seven, she was fifty pounds overweight.

The laboratory in which Sue worked was attached to a medical school that was looking for volunteers to participate in a weight-loss study. She signed up, and after some preliminary exploration of her metabolism and experimentation with her eating habits, the researchers determined that she maintained weight on a mere 800 calories per day, and that any more food than that meant putting on pounds.

They advised her to stick to a 1,000-calorie diet and to carry out an exercise program that burned up 300 calories per day. This she did, and four years later she is only five pounds over her ideal weight.

Sue finds keeping her weight down a continuous struggle. She gains weight during the holidays, and has to work extremely hard at the health club to lose it again. The Weight Watchers organization has been helpful, but Sue will always have to watch what she eats.

Dietary and Life-style Recommendations

Calculate Your Ideal Weight for Height and Frame Size

To plan your weight program, you must first determine how overweight you are.

Strategy First, measure your frame size. To do this, extend one arm and bend the forearm upward at a 90-degree angle. Keeping the fingers straight, turn the inside of your wrist toward your body. Place the thumb and index finger of the other hand on the two prominent bones on either side of your bent elbow. Pull your fingers away and measure the space between them. If the measurement for a person your height is lower than the measurement shown in the table below, you have a small frame; if it is bigger, you have a large frame.

MEASURING YOUR FRAME SIZE

Height in 1" Heels	Normal Elbow Width	Height in 1" Heels	Normal Elbow Width
MEN		WOMEN	
5'2"–5'3"	2½"–2⅞"	4'10"–4'11"	2¼"–2½"
5'4"–5'7"	2⅝"–2⅞"	5'0"–5'3"	2¼"–2½"
5'8"–5'11"	2¾"–3"	5'4"–5'7"	2⅜"–2⅝"
6'0"–6'3"	2¾"–3⅛"	5'8"–5'11"	2⅜"–2⅝"
6'4"	2⅞"–3¼"	6'0"	2½"–2¾"

(Used by permission of Metropolitan Life Insurance Company)

IDEAL WEIGHT FOR HEIGHT

MEN

Height Feet	Inches	Small Frame	Medium Frame	Large Frame
5	2	128–134	131–141	138–150
5	3	130–136	133–143	140–153
5	4	132–138	135–145	142–156
5	5	134–140	137–148	144–160
5	6	136–142	139–151	146–164
5	7	138–145	142–154	149–168
5	8	140–148	145–157	152–172
5	9	142–151	148–160	155–176
5	10	144–154	151–163	158–180
5	11	146–157	154–166	161–184
6	0	149–160	157–170	164–188
6	1	152–164	160–174	168–192
6	2	155–168	164–178	172–197
6	3	158–172	167–182	176–202
6	4	162–176	171–187	181–207

WOMEN

Height Feet	Inches	Small Frame	Medium Frame	Large Frame
4	10	102–111	109–121	118–131
4	11	103–113	111–123	120–134
5	0	104–115	113–126	122–137
5	1	106–118	115–129	125–140
5	2	108–121	118–132	128–143
5	3	111–124	121–135	131–147
5	4	114–127	124–138	134–151
5	5	117–130	127–141	137–155
5	6	120–133	130–144	140–159
5	7	123–136	133–147	143–163
5	8	126–139	136–150	146–167
5	9	129–142	139–153	149–170
5	10	132–145	142–156	152–173
5	11	135–148	145–159	155–176
6	0	138–151	148–162	158–179

Note: The above figures give the weights of people who live the longest. (Used by permission of Metropolitan Life Insurance Company)

Determine How Many Calories to Cut Out to Lose Weight

Calculate how many calories you need to sustain your present weight.

Strategy Make this simple calculation. Take your current weight and multiply it by ten to determine the number of calories you need to maintain your *basal metabolism*, that is, to keep your heart and lungs and other systems functioning normally. Add in 30 percent of the calculated figure for your various physical activities if you are a sedentary person who does not take any regular physical exercise. The combined figures are what constitute the caloric requirement to maintain your present weight.

If, for example, you weigh 150 pounds, then the number of calories you need to maintain your basal metabolism is

$$150 \times 10 = 1,500 \text{ calories.}$$

Your caloric requirement for physical activity is

$$1,500 \times .3 = 450 \text{ calories.}$$

Therefore, the energy you need to maintain your weight is the number of calories you need to maintain your basal metabolism plus your caloric requirement for physical activity, or

$$1,500 + 450 = 1,950 \text{ calories.}$$

Now that you know how many calories are required to maintain your weight, consider how many calories you must eliminate to lose weight.

For you to lose one pound of weight in a week, you need to reduce your caloric intake by 3,500 calories, or increase your energy expenditure by that much. Hence, if you are to lose that pound by dieting alone, you need to cut down by 500 calories a day. If you use up to 300 calories in an exercise program, then you have only to reduce food intake by 200 calories. To lose two pounds per week, you need to cut out 1,000 calories a day, and so on.

Adopt a Balanced Weight-Loss Diet

The golden rule of diets is to set yourself reasonable goals and to pursue them in a sensible manner. Drastic changes in the amount or type of food you eat will only cause you stress and make it more difficult for you to stick to a diet. Remember, it took you a long time to put the extra weight on, and it is reasonable that it should take you some time to lose it. Don't make dieting a nightmare, but try to eat foods that you like and include things like ice cream as occasional (once a week) treats.

Strategy The best kind of diet to follow is one high in complex carbohydrates such as pasta, bread, cereals, and starchy vegetables. You should include at least two three-ounce portions of protein-rich foods, meaning lean meat, skinless poultry, and fish, as well as low-fat dairy products.

You also need plenty of fillers in the form of low-calorie vegetables such as leafy greens, carrots, cauliflower, broccoli, and green beans and fruit. In addition, anybody on a diet should take a daily supplement containing the Recommended Dietary Allowances for vitamins and a 1,000-milligram (one gram) calcium supplement.

High protein/low carbohydrate diets can allow you to lose weight quickly, but most of the early weight loss is water. This will return as soon as you begin to eat normally again. By following a high-complex-carbohydrate diet, you also eat much less fat. Fat calories are harder to burn than carbohydrate calories and make weight loss more difficult. Consult the table on page 332 to see how much of the various food groups you can incorporate in your diet to achieve the caloric level you are following. The table on page 329 gives you your choices for each group.

Eat smaller portions of food five times a day instead of larger ones three times a day. This not only ensures that you do not get too hungry, but it also means that your body uses the food less efficiently. Every time you eat a meal, the body uses a certain amount of energy in preparing the digestive system to receive and digest the food in that meal. This energy is called *thermogenesis*. By eating your food in five meals instead of three, the body gears itself up five times a day instead of three and much more energy is used up.

The table on page 332 gives an example of a typical day's menu of somebody on a 1,500-calorie-a-day diet. This is the most suitable diet for most men and women. Not only will it permit a steady weight loss, but it will also show you how to make wise choices about everyday foods, which is what you will have to remember when you go off the diet and attempt to stay thin.

Losing weight by diet alone has its limitations. The body adjusts to the lower caloric intake after a while (usually two to three weeks) by lowering its metabolic rate. This is because the body resists changes in weight. When you restrict your caloric intake, the body begins to use calories more efficiently in order to maintain the original weight or "set point." By three weeks into your diet, your body is working at 30 percent greater efficiency. This is sufficient to prevent you from losing additional weight.

You can overcome this by exercising, though even with exercise your weight loss will be slower than at the beginning. When you get down to your ideal weight, you must maintain it for at least three weeks by restricting your intake so that you can change your set point to a new level. Once that new set point is achieved, the body will defend it rather than the old level. It will resist any gain in weight as well as loss in weight.

The yo-yo effect of weight gains and losses occurs when people do not maintain their ideal weight for long enough by restrictions before they resume a normal diet. They go on a diet, lose the weight needed to bring them down to the ideal level, then go back to eating normally. No new set point has been achieved, so they gain the weight back again. Unfortunately, the more times you do this, the more difficult it seems to lose weight.

People who have been heavy since childhood need to diet their entire lives. For them, life is a continual battle to maintain ideal weight.

Keep a Food Diary

Short-term weight loss is not difficult, but lasting weight loss is a problem. Of course, this is the only kind that improves your health. Permanent weight loss requires a commitment to modifying your patterns of physical activity as well as eating.

Strategy   The first step in this direction is to find out where you are going wrong. This is most easily done by using a food diary in which you list everything that has anything to do with eating. As you compile it, you should be answering the following questions:

• What did you eat, and in what quantities? (Cite exact number of calories.)
• What time of day, where, and with whom did you eat?
• What was your mood at the time you ate?
• How hungry were you at the time you ate?
• Were you reading or watching TV or involved in some other activity as you were eating?

Recording these facts enables you to pinpoint the situation where you tend to overeat, and you will be able to devise a schedule of resolutions like the following:

- I will not overeat when I am tired.
- I will not eat as a response to stress at work.
- If I miss a meal because of a busy schedule, I will not overeat at my next meal.
- I will eat less when I miss my regular workouts.
- I will not binge in response to family or emotional pressures.
- I will not eat out of boredom, loneliness, or frustration.
- I will not eat at those times of the day when my diary tells me I tend to overeat.
- I will not eat at times when I tend to eat food only half-consciously, such as when I am watching TV or reading.
- I will limit my food consumption when with friends or in a favorite restaurant.

If you can recognize food cues (situations of specific foods that tend to cause you to overeat), you can develop a behavior-modification program to help you diet. By charting your meals in this way, you will also learn the relationship between portion size and caloric value, and be able to determine which foods give you the most satisfaction at the least caloric cost.

Adopt a Behavior-Modification Program

Behavior modification is a set of strategies to deal with the food cues discovered from keeping an accurate and detailed food diary. These are some suggestions to help you break your own individual food cues.

- Eat meals and snacks only at set times.
- Eat only in one place.
- Store food out of sight.
- Don't keep high-calorie foods in the house. Stock up on fresh fruit and vegetables, unbuttered popcorn, clear soup, fiber crackers, and plain yogurt for snacks.
- Don't put serving dishes on the table. Serve food in the kitchen and take the filled plates into the dining room.
- Keep low-calorie foods at hand, such as raw carrots and celery just in case you feel desperate.
- Develop a "buddy system" so that you have somebody to talk to when you are in a stressful situation that would normally make you eat. This could be somebody else you know who is trying to lose weight or a member of your family.

- Stay busy. When you feel very hungry at unscheduled eating times, go for a jog or a walk, take a hot bath, call a friend, brush your teeth, or take a nap.
- Change your eating behavior by being aware of every bite you take, and you will eat less. Try putting down your knife and fork between bites. Take a pause of several minutes in the middle of each meal. Leave some food on your plate. Avoid doing other things at the same time as you are eating.
- Whenever you make a change in your habits, give yourself a reward. (Since most obese people reward themselves with food, it is not always easy to find the appropriate rewards. A crying infant not only obtains food, but also attention and the comfort of being cuddled. Babies will cry as much to get attention as for food, and often one is associated with the other in a baby's mind. This is a lesson well drummed into our brains, because, as adults, instead of eating only when we need food, we eat to appease our other hungers and to reward ourselves when we get something right. We often celebrate over a meal, but a better reward for the person trying to lose weight would be to go to the movies, have a family member do the laundry, or buy a new dress.)
- If stress on the job causes you to gobble, eat carrot sticks instead of candy.
- Try to enlist the help of your whole family. This will make you feel less isolated and less likely to break your diet.
- Use a smaller plate so that your decreased portions don't seem too small.
- Do not miss meals or fast. (If you force yourself to eat nothing for a day or more, you may end up gorging yourself because of your ravenous hunger, and taking in more calories than you would have by eating normally. Evenly spaced meals ensure that your blood glucose levels never fall too far below normal, and thus few hunger pangs result.)
- Allow yourself a treat once a day.

Behavior modification is best for people who have a moderate weight problem. For those who are 50 pounds or more overweight, it is usually not sufficient.

After Consulting with a Doctor, Start an Exercise Program

Once you have selected the right level of calories for you to lose one or two pounds per week, you may think that this will enable you to lose those extra pounds. Unfortunately, as we discussed earlier, your body is likely to adjust to the decreased intake of food, and after about three weeks your weight losses may cease altogether, regardless of how disciplined you are.

The reason you reach this plateau is that the body's basal metabolic rate drops by as much as 29 percent. This means that you require 29 percent fewer calories to maintain your weight. However, by exercising 20 to 30 minutes at least three times a week, you will increase your metabolic rate sufficiently to burn off the extra calories, and your weight loss will continue.

Strategy The kind of exercise you take should be some form of aerobic exercise that burns at least 300 calories at least three times a week. To do this, the exercise must be in a form that employs large muscle groups, such as walking, running, cycling, or swimming. To maximize the effect on metabolic rate, you should do the exercise about two hours after eating. Walking expends 100 calories per hour, and is perhaps the gentlest form of exercise (unlike jogging, it is easy on the bones and joints). But whatever exercise you take, you must embark on your workout program gradually.

Apart from keeping up the metabolic rate, exercise has many other benefits for the dieter. It enables you to eat more and still lose weight. This means that you have less chance of developing nutrient deficiencies. Exercise also helps to preserve lean body tissue. Loss of muscle and protein from the vital organs weakens the body and can be life-threatening.

Another psychological outcome of exercise is that many people feel less hungry, though this varies greatly among individuals. It has psychological advantages, too, in that it improves the sense of well-being and helps to relieve stress.

The more exercise a person does, the more calories he will burn off and the greater will be the weight he loses. The table on page 336 shows how many calories are used up when doing any form of exercise. Remember, overweight individuals expend more energy for a given activity than do people of normal weight, because they have to move their extra pounds.

By making small changes in your daily activities, you can add a significant amount of exercise. For example, walk upstairs instead of using elevators; park in a lot farther away from the office than is your usual practice; or take a brisk walk around the block during lunch hour.

Avoid All Fad Diets

In the past few years, a virtual mountain of "popular" diets have been published in book form, many of which promise total health and quick weight loss. Although the latter may be true (for a short period of time, anyway), the former rarely is.

Diets that provide inadequate amounts of nutrients can produce symptoms of malnutrition. A diet low in protein, for example, can result in hair loss, fatigue, and lethargy, while also depleting the body of amino acids needed for the manufacture of tissue protein. Low-carbohydrate diets can cause elevated uric acid levels in the body, which can, in turn, lead to kidney stones as well as fatigue, headache, nausea, vomiting, and dizziness. Even more significant are disturbances in the acid-base balance of the body, a condition known as *ketosis*. Ketosis can be extremely dangerous, especially for pregnant women and diabetics.

There is no such thing as a miracle diet that lets you lose vast amounts of weight quickly and safely. A sound weight-reduction program is one that contains all the essential nutrients in the required amounts, is easily digested, and includes foods that are good to eat.

Strategy An excellent diet is the Weight Watchers program. It is a sensible, healthy diet because it provides a well-balanced food plan tailored to the needs of different ages and both sexes; it allows flexibility in meal planning within basic dietary guidelines; it includes behavior-modification information and techniques to overcome problem eating habits; it includes a safe and effective exercise program to enhance weight reduction; it promotes a healthy approach to eating that then serves as a good foundation for the future, once the desired weight loss is achieved; and it includes a maintenance program that gives lifetime support to help successful Weight Watchers stay thin.

Avoid the Use of Weight-Loss Drugs

Do not rely on any pharmaceutical preparations to guide you to weight loss unless under the strict guidance of your physician.

STRATEGY

AMPHETAMINES Weight-loss drugs like this one can cause a person to drop one-half to a full pound per week for a couple of months. Once the drug is stopped, however, weight loss not only ceases but is poorly maintained. Amphetamine drugs are also addictive and have numerous side effects including nervousness, restlessness, irritability, euphoria, insomnia, and elevated blood pressure. Amphetamines can be useful as an adjunct to other means of weight loss in the short term but, again, should be used only under the strict supervision of your physician.

BULK PRODUCERS   When the stomach is severely distended, as it can be when you eat a very large meal, the stretched walls of the stomach send messages to the brain that you are full. However, this mechanism doesn't work unless the stomach is so full that you feel uncomfortable. There are many dietary "aids" on the market that are essentially indigestible fiber; when eaten, these products, which contain guar gum or pectin, swell as they absorb water in the stomach and thereby stretch it and make you feel full. Products containing cellulose, bran, or other types of fiber are much less effective, as they do not absorb very much water. In short, these products may help you combat hunger in the first stages of a diet, but are not long-term solutions.

PHENYLPROPANOLAMINE   Popular over-the-counter diet pills containing phenylpropanolamine are believed to work by causing the brain to make you feel less hungry. They may help you lose up to one pound per week for a two-month period. After that, however, their effectiveness wears off. Like the amphetamines, these drugs are addictive and, at daily dose levels above 50 to 75 milligrams, may cause irregular heartbeat, liver damage, headaches, dizziness, and dangerously high blood pressure.

OTHER DRUGS   Avoid exotic-sounding preparations, herbals, and amino acid mixtures. They do not cause weight loss. Although thyroid hormone speeds up the metabolism and causes more calories to be used up, it also causes you to break down your own body muscle and vital organs. Excessive losses of calcium and sodium will also result, so thyroid hormone should not be used for weight loss.

Avoid Surgical Means of Losing Weight

Surgical methods for losing weight are getting increasing press coverage, but only in rare instances are they a suitable substitute for a sensible diet and exercise program.

STRATEGY

BYPASS OPERATIONS   Most of the small intestine is bypassed in an *iliojejunal bypass*. As a result, a person absorbs less of the food he or she eats.

Although 50 to 60 percent of the weight needed to be lost is lost by people who undergo this procedure, only people who are over 100 percent overweight before the operation should be considered as candidates.

Such operations are not to be encouraged. They can lead to diarrhea, liver disease, kidney stones, arthritis, and undernutrition owing to the body's inability to absorb essential nutrients. Also, these are major operations, and obese people are not good risks for surgery. Gastric bypass and jaw-wiring have also been done in grossly obese patients, but are not recommended because of the complications associated with them.

STOMACH REDUCTION   Part of the stomach is stapled closed so that it is much smaller. Consequently, the stomach fills up more quickly and you feel full sooner. This is not such a major operation as a stomach bypass, and it has fewer side effects, but evidence suggests that although patients lose weight initially following the procedure, they soon gain it back.

LIPECTOMY   In a lipectomy, fat is removed by suction from underneath the skin. Only small amounts may be removed this way, perhaps five pounds or less. It is useful for getting rid of particularly hard and unsightly subcutaneous fat, but the fat often returns.

Other Advice

If you would like additional information about obesity and overweight, contact the American Dietetic Association, 430 North Michigan Avenue, Chicago, Illinois 60611.

38
Osteoarthritis

Osteoarthritis is a progressive deterioration of the joints owing to simple wear and tear combined with hormonal, biochemical, and metabolic factors.

"Wear and tear" is a useful term for understanding the nature of the ailment. The cartilage found between the surfaces of connected bones usually provides a cushion between the two joints. It acts as a sort of sponge, absorbing shock and performing a multitude of other tasks involved with keeping the joint healthy and functioning normally.

Sometimes, however, the cartilage's capacity for self-repair does not keep pace with the normal degeneration it undergoes through daily use. In such cases, the cartilage eventually becomes worn away, allowing the two connecting bones to grate on one another. This can also lead the cartilage and bone at the margins of the joints to become enlarged and deformed, and can cause fluid to develop in the joint, making it swollen and inflamed. One or a combination of these consequences leads to the discomfort of osteoarthritis.

Warning Signs

- Virtually any joint in the body may be affected by osteoarthritis, but the joints most often affected are those of the fingers and thumbs, the cervical or neck area and lumbar region of the spine, the knees, and the hips.
- Pain is usually the first symptom experienced; it worsens with

movement or exercise, especially toward the end of the day; the joints are stiff and difficult to move, though the stiffness does tend to wear off after ten to fifteen minutes of exercise.

• Joints may be warm, tender, and red, and sometimes are swollen with fluid.

• In the fingers, the last joint in each finger is the one usually affected, often becoming enlarged.

• Osteoarthritis at the base of the thumb causes pain and limits the use of the thumb; in the knee it will produce pain, swelling, and unsteadiness; in the hip, pain and a limp. It is very common in the spine, too, though even in the presence of severe osteoarthritis, symptoms may not be apparent. It is most common in the mid-neck and lower back regions.

Epidemiological Data

Everybody over the age of 55 has some degenerative joint disease. Half of the adult population over the age of 30 have some degree of osteoarthritis.

Many athletes have osteoarthritis in joints they have injured severely or repeatedly. Women are affected with osteoarthritis of the fingers and toes ten times more frequently than men.

Eight million of the 36 million Americans with diagnosed arthritis are under the age of 45. Below that age, the prevalence is greater in men, while over 45 the prevalence is greater in women.

Arthritis is America's number-one crippling disease. One million new cases are diagnosed each year in the United States, though the vast majority of cases are not crippling.

Prevention and Treatment

• Overweight patients should lose weight to lessen the pressure on the weight-bearing joints.

• Get adequate amounts of calcium and protein.

• Avoid fad cures.

• Exercise the joints and use hot packs or electric heating pads, or take warm baths.

• Supplement your diet with the appropriate nutrients that the drugs you are taking rob from the body.

• Eat fish at least three times a week.

CASE HISTORY: Jane Freedman

Jane Freedman had been a secretary for twenty years when she began to experience a little pain in her fingers at the end of a day filled with typing. Her fingers would become stiff for the first ten to fifteen minutes of the workday. The first joints of her fingers had developed bumps that were unsightly in addition to being uncomfortable. Over time, she found that the pain no longer tended to lessen as she typed, but rather grew in intensity.

Her doctor told her she had osteoarthritis. He said that the bumps were called *Heberden's nodes*, and that they wouldn't go away. The good news, however, was that it was likely that after about six months the pain in them would lessen.

Nevertheless, he advised her to change her job, since X-rays showed that the end joints of the fingers on her right hand showed signs of degeneration. Jane, however, knew only one way to earn a living and her youngest child was just entering college, so she continued working as a secretary. Over the next several years her hands got worse, so when the college bills were paid she was relieved to take early retirement.

By then, her right index finger had become very swollen and enlarged owing to substantial degeneration of the joint at the end of the finger. Her doctor put her on an anti-inflammatory medication, and although the joint is still enlarged, she is relatively free of pain.

Dietary and Life-style Recommendations

If You Are Overweight, Lose Weight

Although there are no diets proven to alleviate or cure arthritis, despite the claims of many faddists to the contrary, there is evidence to suggest that if a patient is obese, the extra weight puts abnormal pressure on the weight-bearing joints and seems to worsen the arthritis since, over time, this can cause more rapid than normal degeneration of the joints.

Strategy Your first order of business must be to lose those extra pounds. This is particularly true if such weight-bearing joints as those in the spine, knees, or hips are involved. (See chapter 37 for a sensible weight-loss plan to follow.)

Be Sure to Eat Adequate Calcium and Protein

Both calcium and protein are required to help maintain cartilage and bone in a healthy state.

Strategy Make sure you get at least 1,000 milligrams (one gram) of calcium daily in your food. (See table on page 301 of calcium-rich foods.) If you are not getting at least that quantity, take a 1,000-milligram daily supplement of calcium (two and a half grams of calcium carbonate). Skim milk is a lower-calorie source of calcium than whole milk for those trying to lose weight and maintain their calcium intake.

Eat three to four portions of protein daily (see table on page 313 for a list of protein-rich foods). This may mean reducing fats and carbohydrates if they prevail in the diet.

Eat Fish at Least Three Times a Week

There is some preliminary evidence to suggest that fish oils tend to prevent inflammatory reactions in the body.

Strategy You can take advantage of this new information by eating fish at least three times a week. On the other hand, fish oil supplements bought in health-food stores could be dangerous. They have been reported to interfere with blood clotting to such an extent that bleeding problems could conceivably occur in some people. If you are considering taking such supplements, check with your doctor first, and then only take them in limited amounts. Any benefit should be felt within a day or two of taking them; if none is felt, discontinue the supplements.

Other Advice

Americans spend $2 billion a year on unproven remedies for different types of arthritis. Because arthritis patients may have unpredictable periods of remission during which pain and disability are substantially relieved, quack remedies often receive undeserved credit for these remissions. The power of suggestion (the *placebo effect*) also explains why these products sometimes help.

Although for the most part these "cures" are harmless, they may distract the patient from the necessary treatment programs. (For more information about these "cures," write to the Arthritis Foundation, see below for address; and see chapter 46, "Rheumatoid Arthritis.")

Isometric exercises help maintain muscle tone and strengthen them, while isotonic exercises may damage the joints further. Isometric exercises are those in which the muscles are tensed without causing any motion at the joints (yoga is an example); isotonic exercises maintain uniform muscle tone but cause movement at the joints, like walking and running. The exercises should be done for 15 minutes to a half hour a day, starting with a few minutes a day and then gradually building up the length of time. (For further information about exercise, once again the Arthritis Foundation is an excellent source.)

Warm soaks, hot packs, and electric heating pads all tend to relieve pain and tightness in the muscle because of the heat they supply. These should be applied twice a day for 15 to 30 minutes if they are to be effective.

Supplement your diet with the nutrients that your medication may be causing you to lose.

ASPIRIN   Consumption of aspirin results in increased excretion of folic acid and vitamin C, and bleeding in the digestive tract, leading to iron losses. Also, take aspirin with meals to avoid gastrointestinal upset.

ACETAMINOPHEN   Do not take more than 500 milligrams of vitamin C with acetaminophen, because it prevents the body from excreting the drug. In the habitual user, this can lead to a toxic buildup, and may damage the kidneys and liver.

PROPOXYPHENE HYDROCHLORIDE, MECLOFENAMATE, IBUPROFEN, NAPROXEN, TOLMETIN, SULINDAC, AND FENOPROFEN   To minimize the chances of gastrointestinal discomfort, all of these medications should be taken with meals.

DIAZEPAM   This medication should be taken with meals; while taking it, be wary of an increased appetite and the potential for weight gain.

INDOMETHACIN   This medication causes bleeding in the digestive tract and may lead to an iron deficiency. To reduce this risk, take the drug with meals and be sure to get plenty of foods rich in iron in your diet.

If you would like additional information about osteoarthritis, contact the Arthritis Foundation, 1314 Spring Street N.E., Atlanta, Georgia 30326, phone (404) 266-0795.

39
Osteoporosis

Osteoporosis makes a once-strong skeletal structure brittle and is responsible for the compression of the spinal cord that results in a "widow's hump" and loss of height. It can occur in anyone over the age of 45, and is particularly prevalent among postmenopausal women, especially those of British, Northern European, Chinese, Japanese, or Jewish extraction. Black women are at low risk.

Although bones seem to be hard and static, they are continually being broken down and reformed. In the early years of growth, bone formation proceeds at a faster rate than bone breakdown. The skeleton grows and strengthens until it reaches full maturity sometime during the early part of the fourth decade. Beyond age 40, however, we lose more bone than we make, and henceforth the bones become progressively more porous and brittle. In people who develop osteoporosis, this process proceeds at a faster-than-normal rate.

Warning Signs

• Women who go into menopause early
• Women who have both ovaries removed
• Lower back pain
• Fractures of the hip, wrist, and vertebra
• Periodontal disease
• Lack of exercise, which promotes bone loss
• Cigarette smoking, which accelerates the loss of bone calcium

• Excessive alcohol consumption, which also leads to the loss of bone calcium

Epidemiological Data

Fifteen to 20 million Americans, or one in every three or four people middle-aged or older, have osteoporosis.

Every year, 1.3 million fractures owing to osteoporosis cost the nation $4 billion.

Forty thousand deaths per year are attributed to osteoporosis.

Prevention and Treatment

• Be sure your diet has a sufficient quantity of calcium (1,000 milligrams a day or more).
• Beware of an imbalance of calcium/phosphorus intake.
• Meat consumption should be limited to one meal a day.
• Limit alcohol, caffeine, and salt.
• Take or eat 400 to 800 international units of vitamin D and 100 milligrams of vitamin C.
• Be sure to get frequent, weight-bearing exercise.
• Stop smoking.
• Avoid aluminum- and magnesium-based antacids.

CASE HISTORY: Jenny Lee

Jenny was sixty-five and of Chinese descent. A writer who was something of a bookworm, she had invested her energies in the life of the mind to the exclusion of physical activity throughout her life.

Her frame had always been small and frail. She was also unable to digest milk because she was lactose intolerant, as are many of her race. Her calcium intake was less than half the Recommended Dietary Allowance of 800 milligrams.

Jenny spent many lonely hours at her typewriter, often drinking alcohol and smoking cigarettes. The alcohol, in fact, along with too many tight deadlines, gave her a hyperacidic stomach that she kept in check with an aluminum hydroxide–based antacid.

She went through menopause at forty-one. Her doctor said it was early because she smoked too much. She never married and had never had children. Over the last few years, she had suffered from chronic backache and had noticed that her posture wasn't as straight as it used to be, but she had not consulted a doctor, assuming it was due to all those hours bent over her books and typewriter.

One December day she slipped on some ice at her garage door. When she fell, she hit the base of her spine on the pavement. She was able to get up, but she felt a great deal of pain in her back. An X-ray revealed that she had sustained a fracture of two of her vertebrae—and that she had osteoporosis.

Her doctor gave her a calcium carbonate supplement and put her on a medication that contained the hormones progesterone and estrogen. When the fractures healed, he encouraged her to walk as much as possible rather than driving, to climb stairs instead of taking elevators. He encouraged her to cut down on her smoking and drinking. He also took her off aluminum-based antacids and switched her to calcium-based antacids.

Dietary and Life-style Recommendations

Eat a High-Calcium Diet

The Recommended Dietary Allowance for calcium is 800 milligrams per day, but the daily average in the United States is between 450 and 550 milligrams. To make matters worse, it is now believed that all women should consume at least 1,000 milligrams daily; in the years immediately prior to menopause 1,200 milligrams is the minimum; after menopause, 1,500 milligrams is a healthier allowance. The RDA is adequate for young men, though elderly men need the same as postmenopausal women.

Young people, especially, should strengthen their bones as much as possible with a high-calcium diet (as well as plenty of exercise). This will enhance their stores so that they will have more to lose before the bones become brittle; according to recent research, the losses are significant for all women over the age of 25.

We get most of our calcium from milk, cheese, and yogurt; canned sardines and salmon are other good sources. (See page 301 for a table of calcium-rich foods.) Some vegetables, particularly spinach, kale, and collards, contain good amounts of calcium. Unfortunately, these vegetables also contain *phytic acid*, which binds to the calcium and reduces the body's ability to absorb it.

Many factors may enhance or inhibit the body's ability to absorb dietary calcium. In general, the average healthy adult absorbs only 20 to 30 percent of the calcium ingested. Rapidly growing children, however, absorb as much as 75 percent of the mineral they eat. At the other extreme, postmenopausal women may absorb only 7 percent of their dietary calcium.

Conditions that enhance calcium absorption include exposure to sunlight and adequate vitamin D, and eating foods containing lactose (milk sugar) and vitamin C. Excessive phosphorus tends to hinder its absorption.

Strategy Three glasses of milk daily provide 800 milligrams of calcium (low-fat or skim milk is preferable to minimize calories and cholesterol). Americans normally get 80 percent of their calcium from dairy products; however, by making careful choices, it is possible to get the same amount of calcium with a much lower percentage coming from milk and milk products. For example, a daily menu that includes single portions of any two of the following will supply more than 400 milligrams of calcium: almonds, broccoli, canned fish (with bones), kelp, tofu, tortillas, kale, turnips, collard greens, macaroni and cheese, pizza, beef tacos, and cheese or meat enchiladas. Although the rest of the diet will supply some calcium, it will still be necessary to include some dairy foods to reach the minimum requirement of 800 milligrams.

Getting more than 800 milligrams of calcium in your regular diet is difficult, especially if you are among the million or so people who have trouble digesting milk (some 70 percent of whom are blacks, only 20 percent of European ancestry). Therefore, many physicians recommend calcium supplements. Until recently, most calcium pills were about the size of a quarter and up to six or more a day were required. Today, however, smaller, more convenient pills are available.

Calcium carbonate and calcium malate are the most absorbable of the supplements. You should take 500 milligrams of calcium as a supplement before you go to bed and 500 milligrams at midmorning. If the supplement constipates you, switch to one that contains magnesium with the calcium. Do not take calcium as bone meal or dolomite, both of which may be contaminated with lead.

Limit Dietary Phosphorus

A diet high in phosphorus will inhibit adequate calcium absorption. Phosphorus combines with calcium to form calcium phosphate, which cannot be absorbed and thereby effectively reduces the amount of calcium getting into the body. For optimal calcium absorption, strive for a dietary pattern that supplies one to two times as much calcium as phosphorus.

Strategy The major sources of phosphorus in the diet are red meats and carbonated soft drinks. But since these foods contain little calcium, their calcium-to-phosphorus ratio is very low. Foods such as beef liver, bologna, fried chicken, corn on the cob, frankfurters, ground beef, ham, lamb chops, and pork chops have a calcium-to-phosphorus ratio ranging from 1:15 to 1:45, which is very bad for calcium absorption. Some of the carbonated soft drinks containing phosphoric acid contain no calcium at all. By contrast, many of the green leafy vegetables such as spinach and lettuce have more calcium than phosphorus and hence favor calcium absorption. Dairy products contain approximately equal amounts of calcium and phosphorus.

Those meals that emphasize calcium-rich foods are better if they avoid phosphorus-rich foods. Thus, calcium from the sour cream in the baked-potato-and-steak meal is not absorbed as well as from the late-evening ice cream snack. A good idea is to emphasize calcium in snack foods, which are often eaten by themselves.

Another point to remember is to take your supplements with fruit juice. Both its acid and vitamin C content will aid absorption.

Beware of an Excess of Dietary Protein

The very high protein diet consumed by most Americans will result in more calcium being excreted in the urine than is the case in people who consume less protein.

Strategy Like phosphorus, the main source of dietary protein is meat. The more meat a person eats, the more calcium she will lose, and so the greater the risk of osteoporosis. This does not mean that meat must be eliminated from a diet designed to lower the risk for osteoporosis. However, meat consumption should be limited to one meal a day; portion size should also be reduced. Remember, if dairy products are being used to supply dietary calcium, they also contain significant amounts of protein, and so there is no need to worry about protein deficiency.

Vegetarians, particularly *ovo-lacto* vegetarians (those who consume eggs and dairy products but no meat) have a lower incidence of osteoporosis than meat-eaters. This is probably because of the lower protein and phosphorus content of their diets. A well-balanced vegetarian diet that allows milk and milk products is probably the best diet for the prevention of osteoporosis. The closer we all come to eating such a diet, the better. More restrictive vegetarian-type diets tend to be too low in calcium to supply the body's needs.

Limit Salt

Too much salt will force the kidneys to excrete the excess, and in the process to excrete calcium as well.

Strategy A low-sodium diet need not be followed to protect the bones from osteoporosis, but a "salt-oholic" should cut back. A mildly sodium-restricted diet in which one simply reduces the amount of table salt used is a good place to start. Up to one-half teaspoon a day can be used during cooking. Pickled and other extremely salty foods should also be eliminated.

Get Sufficient Vitamin D

Most American diets, particularly those that are adequate in calcium, are adequate in vitamin D, which, along with vitamin C, promotes calcium absorption.

Strategy We get most of our vitamin D from dairy products made from fortified milk. In the event of milk intolerance, other good sources, such as calf's liver, fish oils, and eggs, must be included. Remember, vitamin D in excessive amounts can be very dangerous, and since it is stored in the body, its effects are cumulative. Supplements should never contain more than 400 international units.

Eat a Calorically Balanced Diet

Calories are important for two reasons. If a person is too thin, the risk of osteoporosis is increased, and if she is consuming very few calories she is unlikely to be able to fulfill her calcium requirement.

Women who consistently consume under 1,500 calories a day (which often means they are 10 or 20 percent below their ideal weight) are endangering their bones. We often hear about the problems of being overweight and assume that the thinner we are, the better. Clearly, this is not true if a person is at high risk for osteoporosis. Too thin may be just as much of a health risk as too fat.

Strategy If a person is obese (that is, 20 percent or more above her ideal body weight) and at the same time at increased risk for osteoporosis, she should avoid crash or fad dieting.

Foods should be emphasized that have a high nutrient density with specific attention to calcium. Go for a low calorie and high calcium content. For example, skim milk is much better than whole milk; low-fat yogurt is better than sour cream; cottage cheese is preferable to cream cheese. Finally, goals should be set that can be met and maintained without constantly restricting calories to unrealistically low levels (below 1,000 calories daily).

Exercise Can Be Preventive

If a woman has been confined to bed for long periods of time or has spent a significant amount of time in a wheelchair, she is at increased risk for osteoporosis. Leading a sedentary life also increases the risk.

Exercise that emphasizes weight-bearing is beneficial for several reasons. First, stress makes the bones respond by becoming bigger and stronger. (This is why astronauts, when in a state of weightlessness, lose a good deal of calcium from their bones.) Second, exercise will increase the flow of blood to the bones, thereby increasing the availability of bone-building nutrients. Third, exercise generates mini-electrical currents within the bones that stimulate bone growth. Finally, exercise alters the hormonal balance, favoring those hormones that protect the bones. Taking calcium supplements without exercise does absolutely nothing to strengthen the bones.

Strategy The type of exercise that protects the bones from calcium losses consists of movements that put stress on the bones. Walking, jogging, cycling, gymnastics, basketball, and tennis all fit the bill. Swimming, an excellent exercise for cardiovascular fitness, is a poor exercise for lowering the risk of osteoporosis because the water, rather than the bones, supports the weight of the body. Modest increases in weight-bearing activity can preserve bone mass, even in frail, elderly men and women. That's why simply maintaining an active life-style, walking rather than driving, climbing stairs instead of taking elevators, standing rather than sitting, can significantly lower the chances of developing osteoporosis.

Stop Smoking

Smoking constitutes an independent risk factor for osteoporosis in both men and women by increasing calcium losses from the bone. Women who smoke also reach menopause several years earlier than nonsmokers.

Strategy Quit smoking. If you find this impossible, take a one-gram (1,000-milligram) calcium supplement.

Limit Alcohol Consumption

Alcohol is a diuretic and causes increased excretion of calcium. It also directly impairs its absorption.

Strategy Reduce your alcohol consumption to less than two drinks per day. If you drink, take a 1,000-milligram daily calcium supplement. Do not drink alcohol when consuming calcium-rich foods.

Limit Caffeine

Caffeine is a diuretic and causes increased excretion of calcium.

Strategy Limit as much as possible your intake of beverages, foods, and medications containing caffeine. No more than two cups of coffee or tea should be drunk daily. (See table on page 300 of foods and drinks high in caffeine.)

Consume Adequate Vitamin C

Vitamin C aids calcium absorption.

Strategy Try to eat foods rich in vitamin C, such as citrus fruits, berries, and cantaloupe, at the same time as you consume calcium-rich foods. (See pages 301 and 321 for tables of foods high in calcium and vitamin C.)

Avoid Aluminum- or Magnesium-Based Antacids

Aluminum- and magnesium-based antacids cause increased excretion of calcium. They lower blood phosphate levels and hence cause phosphorus to be liberated from the bones to maintain blood levels. Because phosphate cannot be taken from the bones without being accompanied by calcium, this leads to bone calcium reduction.

Strategy Switch to a calcium-based antacid.

Other Advice

If you suffer from osteoporosis, talk to your doctor about the possibility of hormone therapy.

If you would like more information about osteoporosis, contact the American Geriatric Society, 10 Columbus Circle, New York, New York 10019, phone (212) 582-1333.

40
Overactive Thyroid

Overactive thyroid, or *hyperthyroidism,* is the overproduction of thyroid hormones (*thyroxine* and/or *triiodothyronine*). The excess hormones result in a speeding up of all the reactions in the body and the wasting of tissues. The most common cause of it is Graves' disease, which is a condition in which a person's own immune system causes the thyroid gland to produce abnormally large amounts of thyroid hormone. Less common causes of the disease include tumors of the thyroid, pituitary, and placenta.

Warning Signs

- Excessive sweating and warm, smooth skin; also, a preference for cold weather
- Weight loss and increased appetite
- Nervousness and tiredness
- Physical manifestations may include bulging eyes, palpitations, swollen neck (goiter), tremor, and muscle weakness
- Increased frequency of urination and bowel movements and sometimes diarrhea
- Fine and thin hair
- Bone loss predisposing to osteoporosis
- Moodiness and anxiety, inability to sleep, and, in elderly patients, apathy

• In women, a decrease in the frequency or cycle length of menstruation, perhaps to an excess of 40 days

Epidemiological Data

Graves' disease usually runs in families; .4 percent of the American population has it.

Hyperthyroidism is five times more common in women than men.

Forty percent of people receiving antithyroid drugs will go into remission within two years of receiving the drug.

Prevention and Treatment

• Increase your calories by 50 percent, and be sure to include large quantities of carbohydrates and protein (90 to 120 grams).
• Increase the amount of fluids you drink to three to four quarts per day, unless you have accompanying heart or kidney problems.
• Drink a quart of milk a day, or take a 1,000-milligram calcium supplement.
• Reduce your consumption of spicy and highly seasoned foods, fiber, and caffeine-containing beverages and foods.
• Supplement your diet with vitamin C and the B-complex group and potassium.
• If you're taking antithyroid medication, eliminate foods containing goitrogens.
• Cut back on alcohol as much as possible.
• If you have bulging eyes, reduce your intake of salt to prevent or reduce the swelling behind the eyes and help the condition.

CASE HISTORY: Henry Felker

One day in the shower, Henry Felker noticed that his lower legs were swollen. They were not painful or tender, and he couldn't remember doing anything to injure them.

He had recently celebrated his thirty-fifth birthday, and Henry had remarked to himself how lucky he was to have enjoyed good health virtually all his life. Then, to compound his concern at the swelling in his legs, he also noticed that, though he had an excellent appetite, he was losing weight rapidly. In fact, he lost twelve pounds in the following month.

He also found he had to go to the bathroom nine or ten times a day, and that he would usually have a loose bowel movement. Though not normally a nervous person, he seemed suddenly to become one, to the degree that he found himself sweating profusely. He decided it was time he saw a doctor.

When he arrived at his doctor's office, the doctor noticed immediately that Henry's eyes were more prominent than normal. He gave Henry a complete physical examination, and also analyzed his blood for thyroid hormones. His preliminary diagnosis based upon Henry's bulging eyes was confirmed. Henry had hyperthyroidism. As a treatment, the doctor prescribed low doses of antithyroid drugs and advised him to increase his intake of liquids, including milk, to take a vitamin supplement, and to limit the salt in his diet. Gradually, over the next eighteen months, all of Henry's symptoms lessened and eventually disappeared.

Dietary and Life-style Recommendations

Increase Your Caloric Intake

If you suffer from hyperthyroidism, the number of calories you get should be increased by 50 to 60 percent, to compensate for the increase in your metabolic rate that results from the extra thyroid hormone produced by the thyroid gland.

Strategy This usually means a diet of approximately 3,500 to 4,000 calories (see chapter 50 for a balanced diet for underweight people). Such a diet must contain 50 to 60 percent carbohydrates to replace the depleted carbohydrate stores in the liver and muscles. This will also ensure a sufficient supply of carbohydrates for the brain between meals. Carbohydrates are the chief source of energy for the brain.

In addition, the diet should contain six ounces of protein-rich food every day to provide the materials needed to replace wasted muscle. (See page 313 for table of protein-rich foods and the chart on page 7 for advice on how to combine vegetable proteins to improve their quality.) Once the condition is under control, watch your weight carefully, as you may need to cut back on your calories to prevent unwanted weight gain.

Drink a Quart of Milk Daily or Take a Calcium Supplement

Excess thyroid hormone tends to weaken the bones by causing calcium to be freed from them. This will increase your risk of osteoporosis.

Strategy Drinking a quart of milk a day will provide all the calcium, phosphorus, and vitamin D you need to limit calcium losses to a minimum. If you find milk unpalatable or are intolerant of lactose (see chapter 35), a 1,000-milligram (one gram) calcium supplement should be taken. This is best taken as calcium carbonate (2½ grams). Half should be taken at midmorning and half just before retiring at night.

The vast majority of Americans have adequate vitamin D and phosphorus in their normal diet, but consult with the tables on pages 312 and 321 for the amounts of phosphorus and vitamin D found in the foods you eat. You need 1,000 milligrams of phosphorus and 400 international units or 10 micrograms of vitamin D daily. If you are not getting what you need, adjust your diet accordingly, or take a supplement of no more than 400 international units.

Increase Your Intake of Fluids

Because this condition tends to increase the amount of body fluids you excrete as urine, you need to increase the amount you drink. This will also help you excrete the excess calcium in your blood to reduce the risk of kidney stones.

Strategy Drink three to four quarts of liquids per day. However, if you have high blood pressure or other heart or kidney problems, this may not be a suitable strategy. Ask your doctor first.

Limit Spicy, Seasoned, Fibrous, and Caffeine-Containing Foods

All of these sorts of foods tend to increase the frequency of your bowel movements, and should be restricted in the diet.

Strategy Consult the tables on pages 300 and 303 for foods rich in caffeine and fiber. Avoid them whenever possible.

Take Vitamin C and B-Complex Supplements

Since excess thyroid hormone tends to speed up the metabolic rate, your requirements for all nutrients are increased. The extra stress imposed on the body will especially increase the need for vitamin C and the B-complex vitamins, as well as potassium, calcium, and protein.

Strategy Take a daily vitamin supplement containing the Recommended Dietary Allowances for vitamin C and the B-complex vitamins, or be sure to get plenty of foods rich in these nutrients in the diet, and include at least two grams of potassium as food. (See pages 307, 313, and 318–321 for lists of foods rich in these nutrients.) But do not take potassium supplements unless under the direction of a physician.

While Taking Antithyroid Medications, Reduce Your Intake of Foods Containing Goitrogens

Certain foods contain substances called *goitrogens*, which prevent the thyroid gland from producing thyroid hormones. Consequently, this will add to any antithyroid drug's effects and will necessitate a reduction in the level of medication being taken.

Strategy People taking antithyroid medication should limit foods containing goitrogens. These include produce in the cabbage family, such as Brussels sprouts and cauliflower, and peaches, pears, spinach, and turnips. (See table on page 308 for other goitrogen-rich foods.) Keep in mind, however, that cooking these foods renders the goitrogen harmless, making them safe to eat even while taking antithyroid drugs.

Avoid Alcohol

People with hyperthyroidism have a tendency to deplete the carbohydrate stores in their livers. This makes it more difficult for them to maintain their blood glucose level within normal limits.

Strategy Because alcohol prevents the liver from producing glucose in the normal way, its presence makes it even more difficult for the body to maintain blood glucose levels. If blood glucose levels drop below normal, the result can be light-headedness or fainting. Avoid alcoholic beverages.

If Your Eyes Bulge, Reduce Salt Intake

Bulging eyes are caused mainly by water retention. Some people who eat a lot of salty foods are not able to excrete it, so the salt is retained in the body. Whenever salt is retained, so is water, which tends to exacerbate any kind of swelling.

Strategy Restrict salt to less than three grams (3,000 milligrams) a day. This means not adding salt at the table and using no more than one-half teaspoon in cooking. In addition, pickled foods (such as sauerkraut) and extremely salty foods (such as luncheon meats, snack chips, and processed cheeses) should be eliminated. (See table on page 315 for sodium-rich foods.)

Other Advice

The drug *propranolol* (sold under the brand names *Inderal* and *Inderide*) is sometimes prescribed for hypertension associated with hyperthyroidism. If your doctor prescribes this drug for you, take it with meals or milk to avoid gastrointestinal upset.

Long-term use of thyroid hormone as an aid to weight loss is extremely dangerous and may make the thyroid gland less able to produce thyroid hormone. Consult with your physician.

If you would like additional information about overactive thyroid, contact the National Health Information Clearinghouse (NHIC), P.O. Box 1133, Washington, D.C. 20013, phone (800) 336-4797.

41
Parkinson's Disease

Parkinson's disease results from a problem with a group of nerve cells in the brain. These nerves form the *substantia nigra*, which is a part of the brain that helps to control movement.

The substantia nigra produces and stores the neurotransmitter *dopamine*, a "brain messenger" that carries messages of movement to other parts of the body. In patients with Parkinson's disease, the substantia nigra cannot make dopamine and a deficiency occurs. As a result, the limbs tremble, muscular stiffness and slow body movements prevail, and the sufferer walks with short, shuffling steps.

Though many scientists say that the symptoms of Parkinsonism are a result of the depletion of brain dopamine, the cause of the disease is still unknown. Some researchers speculate it is a virus, but others theorize that it is a premature aging process that attacks the cells of the substantia nigra. Despite popular belief, however, the disease does not appear to be genetically linked.

Warning Signs

- Rapid fatigue
- Tendencies to carry one arm bent at the elbow while standing or walking, to swing the arms less than usual when walking, to walk in a stooped posture and with short, shuffling steps
- When standing, a tendency to hold the foot turned in slightly

- An increased liking for sweet foods, and difficulty in chewing and swallowing
- Aching soreness in an arm or leg, and swelling of the feet
- Feelings of cold or warmth in some part of the body such as a hand, the throat, one side of the body, or the stomach or rectum
- Constipation and frequent urination
- Dizziness on standing
- Oily skin on the forehead, face, sides of nose, and scalp, especially in warm weather, that may lead to redness, itching, and scaling of the skin and dandruff on the scalp
- Excessive sweating
- Reduced blinking of the eyes, leading to burning, itching, and bloodshot eyes; impaired vision may also result
- Legible handwriting, but much smaller than usual; soft manner of speaking, with a rapid but even tone at all times
- Slow body movements owing to a hesitancy to initiate new movements
- Muscular stiffness
- Trembling of the limbs when at rest in a relaxed position, which disappears when the limbs are moving
- Sexual dysfunction

Epidemiological Data

Patients tend to develop the disease between the ages of 50 and 65. One percent of all Americans over the age of 50 suffer from the disease, which means that there are one-half million cases of Parkinson's disease in the United States. The prevalence of the disease has not changed over the last century.

Prevention and Treatment

- Limit your protein consumption.
- Be sure to get adequate salt in your diet.
- Avoid faddist nutritional cures such as tyrosine, vitamin B_6, tryptophan, or phenylalanine supplements.
- Supply dopamine to the brain with drugs.
- Maintain optimal physical and emotional health.
- Provide adequate calories to prevent weight loss, but obesity should be avoided.

CASE HISTORY: Jane Dolittle

Jane became a lawyer in the days when not many women did. As well as enjoying a challenging working life, she had always been active and in good health.

She had recently entered her sixties when her husband, Philip, noticed that she had developed a new habit of holding her right arm bent at the elbow and close to the body while walking. When he asked her about it, she said she had not been aware of doing it, and that her arm was fine. As the habit persisted, she mentioned it to her family physician when she went for a checkup.

Her doctor was able to see that something was wrong, but the telltale signs of Parkinsonism were not present. He ordered the usual battery of tests given for a checkup, including a blood count and other blood tests, an electrocardiogram, a chest X-ray, and a routine analysis of the urine. Since all were normal, the doctor told Jane to come back in a couple of months if the problem persisted.

Apart from the bent arm, nothing more developed in the two-month period, so Jane did not bother to go back to her doctor. However, over the next year or two she developed persistent tiredness, minor aches and pains, and a vague sense of just not feeling well. Things that she had once found easy to do now seemed to require a concerted effort. She was getting older, but she wasn't ready to concede so much, so soon. She returned to her doctor.

He again found nothing wrong and suggested that she get more rest. When she got no better, she sought a second opinion. The second doctor, noting that she was a little depressed, suggested an antidepressant. He told her that overwork, lack of sleep, nervousness, depression, arthritis, and poor dietary habits are common causes of her symptoms and counseled her on improving her life-style.

During the next year, Jane developed soreness in the right arm. She returned to her family doctor, who, familiar with the history of her illness, knew that something was definitely wrong and suspected Parkinson's disease. Since there is no specific test for the disease, however, he could not diagnose it conclusively. But over several years she developed the three characteristic signs of the disease. First her right hand began to shake when at rest—minimally at first, and only when she was tired. The shaking gradually became more pronounced, especially when she was under stress or nervous. She also became very stiff and took much longer to do simple household tasks than she used to. Her doctor was finally confident of his diagnosis of Parkinson's disease after a neurologist did a battery of tests to rule out other neurological disorders causing the same symptoms.

Unfortunately, there is no cure for the disease, but the symptoms may be kept under control with medication for many years. When Jane's symptoms began to affect her activities seriously, her physician put her on a drug called *levodopa*, and suggested that she limit protein to no more than two three-to-four-ounce portions a day. This corrected her symptoms and she is still enjoying life as she prepares to celebrate her seventy-seventh birthday.

Dietary and Life-style Recommendations

Limit Protein

A high-protein meal, like a steak dinner, can reduce the effectiveness of the drug levodopa.

Strategy Your doctor must adjust your dosage to conform to your normal diet, and the lower the protein, the lower the dosage. Four ounces of protein-rich food per day is ideal.

Meals should also be eaten at regular times and all excesses or surprises should be avoided. (See table of high-protein foods on page 313 for guidance in adjusting your diet.)

Consume Reasonable Quantities of Salt

Salt is a must. Sodium chloride (table salt) may be helpful in combating one of the side effects seen in some patients who take levodopa, i.e., low blood pressure, which results in fatigue and/or dizziness.

Strategy Usually, one to two grams of salt per day should do the trick. The average American (unless on a salt-free diet) takes in much more than this through normal meals.

However, exercise caution. Excess salt intake can be dangerous to overall physical health, as it may increase high blood pressure, can exacerbate chronic congestive heart failure, and may result in kidney problems. Therefore, older people with this disease should let their doctors decide whether or not they need to increase their intake of salt.

Avoid Faddist Cures

There are a number of treatments for Parkinson's disease that are not, in fact, cures at all, and may even be dangerous to your health.

STRATEGY

Avoid the following faddist treatments:

TYROSINE Some practitioners claim that taking large amounts of tyrosine, an amino acid found mainly in the protein we eat, will cure the disease, since the brain makes levodopa from tyrosine. This treatment doesn't work for two reasons. First, the cells in the substantia nigra of patients with Parkinson's disease are not able to convert tyrosine into levodopa efficiently because many of these cells are dead. Second, most of the tyrosine we get from foods is used in building new protein, and only a very small amount is taken up from the blood by the neurons in the substantia nigra that make dopamine. Thus, tyrosine has little effect in treating the disease.

VITAMIN B6 Don't believe it if you hear that this vitamin helps cure the symptoms of the disease; it actually makes them worse, and should be avoided as much as possible.

Vitamin B6 is essential for the optimal function of the enzymes (located in the nerve tissues throughout the body) that control the conversion of levodopa to dopamine. If a patient with Parkinson's disease takes vitamin B6 supplements, this action of the enzymes will convert levodopa to dopamine at a much faster rate. So, what's wrong with that?

The problem is that the extra B6 will convert the levodopa so quickly that the dopamine is converted before it reaches the brain. Unfortunately, after it has been converted it cannot enter the brain.

Avoid vitamin supplements that contain more than the minimum daily requirement of B6, which is one-half to one milligram per day. Limit foods rich in vitamin B6, including wheat germ, dry skim milk, peas, beans, sweet potatoes, yams, avocado, fortified cereal, bran, oatmeal, yeast, pork, beef organ meats, tuna, and fresh salmon.

TRYPTOPHAN Many people use tryptophan supplements to relieve common depression and help them sleep, but this form of supplement should be avoided by the Parkinson's patient if taken within four hours of taking levodopa, as it reduces the amount of the medication entering the brain by direct competition. However, it may be used to help the patient sleep if the last dose of levodopa is taken at dinnertime (see chapter 32).

PHENYLALANINE Some sufferers of Parkinson's disease have tried taking an amino acid found in health-food stores called phenylalanine. This is because of findings of Dr. George Cotzias of Buenos Aires, who reported that D-phenylalanine was somewhat effective in controlling the tremors in several patients.

There are two problems here, however. First, we know little about the toxic effects on the body of taking D-phenylalanine for any period of time. Second, health-food stores do not carry D-phenylalanine, they carry L-phenylalanine. The D-form is not naturally found, but is a manufactured chemical agent that is quite expensive. The L-form is found as a natural part of the proteins in the diet and is converted to tyrosine in the body. The L-form has no beneficial effects on the symptoms of Parkinson's disease. There have been no scientific trials either confirming or disproving Dr. Cotzias's theory.

Other Advice

It is important to try to maintain optimal physical and emotional health despite the presence of Parkinson's disease. Patients with the ailment tend to avoid exercise and withdraw from society, and that only serves to worsen the overall effect of the disease on the patient. It may be difficult, but try to maintain as normal a pattern of exercise and socializing as possible.

The best way to improve the function of the "sick" dopamine-producing nerve cells is to give these patients levodopa, which is converted in the brain to dopamine. The drugs used in the treatment of the disease act either by replenishing brain dopamine or by modifying brain function to compensate for dopamine deficiency.

The presence of *acetylcholine*, another brain chemical messenger, is another contributing factor to the disease. There seems to be a reciprocal seesaw relationship between these two chemical messengers and their nerve cells. Dopamine normally restrains the acetylcholine-containing cells, but the absence of dopamine in Parkinson's disease results in the release of these nerve cells from their restraints. Their improperly regulated activity appears to contribute to the symptoms of the disease. Therefore, drugs like *trihexyphenidyl* and *benztropine*, which inhibit the action of acetylcholine, ease the symptoms of the disease.

The following table gives brand and generic names of commonly prescribed anti-Parkinsonism drugs, along with the interactions common between the drugs and foods commonly consumed.

Brand	Generic	Food-drug interactions
ARTANE	trihexyphenidyl	Take with meals and increase dietary fiber
KEMADRIN	procyclidine	Same as above
AKINETON	biperiden	Same as above
COGENTIN	benztropine	Same as above
SYMMETREL	amantadine	Same as above
PARSIDOL	ethopropazine	Same as above
BENADRYL	diphenhydramine	Avoid alcohol and antacids
DISIPAL	orphenadrine hydrochloride	Avoid alcohol and antacids

Brand	Generic	Food-drug interactions
PARLODEL	bromocriptine	None
LARODOPA DOPAR	levodopa	Reduce protein intake, avoid B_6 supplements
SINEMET	carbidopa/levodopa	None

If you would like additional information about Parkinson's disease, contact the American Parkinson's Disease Association, 116 John Street, New York, New York 10038, phone (212) 732-9550; or the United Parkinson Foundation, 220 South State Street, Chicago, Illinois 60604, phone (312) 922-9734.

42
Peptic Ulcer

A *peptic ulcer* is a sore extending through the lining of the digestive tract and into the muscle surrounding it. Generally, ulcers are caught long before they burn right through the muscle, leaving an open passage for the contents of the digestive tract to pass into the abdominal cavity. An ulcer may also burn through the muscle wall and make a hole in one of the large arteries supplying the digestive system. If this occurs, the patient may develop a very serious hemorrhage and die.

Ulcers most frequently occur in the first few inches of the duodenum, which is the upper part of the small intestine that attaches to the stomach, and are called *duodenal ulcers*. Less common are *gastric ulcers*, those found in the upper part of the stomach wall. Rarer still are ulcers found in the narrow part of the stomach at its base where it joins to the duodenum *(channel ulcers)*, and lower in the duodenum *(post-bulbar ulcers)*. Occasionally, ulcers are found in the esophagus (the tube leading from the mouth to the stomach).

Ulcers are caused by the acid in the stomach and an enzyme produced by the stomach, *pepsin*, which is involved in protein breakdown. We all produce acid and pepsin in our stomachs, but although some people produce more acid than others, there is no correlation between the amount of acid produced and the development of ulcers.

The cause seems more likely to be an imbalance between the production of acid and mucus in the stomach. The linings of the stomach and intestines are coated with a covering of mucus. If too little is produced, the acid can directly bathe the wall of the stomach or duodenum, leading to the formation of an ulcer.

Warning Signs

- Burning, gnawing or aching pain that is steady, mild to moderately severe, and located in a limited area in the abdomen.
- The pain may also appear as a soreness, an empty feeling, or hunger pangs.
- Discomfort is relieved by antacids or milk.
- DUODENAL ULCERS: The pain is absent on waking, but appears in midmorning and may often awaken you at 1:00 or 2:00 A.M. It is relieved by food, but recurs two to three hours after eating. It may occur one or more times a day for several weeks and then disappear. It may recur frequently during the following one to two years and occasionally after that. The recurrences usually occur in the spring or fall or during periods of stress.
- GASTRIC ULCERS: Eating causes pain rather than relieving it.
- CHANNEL ULCERS: There is a bloated sensation after eating, or even nausea and vomiting.
- POST-BULBAR ULCERS: The pain is unrelated to eating meals.
- ESOPHAGEAL ULCERS: The discomfort is most noticeable when lying down or swallowing.

Epidemiological Data

Males are more susceptible to all types of ulcers than are females, though in recent years the frequency with which the problem is found in women has increased at a rapid rate.

Ulcers can occur at any age, but gastric ulcers are more likely to appear in later life. Duodenal ulcers are most common between ages 20 and 30 in men, and between 40 and 50 in women. Gastric ulcers appear between ages 50 and 60 in men and women.

Only half of ulcer patients report to their doctors with characteristic symptoms. Complaints among the elderly are minimal.

Fifty percent of ulcer patients are not aware of the problem until gastrointestinal bleeding (black, sticky stools or red blood in the stool) or obstruction occurs (an inability to get food down). Any pain they have may be mistaken for indigestion or irritable bowel syndrome (see chapter 33).

Within two years of completing treatment for an ulcer, 50 percent or more patients will have a recurrence. Most patients will have trouble of some sort related to the ulcerous condition during the next ten years.

The condition tends to run in families; in fact, ulcers are three times more common among blood relatives of ulcer patients.

Five to 10 percent of gastric ulcers are cancerous.

Prevention and Treatment

- Eat three well-spaced meals per day.
- Include plenty of protein and vitamin C to promote healing.
- Omit substances that stimulate gastric acid secretion, such as caffeine, alcohol, pepper, garlic, cloves, and chili powder.
- Avoid large amounts of milk.
- Stop smoking.
- Try to avoid stressful situations.
- Be aware of the side effects of drugs taken for ulcers, and avoid taking aspirin, reserpine, corticosteroids, and other drugs that irritate the lining of the digestive system.
- Get plenty of rest during healing stages.

CASE HISTORY: Philip Redman

Phil Redman was a hard-driving businessman who had developed a very successful data-processing firm in a period of five years. His life was extremely stressful, and he worked many late nights and smoked far too many cigarettes. Meals were often missed or used as a vehicle for business deals.

For some time Phil had experienced a gnawing pain in his abdomen. It was fine when he woke up, but by midmorning the pain was back. At first he mistook it for hunger pangs, as he discovered that relief could be obtained by eating something. However, when he started waking up in pain between 1:00 and 3:00 A.M., he decided it was time to seek help from his doctor.

His doctor gave him a barium X-ray. He performed an endoscopy, a procedure in which a tube is passed down the throat to allow a visual examination of the lining of the digestive tract. The doctor found a duodenal ulcer in the upper part of Phil's duodenum.

Phil was prescribed Zantac, which prevents the stomach from producing acid, and was told to eat three well-spaced meals a day and to take liquid antacids one hour and three hours after each meal and at bedtime. During the next week the symptoms totally disappeared, although his doctor kept him on the drug for the eight weeks it usually takes for an ulcer to heal.

Dietary and Life-style Recommendations

Eat Three Well-Spaced Meals a Day

It was once common practice for doctors to prescribe very bland foods for patients with ulcers, including lots of milky foods. However, this led to three kinds of problems.

First, milk-based foods do not work as antacids. In fact, being rich in both protein and calcium, dairy products tend to stimulate acid production in the stomach. Such a diet also excludes fiber, which is now believed to help the healing process, though how it helps ulcers heal is not known. Third, bland diets are low in iron and vitamin C, both of which are essential nutrients.

Strategy Eat normally, but space your three meals out over the course of the day. You may eat most foods, as long as they do not cause stomach upset. Small, frequent meals may help to buffer the lining of the stomach, but they also increase acid secretion, so many doctors now do not advise between-meal snacks.

Rather than eating when you feel stressed, try taking an antacid. Consuming food at such times will only increase the acid secretion.

Include Vitamin C and Protein-Rich Foods in Your Daily Diet

Both vitamin C and protein are important to your body's healing processes.

Strategy Eat three to four portions of protein daily and 100 milligrams of vitamin C (see tables on pages 313 and 321 for foods rich in protein and vitamin C). If you are a vegetarian, consult the chart on page 7 for advice on how to combine foods to improve their protein quality.

Avoid Substances that Promote Gastric Acid Secretion

Treatment of ulcers is designed to neutralize or decrease acid secretion.

Strategy Since caffeine, alcohol, black pepper, chili powder, and decaffeinated coffee all stimulate acid secretion and worsen the condition, you should avoid these foods. Most other seasonings and carbonated beverages will not cause an ulcer to act up in most people, and can be used.

Other Advice

Smoking tends to exacerbate an existing ulcerous condition by increasing acid secretion and slowing down the healing process. Cigarette smoking is especially linked to the recurrence of duodenal ulcers, and should be avoided.

Try to avoid stressful situations. Being high-strung and a bit of a perfectionist (indications of Type-A personality) definitely seems to increase the risk of getting an ulcer. But it should be mentioned that not all Type-A's develop ulcers and not all ulcer sufferers are high-strung people. (See table on page 334 for some ideas about stress management.)

Get plenty of rest. Early nights, when recovering from an ulcer attack, will help the healing process.

Be aware of the side effects of drugs taken for ulcers. Among them are the following:

ANTACIDS   Aluminum hydroxide and magnesium hydroxide may cause phosphorus malabsorption and predispose a person to osteoporosis. Get plenty of phosphorus in your diet (see table on page 312) and at least 1,000 milligrams (one gram) of calcium daily (see page 301). It is also a good idea to take 1,000 milligrams of calcium as calcium carbonate (2½ grams daily). Take half at midmorning and half at bedtime.

TAGAMET AND ZANTAC   These medications, known generically as *cimetidine* and *ranitidine hydrochloride*, reduce iron absorption, so you should be careful to include iron-rich foods in your diet (see page 309).

You should also avoid taking drugs that irritate the lining of the stomach if you have a tendency to develop ulcers. When taken over an extended period aspirin, *indomethacin, corticosteroids*, and other drugs that irritate the stomach wall may cause an ulcer in the lining of the stomach. However, unlike peptic ulcers, this type of ulcer will not penetrate the muscle. Furthermore, the ulcer will tend to heal when the drug is discontinued, and will not recur unless the drug is taken again.

If you would like additional information about ulcers, contact the American Digestive Disease Society, Suite 217, 7720 Wisconsin Avenue, Bethesda, Maryland 20014, phone (301) 652-5524; or the National Digestive Disease Education and Information Clearinghouse, Suite 600, 1555 Wilson Boulevard, Rosslyn, Virginia 22209, phone (703) 522-0870.

43
Periodontal Disease

Periodontal disease involves the loss of bone from around the roots of the teeth, leading to the loss of teeth. This is the number-one cause of tooth loss. The two terms most often associated with periodontal disease are *gingivitis* (meaning swollen, inflamed, and bleeding gums) and *pyorrhea* (bone loss and generalized infection of the gums).

Warning Signs

• Red, sore, sensitive, receding, or swollen gums that may bleed
• Teeth that are loose, and may be allowing spaces to develop between them
• Bad breath

Epidemiological Data

At least 75 percent of all adults have some degree of gum disease; in fact, by the teenage years, most people have the beginnings of periodontal disease.

Periodontal disease is often evident about ten years before osteoporosis, although it is not always present in osteoporosis sufferers.

Prevention and Treatment

• Get adequate calcium, phosphorus, and vitamin D.
• Get adequate vitamin C, folic acid, and the other B-complex vitamins.

- Cut down on foods that cause plaque on the teeth, and stop smoking.
- Floss and maintain meticulous oral hygiene; for those suspected of having periodontal disease, this includes using a 5-percent solution of hydrogen peroxide once a week as a mouthwash, on the advice of your dentist.

CASE HISTORY: Laurie Davidson

Laurie was a twenty-nine-year-old busy executive. She was always eating on the run and did not follow a balanced diet. She had been taking oral contraceptives for about ten years off and on, and smoked heavily.

Laurie's gums were always sore and red and sometimes swollen, and bled frequently. She collected a lot of plaque on her teeth, despite the warnings of her dentist. She never managed to visit him more than once every other year to have her teeth cleaned.

After a particularly painful episode when her gums swelled so much that she had difficulty in closing her mouth, she visited her dentist. He scraped her teeth and showed her how to brush them properly to remove much of the plaque where the bacteria grew, which caused her gums to bleed in the first place. He advised her to floss each evening.

He also suggested that she take a daily vitamin supplement that contained the Recommended Dietary Allowances for all the vitamins, but especially folic acid and vitamin C (400 micrograms and 60 milligrams respectively). He explained that since she was taking birth-control pills, her dietary needs for these nutrients were increased. This was important in her case, as both are crucial to the health of the gums.

Her gums soon became a lot better except when the plaque built up on her teeth. She did feel it was impossible to stop smoking or to eat more regularly, but she found that if she visited her dentist every three months, plaque rarely accumulated and she had little trouble with her gums.

Dietary and Life-style Recommendations

Be Sure You Get Adequate Amounts of Calcium, Phosphorus, and Vitamin D

Calcium, phosphorus, and vitamin D are all important for maintaining the calcification of bone. When there is inadequate calcium in the diet, it is liberated from the bones to supply the body with what it needs for metabolism. The jawbone is one of the first bones to give up its calcium for this purpose.

Strategy By ensuring that your diet contains the Recommended Dietary Allowances for vitamin D, calcium, and phosphorus, you can maintain proper blood calcium levels and prevent bone loss. The average American diet contains plenty of phosphorus, but is often lacking in calcium. If you do not eat lots of dairy products, take a 1,000-milligram calcium supplement each day as 2½ grams of calcium carbonate. Half should be taken at midmorning and half before bed. In addition, try to get as much in the way of calcium-rich foods in your daily menu as you can. (See page 301 for a list of calcium-rich foods.)

Get Ample Vitamins A and C, Folic Acid, and the Other B-Complex Vitamins

The tissues of the mouth are shed and replaced more rapidly than any other tissues in the body. In fact, they are replaced every three days. Vitamin C is an essential nutrient for the development of *collagen*, which is the connective tissue that holds the cells together. Without an adequate supply of vitamin C, the gums become weakened and prone to infection, and the blood vessels supplying the gums (capillaries) fracture and bleed.

Strategy   Incorporate good sources of vitamin C into your diet. Such sources are citrus fruit, berries, and dark green vegetables. (See page 321 for table of other vitamin C–rich foods.)

Smokers are especially at risk for vitamin C deficiency, as they have an increased need for the vitamin. It is very difficult for them to get enough vitamin C from their diet, and they should take a 100-to-500-milligram daily supplement. Anyone smoking a pack of cigarettes a day or more should be taking 500 milligrams of vitamin C daily.

The B-complex vitamins, including thiamine, riboflavin, niacin, vitamin B_6, folic acid, and vitamin B_{12}, and vitamin A, help build and maintain oral tissues. Cracked lips, sores in the corners of the mouth, a sore tongue, and sore and bleeding gums can all be caused by B-complex deficiencies.

Folic acid seems to have a special role in keeping the gums healthy. One-third of all young women in the United States have folic acid deficiency, which is partly a result of the fact that oral contraceptives tend to reduce its absorption from foods. Folic acid deficiency combined with vitamin C deficiency is a main cause of gum disease.

Anybody with sore gums should take a 400-microgram supplement of folic acid per day, as should all oral contraceptive users to prevent this problem. For the other B-complex vitamins, be sure to get lots of B-complex-rich foods in your diet, such as whole grains and liver (see pages 307 and 318–321) or take a daily vitamin supplement containing the Recommended Dietary Allowances.

Cut Down on Foods that Cause Plaque, and Quit Smoking

The presence of plaque on the teeth seems to be a catalyst that speeds up periodontal disease.

Strategy By avoiding a lot of sweet foods between meals, you can greatly reduce plaque buildup (see chapter 16). Smoking will also accelerate plaque buildup, which is yet another reason for not smoking.

Meticulous oral hygiene will also reduce plaque buildup. This means frequent visits to the dentist, and flossing at least once a day. Studies have shown that using a 5-percent solution of hydrogen peroxide once a week as a mouthwash also makes a significant impact on plaque. A word of warning, though: do not use it more frequently, as it will upset the natural balance of bacteria in your mouth, which could cause an infection.

If you have mouth ulcers, avoid foods high in acid, such as citrus juices, and supplement the diet with vitamin C and plenty of protein-rich foods. Very acidic foods can also erode tooth enamel. Soft drinks that contain phosphoric acid, such as colas, are especially harmful in this respect.

If you would like additional information, contact the American Dental Association, 211 East Chicago Avenue, Chicago, Illinois 60611, phone (312) 440-2500.

44
Premenstrual Tension Syndrome

Premenstrual tension syndrome, usually called *PMS*, is a group of symptoms experienced by many women that generally occur four to ten days prior to menstruation and end abruptly after the onset of flow. The most common symptoms are depression, sudden mood swings, feelings of hostility and anger, nervous tension, craving for sweets and alcohol, tender breasts, water retention, and weight gain. Such symptoms are often associated with elevated estrogen-to-progesterone ratios in the body.

Warning Signs

Any of the following signs and symptoms may occur during the week prior to menstruation:

• Anxiety, irritability, nervous tension, depression, insomnia, forgetfulness, confusion, or dizziness
• Swollen and tender breasts; swollen joints or muscle stiffness
• Abdominal bloating or cramps
• Weight gain of more than three pounds
• Other possible physical symptoms: backache, cold sweats, constipation, diarrhea, or vomiting, the sudden outbreak of acne or other skin problems, and a ringing in the ears or fuzzy vision
• Palpitations, fatigue, fainting spells, headache, and a craving for sweet foods, sometimes followed by the shakes and other signs of

263

hypoglycemia (see chapter 31); a craving for salt, or an increase in appetite; accident-proneness; a tendency to avoid social activities; distraction or excitability

Epidemiological Data

Up to 10 percent of all women of reproductive age in America suffer from PMS. Sixty percent of women between ages 30 and 40 suffer from PMS.

Sixty percent of the estimated 2 million alcoholic women in the reproductive age group in the United States relate their drinking to PMS.

Perhaps as many as 3 to 5 percent of women with PMS find that its symptoms are so severe that the PMS seriously interferes with their lives or relationships.

Prevention and Treatment

- Avoid water and salt retention by using no salt at the table and adding no more than one-half teaspoon during cooking.
- Increase green leafy vegetables, legumes, whole grains, and cereals.
- Increase complex carbohydrates to 60 percent of total calories, and limit simple sugars.
- Take a daily supplement of 30 milligrams of vitamin B_6.
- Reduce coffee, tea, chocolate, and caffeine-containing soft drinks, and limit your alcohol intake to one drink per day.
- Limit tobacco use, as nicotine tends to exacerbate the breast symptoms.
- Take up some form of aerobic exercise; swimming, in particular, is highly recommended.
- Take tryptophan supplements.
- Get adequate dietary intake of linoleic acid.

CASE HISTORY: Sarah Baines

Sarah is a successful career woman who has risen to the vice-presidency of a stock brokerage firm, though she is only thirty-five years old.

Her job requires her to attend many business luncheons, where she has found that she drinks to excess. Her work is stressful, and she attributes her heavy smoking to its pressures. As if her life were not full enough, Sarah is also the mother of two young children.

Her recent weight gain worried her. She knew that one cause was her uncontrollable bingeing on sweet foods during the week immediately preceding her period. She admitted to her doctor that she might eat a whole cake or a quart of ice cream at one sitting.

But she was even more concerned with the shifts in her moods. During the premenstrual week she sometimes felt alternately lethargic and restless, and was easily distracted.

She would find herself obsessed with order. Sometimes she remained late at her office, compulsively attending to the small details of her job, only to experience a sudden mood swing to acute loneliness. She knew rationally that she wasn't lonely; her marriage was happy, her children wonderful, her job challenging, and her sex life healthy. Strangely, she was also occasionally struck with an almost overwhelming desire to stay in bed or to take a midday nap—something the usually energetic and disciplined Sarah would normally never do.

Sarah is typical of women who are at the highest risk for PMS. Her doctor told her that no one really knows what causes PMS, although most experts feel that it has something to do with hormonal imbalances occurring during the menstrual cycle. She told Sarah that such an imbalance could take place as a result of disturbed rhythms in the hypothalamus and/or pituitary glands, which control the hormonal system of the body, including the sex hormones. An excess of either estrogen or progesterone in relation to one another (both are produced during the menstrual cycle) may be responsible.

Despite a lack of sound scientific data, 60 percent of all physicians treating PMS also recommend some kind of dietary modification or supplement, and sometimes exercise. Sarah's doctor was no exception. Many women say that they experience relief after making such dietary changes, and Sarah was no exception. Although since adolescence she had had several cola drinks a day, she stopped. She took up swimming and found that it made her feel better all month long. She disciplined herself to stop drinking alcohol during her premenstrual period, and found that she has stopped drinking almost entirely. She still feels that she smokes more than she should, but she does try to be especially careful of how much she smokes when her period is imminent.

Dietary and Life-style Recommendations

Eat Large Amounts of Complex Carbohydrates

A tendency to develop hypoglycemia is not uncommon among PMS sufferers. (Hypoglycemia is a condition characterized by low levels of sugar in the bloodstream.) Women who experience cold sweats, dizziness, faintness, headaches, and head-pounding two to four hours after eating a meal high in sweet foods could be hypoglycemic. The cause may be abnormal hormonal changes that cause an increased secretion of insulin after very sweet foods are eaten that, in turn, causes the shortfall of sugar in the blood. (See chapter 31.)

Strategy In practical terms, this means that hypoglycemics should avoid all candy, sugar, jellies, jams, desserts, and soft drinks containing sugar. Sixty percent of dietary calories should be supplied by complex carbohydrates, such as fruits, vegetables, bread, cereals, potatoes, and other starches. Proteins should supply 15 to 20 percent, which means eating generous servings of meat, fish, poultry, and cheese. The balance of the diet should come from fat found in meat, fish, poultry, cheese, cooking oils, milk, and butter. Because milk contains the simple sugar lactose, it must be limited to two cups daily.

If you are hypoglycemic, you should divide your food into three main meals and three snacks. This will ensure that fluctuations in glucose levels are kept to a minimum. Alcohol should be avoided at all times, since it prevents the liver from producing glucose when blood glucose levels drop below normal.

You may also find it helpful always to carry some crackers, just in case an attack of hypoglycemia occurs.

Get Adequate Vitamin B_6 and Magnesium

Both magnesium and vitamin B_6 are essential to the brain's capacity to produce the neurotransmitters *serotonin* and *norepinephrine*. A deficiency in either nutrient could be responsible for the psychological changes seen in PMS, such as mood swings and depression.

Several studies have shown low magnesium levels in PMS sufferers, and it is known that one out of every two Americans consumes less than the Recommended Dietary Allowances of B_6. Women taking oral contraceptives are especially at risk for B_6 deficiency. (It has been reported that 15 to 20 percent of oral contraceptive users are B_6 deficient.) Apparently the estrogen these pills contain stimulates many reactions in the body that require B_6, and also makes the vitamin work less efficiently.

Many physicians believe that these deficiencies reduce brain serotonin levels and account for many of the emotional disturbances and headaches experienced by women with PMS.

People who drink or smoke also need more B_6. There are 2 million female alcoholics in the reproductive age group in this country. Of these, fully two-thirds relate their drinking to the menstrual cycle; they report that their drinking bouts almost always occur in the week prior to menstruation. In many cases, the PMS sufferers report that they drink to relieve anxieties.

Strategy To prevent any PMS symptoms due to inadequate B_6, you should take a 25-to-50-milligram supplement of the vitamin daily throughout the month. However, limit your intake to that range, as a regular daily dose of 250 milligrams has been reported to cause neurological disorders.

If no improvement is seen after taking the supplement through three complete monthly cycles, discontinue it. In any case, do be certain you are getting enough of the vitamin through your diet. (See table of vitamin B_6–rich foods, page 320.)

All women who take contraceptive pills should also take a daily supplement of 5 milligrams of B_6. Women with PMS who are most likely to benefit from B_6 supplements are those with a history of depression whose symptoms increase when put on oral contraceptives.

It is important to get enough magnesium through your diet (see table of magnesium-rich foods, page 311). You need 300 milligrams daily, so you should either change your diet accordingly or take a 200-to-300-milligram supplement of magnesium.

Avoid heavy drinking, which causes the body to excrete a lot of magnesium in the urine. One drink of hard liquor, one or two glasses of wine, or one beer daily should not be a problem, provided you get the Recommended Dietary Allowance of magnesium.

Watch Your Salt

Fluid retention, also called *edema*, is one of the main complaints of PMS sufferers. Edema may take the form of swelling of the breasts, genitals, joints, or abdomen. Some doctors believe that fluid retention in the brain may be another cause of PMS's psychological symptoms.

Although the primary cause of edema is thought to be hormonal imbalances, in some cases a diet high in sodium can make the condition worse. Many people are not even aware of how much sodium they eat. Each teaspoon of salt contains two grams of sodium, and sodium can also be found in many common foods. If salt (sodium chloride) or any compound containing sodium appears as one of the first ingredients on a food label, then the product contains a significant amount of salt. If, on the other hand, it appears very near the end of the list (as with bread), there is no need for concern. Read the labels on the foods you eat, especially if your diet contains many processed foods.

Strategy PMS sufferers with edema should cut back to no more than three grams of sodium a day. This means that no salt should be added at the table, though up to one-half teaspoon can be added per day during cooking. In addition, one should avoid very salty foods, such as luncheon meats, snack chips, canned soups and vegetables, TV dinners, soy sauce, and processed cheeses, as well as pickled foods such as sauerkraut. (See table of sodium-rich foods on page 315; those listed should be eaten only in moderation.)

Reduce Caffeine

Many people believe that caffeine exacerbates the breast symptoms of PMS, but some recent evidence suggests that caffeine can make *all* the symptoms of PMS worse. In a study involving over 200 college-age women, the prevalence and severity of PMS increased with greater intake of beverages containing caffeine. The reason for this is not known.

Strategy PMS sufferers should limit or reduce caffeine for a trial period of three monthly cycles to see if they notice any improvement in their symptoms. Foods and beverages high in caffeine include coffee, tea, colas, chocolate, and many cough and analgesic medications. (See table of dietary sources of caffeine, page 300.)

Include Adequate Linoleic Acid in Your Diet

Prostaglandins are chemicals found naturally in the body that are believed to correct hormonal abnormalities in women with PMS and relieve its symptoms. Prostaglandins are made from linoleic acid found in vegetable oils. Vitamins B_6 and C, niacin, and zinc are all needed by your body to make prostaglandins.

Strategy Vegetable oils rich in linoleic acid should be used to replace other types of fats normally used in food preparation. Oils rich in linoleic acid include those derived from corn, cottonseed, peanut, safflower, sesame, soybean, sunflower, walnut, and wheat-germ.

You should eat plenty of foods rich in niacin, vitamins B_6 and C, and zinc (see pages 320, 321, and 323 for tables). You might consider taking a daily vitamin and mineral supplement containing the RDA for these nutrients.

Take Tryptophan Supplements if You Crave Carbohydrates

A large number of women suffer from carbohydrate craving associated with depression during the premenstrual period. The occurrence of these two symptoms is often associated with low brain serotonin levels.

Strategy For women who fall into this category, one-half to one gram (500 to 1,000 milligrams) of tryptophan taken three times a day with a carbohydrate-rich snack or beverage could be helpful.

Other Advice

Vigorous aerobic exercise is beneficial for women suffering from edema, as it helps to dissipate the fluid retained in the tissues. Exercise also helps to relieve stress and tension by raising brain endorphin levels, which are rather like morphine in their calming effect.

Most women who suffer from edema during the premenstrual days have what is known as *idiopathic edema*. They wake up in the morning with puffiness around the eyes and face. As the day wears on, the swelling gradually moves down to the breasts, the abdomen, and finally the ankles and feet.

The swelling is believed to be the result of the hormone estrogen making the capillaries permeable to water, allowing water to leak into the body's tissues. Once it is there, gravity slowly but surely pulls the water downward. Some researchers believe that water leaking into the brain tissue may even account for the behavioral disturbances experienced by women who suffer with PMS.

If you suffer from idiopathic edema, take up daily swimming to help dissipate the edema. Other types of exercise where the body is upright are not advised, in that they tend to worsen the condition; the extra time spent on the feet will give gravity a greater opportunity to work. You might also try elevating your feet in the evening to limit the swelling in the feet and ankles. If your edema does not worsen over the course of a day, any form of aerobic exercise will be beneficial.

If you would like further information about PMS, contact the American Gynecological and Obstetrical Society, P.O. Box 601, Elmwood Avenue, Rochester, New York 14642, phone (716) 275-5201.

45
Prostate Cancer

The cause of prostate cancer is unknown, but it probably has something to do with an imbalance of male sex hormones. Another theory suggests that a virus may be the cause. When not detected early, it spreads to the skeleton, causing arthritis-like pain in the back of the legs. This is the most common form of cancer in men over 65.

The prostate is a gland attached to the lower end of the bladder at the base of the penis. Its main function is to produce the milky seminal fluid that helps transport sperm from the testes during ejaculation. Without a prostate, a man is sterile but is still able to have intercourse.

Before puberty, the prostate is the size of an almond, but under the influence of sex hormones at puberty, it swells to the size of a walnut. As a man ages, production of testicular hormones decreases and this slowly changes the prostate as scar tissue replaces glandular tissue. The prostate can expand, in some cases, to the size of a grapefruit. When the prostate becomes enlarged in a young man, it is usually the result of an infection, though drugs can have the same effect. One out of five men has an enlarged prostate by the age of 50; by 70 years of age, the rate is one in two; by age 80, the rate is better than four out of five.

If for some reason the prostate is exposed to testicular hormones in an unbalanced ratio, a tumor will sometimes develop. If caught early, the prognosis is excellent and either part or all of the prostate may be removed. This operation has an 85-percent success rate.

Warning Signs

- Weak or interrupted flow of urine
- Difficulty in urinating or in starting to urinate
- Frequent, painful, or burning urination, sometimes interrupting sleep several times during the night
- Blood in the urine
- Urine flow that is not easily stopped
- Continuous pain in the lower back, pelvis, or upper thighs

Epidemiological Data

Twenty to 30 percent of all men are affected by prostate cancer. Each year, 86,000 new cases are diagnosed in the United States; some 20,000 die from the disease annually. Most men over the age of 80 have prostate cancer, but die with the disease rather than of it.

Men who are obese are two and one-half times more likely to get prostate cancer.

Prevention and Treatment

- Eat fewer animal food products, especially those high in fat.
- If you are overweight, lose weight.
- Increase your intake of beta-carotene and vitamins C and E.
- Eat plenty of cruciferous vegetables.
- Be sure you are getting enough selenium.
- Be sure to eat a balanced diet.
- Every man over 40 should undergo a rectal examination each year; for those over 50, the exam should be repeated at six-month intervals.

CASE HISTORY: Tony Phillips

Tony Phillips was an overweight seventy-year-old who loved good food. He was more than pleasantly plump, as he tipped the scales at 210 pounds, more than 30 percent over his ideal weight.

Over a period of several months, he noticed that his urine flow had been growing weaker. He had put it down to age, and thought little of it. However, one morning he awoke earlier than usual to some pain in his groin. When he went to the bathroom to urinate, he was shocked to see that he was passing some blood, too.

He called his doctor immediately. The doctor agreed to see him that day, and only hours later, Tony found himself "assuming the position," bent at waist, gripping the examination table, while his doctor conducted a rectal examination.

The doctor found that Tony's prostate was oversized. But it also had an irregular contour, signifying the presence of a tumor. His doctor gave him a phone number and a piece of advice: "Call this surgeon, and get this removed."

Tony had the operation a week later. Within a matter of weeks, to Tony's great relief, he was able to make love to his wife without discomfort. He was able to reach orgasm, though the climax was dry because no seminal fluid was expelled. And his doctor tells him that although he should have frequent checkups, the chances are that Tony will have no recurrence of the problem.

Dietary and Life-style Recommendations

Eat Fewer Animal Food Products, Especially Those High in Fat

One recent study showed that heavy consumers of animal-food products were over three and a half times as likely to die of prostate cancer as were light consumers. These people were eating cheese, eggs, or meat at least three times a week, and drinking about two glasses of milk every day, whereas the light consumers were eating less than one portion of animal food each day, as well as drinking less than one glass of milk.

The reason for the increased mortality in heavy animal-food consumers is believed to be that the body uses animal fat to make excess sex hormones. In fact, there is good evidence that prostate cancer can be treated by checking production of male hormones with drugs. By reducing your intake of animal food, you will reduce the amount of fat available to be converted to the male hormones.

If you have an average American diet, you consume 40 percent of your calories as fat. This should be reduced to below 30 percent. Too much fat in the diet also leads to obesity, another risk factor for prostate cancer. You can reduce fat by making a few simple changes in your diet.

On the average, men consume 2,700 calories daily, so a 10-percent fat reduction from 40 to 30 percent of total calories would mean about 30 grams less fat per day, or some 900 grams a month. (See the table on page 306 for reducing dietary fat.)

Specific strategies for reducing fat include the following:

• Select lean meats and low-fat products when you shop (see also the table on page 304 for foods low in fat).
• Trim excess fat from meat.

- Change to skim milk products.
- Check labels of prepared foods for fat content.
- Add more salads, low-fat soups, and bean, fish, and vegetable dishes to your weekly menu.
- Bake, broil, or boil rather than frying foods.
- Limit your use of salad dressings, rich sauces, butter, cream, margarine, shortening, and oil in food preparation and at the table; use less cooking oil and fat than is called for in recipes.
- Substitute broth for fat in cooking.

If You Are Overweight, Lose Weight

All evidence points to the fact that being overweight increases your risk of contracting prostate cancer. One study shows that if you are as much as one-third overweight, you are two and a half times as likely to get prostate cancer.

Strategy For a disciplined approach to weight loss, see chapter 37.

Increase Your Intake of Beta-Carotene

The nutrient *beta-carotene* has a protective role to play in all forms of cancer, including prostate cancer. The mechanism by which beta-carotene works is unknown, but one theory suggests that it is an efficient antioxidant that helps prevent the formation of *free radicals*, which are atoms or groups of atoms with unpaired electrons that are highly reactive and are thought by many researchers to be one cause of cancer.

Strategy You should eat foods containing beta-carotene. It is found in dark green and deep yellow vegetables such as cabbage, spinach, carrots, broccoli, tomatoes, and Brussels sprouts. Some people advocate taking a 30-milligram supplement of beta-carotene every other day, but take care not to overdo this or eat too many foods rich in beta-carotene, as in larger doses it will be stored in the skin in sufficient amounts to give it a yellowish discoloration.

Although beta-carotene is converted to vitamin A in the body, you should not take vitamin A supplements. Unlike beta-carotene, which is harmless since the body can only convert a limited amount to vitamin A, vitamin A itself is exceedingly dangerous at doses in excess of 10,000 international units taken over a sustained period (five to ten years).

Eat Plenty of Cruciferous Vegetables

Cruciferous vegetables, like Brussels sprouts, cabbage, broccoli, cauliflower, and other members of the cabbage family, are good sources of vitamins, minerals, and fiber, but in addition, they contain *dithiothiones*, substances that protect against cancer by eliminating the destructive properties of cancer-causing agents.

Strategy Incorporate cruciferous vegetables into your diet.

Increase Your Vitamin C Intake

In a variety of cancer studies, vitamin C has been shown to be beneficial. This could be because it is important in the maintenance of the immune system, which helps to resist cancer invasion. The vitamin, like beta-carotene, may also help to prevent the damaging activities of free radicals.

Strategy You should incorporate quantities of good food sources of vitamin C in your daily diet. These include citrus fruits, berries, peaches, melons, green and leafy vegetables, tomatoes, green peppers, and sweet potatoes. (See page 321 for table of vitamin C–rich foods.)

You may also elect to take a supplement of vitamin C, but keep in mind that megadoses of the vitamin are of no proven benefit over that derived from moderate intakes of 100 to 300 milligrams per day.

Increase Vitamin E

Vitamin E is a powerful antioxidant, which, like vitamin C and beta-carotene, blocks the production of cancer-causing free radicals in cells.

Strategy Vitamin E is found in whole-grain cereals, wheat germ, soybeans, broccoli, Brussels sprouts, and leafy greens such as spinach. (See page 322 for table of vitamin E–rich foods.) Research suggests that 200 milligrams a day of vitamin E is helpful in reducing cancer risk.

Be Sure You Get Adequate Selenium

Selenium is another antioxidant that can block cancer-causing substances in cells. Studies in humans have shown that cancer mortality rates are higher in areas where there is little selenium in the diet. The amount of selenium in food depends on where the food is produced, as the quantities of the nutrient present in soil determine how much will be found in plants and in animals that eat plants.

Strategy A safe and adequate dose of selenium is 50 to 200 micrograms per day, which is the range normally found in our daily diet. Good food sources of selenium include wheat germ, bran, tuna fish, onions, tomatoes, and broccoli. (See page 314 for table of selenium-rich foods.)

Though selenium tablets are popular as a supplement, they are not advised. Selenium is toxic, and a buildup can occur if more than 200 micrograms are taken daily as dietary and supplementary sources combined.

Make Sure You Eat a Balanced Diet

A balanced diet will ensure that you get all the nutrients you need for an efficient immune system to protect you against cancer-causing agents. All nutrients have an impact on the immune system, and any excesses or deficiencies reduce its effectiveness. For instance, too much vegetable fat in your diet significantly impairs the immune system, as does a daily dose of more than two or three grams (2,000–3,000 milligrams) of vitamin C. On the other hand, too little of any of the vitamins and minerals can also compromise your natural defenses.

Strategy   Eat a well-balanced diet, one that contains two servings of protein, two to six servings of vegetables and fruits, four to six of bread and cereals, and two of milk and dairy products per day. (See chart on page 326.)

Get a Regular Rectal Examination if You Are Over Forty Years of Age

Although there is no definite means of preventing prostate cancer at the present time, it is possible to detect problems at an early state of its development through a digital rectal examination.

Strategy   The American Cancer Society recommends that every man over 40 get an exam each year and those over 50 undergo one every six months. The earlier the disease is caught, the better the chances of a complete cure.

Other Advice

If you would like additional information about prostate cancer, contact the Cancer Information Clearinghouse, National Cancer Institute, Office of Cancer Communications, 9000 Rockville Pike, Building 31, Room 10A18, Bethesda, Maryland 20205, phone (301) 496-4070.

46
Rheumatoid Arthritis

Rheumatoid arthritis is an inflammation of the joints. The joints swell and fluid accumulates within them, putting pressure on the nerves, which causes pain, muscle stiffness, and difficulty in moving.

Eventually the joints may be destroyed or become fused and no longer movable. Rheumatoid arthritis affects the whole body, causing fever and involving, in some cases, the eyes, heart, lungs, or muscles.

No one knows for sure what causes the disease, but it does seem to be the result of the immune system attacking the joints. The disease may occur at any age from infancy to old age, but usually begins in the thirties and forties, and is more severe in women than in men. It waxes and wanes, but is progressive, and attacks usually occur at more frequent intervals with the passage of time. Rheumatoid arthritis is the most severe and potentially debilitating form of arthritis.

Warning Signs

- The onset of pain and stiffness in several joints, worse upon rising in the morning and lessening as the day progresses (it usually takes 30 minutes or more for the stiffness to abate)
- Redness, swelling, and warmth in an affected joint
- Symmetrical involvement of the joints (meaning that if the joints of the fingers of the left hand are affected, so will be the joints of the right hand)
- Weakness, restlessness, loss of appetite and weight, and, by three or four o'clock in the afternoon, extreme tiredness and malaise

- The small joints of the hands and feet are most commonly affected, but hips, knees, and elbows are often also involved, and occasionally the ankles (but not usually the first joint on each finger)
- Fever, usually associated with an acute attack of the disease
- Joints eventually becoming fused and sometimes fixed at odd angles

Epidemiological Data

Seven million Americans have rheumatoid arthritis.

Some 250,000 American youngsters have juvenile rheumatoid arthritis, which often begins before age seven; but 75 percent of children with rheumatoid arthritis grow out of it.

Rheumatoid arthritis is two to three times as common in women as in men.

Sixty percent of patients suffer minimal or only mild disability and are able to continue a full, active life; 30 to 35 percent suffer serious disability with various degrees of impairment of movement; 5 to 10 percent progress to a serious and almost complete disability.

Prevention and Treatment

- Maintain a well-balanced diet containing plenty of protein and calcium.
- Try to avoid stress as much as possible.
- Stay active with as much exercise as possible.
- Eat as much fish as possible.
- Avoid quackery and unsound arthritis cures.
- If you are overweight, slim down to your ideal body weight.
- Be aware of the nutritional effects of the drugs you are taking.
- Reduce your carbohydrate intake if it brings on a bout of diarrhea or stomach upset.

CASE HISTORY: Jean French

Jean French's first symptom of rheumatoid arthritis (or RA, as she later learned to call it) was morning stiffness in the fingers on both her hands. She noticed it first because it was difficult for her to put on her makeup. Over the next few months her fingers went from being stiff to being a little painful and swollen. It was about thirty minutes after getting up before she was able to use them properly. Because she was in her early forties, she was pretty sure it wasn't the osteoarthritis from which her father suffered, so she went to see her doctor.

He identified her ailment as RA, and prescribed aspirin. He gave her one gram divided into four doses taken with meals and a bedtime snack. He then adjusted it upward to about four and one-half grams or fourteen tablets a day over the next year to control the pain.

Since Jean experienced some stomach upset, he also advised that she take antacids between meals. With the aspirin, Jean has been able to sustain a full, active life, although she tries to avoid very stressful situations, which always cause a flare-up of her problem. It appears after five years with RA that Jean is among the luckier rheumatoid patients, as her arthritis has not progressed significantly, and she has spent more time without significant pain than with it.

Dietary and Life-style Recommendations

Eat a Balanced Diet

A varied diet of fruits, vegetables, meats, fish, poultry, grains, and dairy products is required to prevent poor nutrition that would compound the other problems RA presents to the sufferer.

Strategy In particular, consuming generous portions of protein- and calcium-rich foods is essential to help the damaged joints repair themselves. This means getting two to three portions of protein per day and 1,000 milligrams of calcium either as food or a 2,500-milligram supplement of calcium carbonate. (See table on page 313 for a listing of protein-rich foods, page 301 for foods rich in calcium). Patients with arthritis seem to have greater nutritional needs, so a daily multivitamin containing the Recommended Dietary Allowances is a good idea.

Eat as Much Fish as Possible

Fish contains *eicosapentaenoic acid (EPA)* and *docosahexaenoic acid (DHA)*, which have been shown to reduce inflammation, thereby ameliorating morning stiffness and pain.

Strategy Eat fish as often as possible, or at least three times a week. (See table of fish rich in omega-3 fatty acids, page 307.) Vegetable oils rich in polyunsaturated fats are also beneficial, so make a habit of using them in cooking.

If You Are Overweight, Lose Weight

If you have arthritis in weight-bearing joints, such as the knees and hips, any extra weight will impose stress on those joints, make the pain worse, and cause the joints to deteriorate more quickly.

Strategy Consult chapter 37 for suggestions as to how you might lose weight.

If Necessary, Reduce Carbohydrates

Be aware that chronic inflammation sometimes causes carbohydrate intolerance, leading to diarrhea.

Strategy If this is the case, do not be alarmed, but reduce your carbohydrate intake until the inflammation is under control, and then gradually reintroduce carbohydrates into your diet. (See table of foods rich in simple and complex carbohydrates, page 301.)

Other Advice

Try to avoid stress as much as possible, since tension can cause flare-ups, perhaps by affecting the immune system. Other things affecting the condition are overexertion, inadequate rest, and changes in day-to-day life circumstances, such as an illness in the family, difficulties at work, or financial problems. (See page 334 for strategies for coping with stress.)

It is important to stay as active as possible, because exercise has both physical and psychological benefits. It fosters a sense of self-reliance and helps to keep the joints mobile. Moderate and regular exercise is the key. Too much exercise will cause pain, but stretching, isometrics (like yoga), and swimming, where the weight of the body is supported, are ideal. But remember that exercise is of no benefit until the inflammation in the joints has gone down. Until then, rest, apply heat to the joint, and gently massage it.

Avoid quackery. There are many arthritis quacks—self-styled nutritionists, chiropractors, or even M.D.'s—who claim to have quick cures for arthritis. Don't believe them, and certainly do not forgo your regular therapy to follow one of these people. The Arthritis Foundation estimates that for each dollar spent on legitimate arthritis research, 25 are wasted on quackery. Here are some common examples:

COPPER BRACELETS It is true that patients with arthritis often have low copper levels in their bodies, but neither copper supplements nor the wearing of copper bracelets has any demonstrable benefit for the arthritis sufferer.

DMSO Dimethyl sulfoxide does nothing for arthritis, despite claims by its adherents to the contrary.

ACUPUNCTURE This can give temporary relief from the pain, but has no long-term benefits.

OTHER TREATMENTS Among the innumerable treatments for which exaggerated claims are made are mussel extracts from the New Zealand mollusk, aloe vera, insect and snake venoms, Chuifing Tonkuwan (herbal medications from Hong Kong), light and heat therapy, and various vaccines, vibrators, and radioactive gadgets. Unfortunately, none of these are of benefit to the arthritic patient.

Such therapies as the above flourish because people with arthritis will do anything to stop the pain and the progression of the disease, even to the extent of convincing themselves that a therapy does some good even when it doesn't. Be aware of the nutritional effects of the drugs you are taking, such as the following:

ASPIRIN Its consumption results in losses of iron, folic acid, and vitamin C, leading to anemia and bleeding gums. Eat plenty of foods rich in these nutrients. Also, take aspirin with meals to avoid gastrointestinal upset.

INDOMETHACIN To minimize the chances of gastrointestinal discomfort and bleeding, this medication should be taken with meals. You should also eat plenty of iron-rich foods (see table, page 309) to replace the iron lost through gastrointestinal bleeding.

PENICILLAMINE Eat plenty of foods rich in zinc and vitamin B_6 while taking penicillamine. The drug makes the body use these nutrients inefficiently.

HYDROXYCHLOROQUINE Take this drug with meals to avoid an upset stomach.

CORTICOSTEROIDS Consume plenty of calcium, protein, potassium, zinc, and vitamins B_6 and C, which are all in high demand when taking this drug. (See tables on pages 301, 313, 323, 320, and 321.)

CYCLOPHOSPHAMIDE Do not restrict your sodium intake while taking this medication, as the drug causes severe losses of body sodium, leading to poor appetite, nausea, mouth sores, impaired taste, and vomiting.

METHOTREXATE Get plenty of foods rich in calcium, vitamin B_6, and folic acid, which are needed in greater quantities when using this drug. (See tables on pages 301, 320, and 307.)

AZATHIOPRINE Take at the end of meals to prevent stomach upset.

If you would like additional information about rheumatoid arthritis, contact the Arthritis Foundation, 1314 Spring Street N.E., Atlanta, Georgia 30326, phone (404) 266-0795.

47
Sluggish Thyroid

Hypothyroidism—sluggish thyroid—occurs when the thyroid gland produces insufficient quantities of thyroid hormones to maintain the blood levels in their normal range. Because thyroid hormone has such widespread effects on the growth and development of the body and the workings of all of its cells, its deficiency leads to many health problems. In the extreme, thyroid hormone deficiency in infants and young children can lead to mental retardation, and in adults to mental confusion, failure to maintain normal body temperature in the cold, and heart failure.

A lack of thyroid hormone can result from an inadequate amount of dietary iodine and/or increased intake of food substances called *goitrogens* that prevent the thyroid from producing its hormone. In response, the gland increases in size to compensate, and *goiter*, characterized by a swollen neck, is produced. The gland can become quite large.

In some African countries, a woman's goiter is considered a sign of beauty; in these places, iodine deficiencies are rampant, and the thyroid may become the size of a tennis ball. Despite its size, however, it still cannot produce sufficient thyroid hormone to satisfy the needs of the body. In America, goiter is quite rare, as iodized salt, which prevents the condition, is readily available.

The second cause of sluggish thyroid is a disease of the immune system called *myxedema*, in which the body's own immune system slowly destroys the thyroid. Other causes include diseases of the pituitary gland and hypothalamus, which normally produce the substances called *thyroid stimulating hormone (TSH)* and *thyrotropin releasing hormone (TRH)*, which stimulate the thyroid gland to produce thyroid hormone. Finally, some babies are born with no thyroid gland or a defective one. It is vital that this be detected at birth, as without adequate thyroid hormone the brain does not grow properly and the child becomes severely mentally retarded. Such babies are very lethargic and do not grow very well.

Warning Signs

- Intolerance to cold, lack of energy, increase in weight
- Dry, rough, and cold skin, sallow complexion, yellowish coloration on the soles of the feet and the palms of the hand
- Dry and unruly hair
- High blood cholesterol levels and hypoglycemia (see chapter 31)
- Dulled sense of taste, constipation
- Water retention and frequent urinary infections
- Muscular pains and pins-and-needles sensations in the hands and wrists
- Lethargy, slow speech, and hoarseness; hearing loss and loss of memory
- Hand and face puffiness
- Reduced heart rate and blood pressure
- Goiter (indicated by a swelling at the front of the neck)

Epidemiological Data

Hypothyroidism is five times more common in women than in men, and tends to run in families.

Prevention and Treatment

- Watch your weight carefully, and reduce the amount you eat so that you stay within your ideal weight range.
- Make sure that you get plenty of fiber in your diet.
- Be sure that you are getting adequate iron and folic acid.
- Cook all foods known to contain antithyroid substances, or eliminate them from your diet and get adequate iodine.
- Reduce the animal fat in your diet, and limit cholesterol to no more than 300 milligrams daily.
- Be sure to get the Recommended Dietary Allowance (5,000 international units) of vitamin A every day.

CASE HISTORY: Rhoda Goldin

Rhoda Goldin's condition had developed almost insidiously over a two-year period, in fact since her retirement. The first thing she noticed was the swelling in her ankles. Shortly after that, she began to suffer from shortness of breath and, on occasion, sharp, angina-like pain in her chest.

These observations prompted her to see her doctor, who found her to be slightly anemic and prescribed an iron supplement, a drug for angina *(Peritrate)*, and a diuretic *(Diuril)*. She took these drugs conscientiously, but didn't seem to get much better. In fact, she developed additional symptoms.

She gained weight despite her loss of appetite and the fact that she was eating less than ever before. In addition, she found that she was always tired, had absolutely no resistance to the cold, and seemed to have terrible trouble remembering things. The situation got so bad that after about two years following her first visit to the doctor, she found herself unable to take care of herself or her home. She checked herself into the hospital, fearing that she was terminally ill.

In the hospital they gave her a thorough physical examination and a number of blood tests and found that she was hypothyroid and had folic acid deficiency anemia. She was given folic acid supplements and thyroid hormone and soon felt much better. On discharge from the hospital, she was kept on thyroid hormone and advised to take a folic acid supplement. Rhoda was told that she would have to take the thyroid medication for the rest of her life. At eighty, she continues to lead a normal and healthful life.

Dietary and Life-style Recommendations

Watch Your Weight

People with a sluggish thyroid have a 30-to-40-percent slower metabolic rate, which means that they require 30 to 40 percent fewer calories.

Strategy Measure your weight frequently to detect any gains. Until the condition is under control with medication, you will need to cut back on calories, but at the same time maintain a balanced diet. (See chapter 37 for guidance in losing weight.)

Eat Plenty of Fiber

Everything tends to slow down in a person with a sluggish thyroid, including the motility of the intestine. This means that patients often suffer from constipation.

Strategy To combat this, get at least 25 grams of fiber in your daily diet. (See table on page 303 for foods rich in dietary fiber; see also chapter 14 for suggestions to help with a constipation problem.)

Get Adequate Iron and Folic Acid

Patients with a sluggish thyroid are frequently found to have anemia owing to iron deficiency or folic acid deficiency.

Strategy Be sure to get at least 18 milligrams of iron in your diet and 400 micrograms of folic acid by eating frequent servings of foods rich in these nutrients. (See tables on pages 307 and 309 for foods high in folic acid and iron.)

Cook All Foods Containing Goitrogens

Certain foods contain substances called goitrogens, which prevent the thyroid gland from producing thyroid hormones and cause hypothyroidism. In a patient with hypothyroidism, goitrogens will exacerbate the condition and necessitate raising the therapeutic dose of thyroid hormone.

Strategy If you suffer from hypothyroidism, do not consume raw foods containing goitrogens. (See table on page 308.) Cooking destroys the active substance called *goitrin*, and so it is a good idea always to cook such foods.

Get Adequate Iodine

At one time, the leading cause of a sluggish thyroid was iodine deficiency. Nowadays, iodine is readily available in foods and is added to salt, so the problem no longer exists even in areas where the soil and natural foods are deficient in this mineral.

Strategy Be sure to include in your diet the foods listed in the table on page 309, so that you get an average of 150 micrograms of iodine a day. This is particularly important for children and for pregnant and lactating women. Thyroid hormone is crucial for normal growth and development, and an iodine deficiency leads to hypothyroidism, which in turn causes growth retardation and mental retardation in an infant or young child.

Limit Cholesterol

People with hypothyroidism tend to have high blood cholesterol levels, which puts them at increased risk for coronary artery disease and strokes.

Strategy To reduce your risk of suffering from these life-threatening problems, you should reduce the animal fat in your diet, and limit total cholesterol intake to no more than 300 milligrams daily. (See also the strategies enumerated in chapter 6.)

Get Sufficient Vitamin A

Patients with hypothyroidism have a reduced capacity to convert carotene, the form of this vitamin found in vegetables, to the active form of the vitamin. This can result in a sallow complexion (as the carotene builds up in the tissues) and a vitamin A deficiency.

Strategy Make sure that you get adequate vitamin A (see table on page 318), and cut down on foods high in carotene. Foods high in vitamin A include beef liver, eggs, whole milk, and yogurt.

Foods rich in carotene are to be limited to no more than one serving per day. Such foods and recommended serving sizes are apricots (six halves); broccoli, cantaloupe, or carrots (one-half cup); a medium-sized peach; or one-half cup of sweet potato, pumpkin, or winter squash.

Since most of the sources of vitamin A are high-cholesterol foods, a daily vitamin containing the Recommended Dietary Allowances (5,000 international units) is advised for people at high risk for cardiovascular disease, who should not be overindulging in eggs and liver.

Other Advice

Do not take thyroid hormone for a prolonged period of time as a means of losing weight, as it can permanently reduce the production of thyroid hormone, and can lead to a hypothyroid state.

People with a hypothyroid problem usually have thyroid hormone (brand name *Synthroid*) prescribed for them. It should be taken first thing in the morning, before breakfast.

If you would like further information about hypothyroidism, contact the National Health Information Clearinghouse (NHIC), P.O. Box 1133, Washington, D.C. 20013, phone (800) 336-4797 or, in Virginia, (703) 522-2590.

48
Stomach and Esophageal Cancer

Research in recent years has indicated that there may be a strong nutritional component in the development of stomach and esophageal cancers. Among the foods thought to play a possible role are smoked foods, which absorb some of the tars that arise from incomplete combustion of carbon during the smoking process. These tars contain several compounds similar to the cancer-causing tars in tobacco smoke. The food processing industry now often uses "liquid smoke" flavoring that is thought to be less hazardous.

Salt-cured or pickled foods may increase risks of stomach and esophageal cancers as well, and nitrate and nitrite have been shown to enhance the formation of *nitrosamines*, many of which are potent cancer-causing agents.

Warning Signs

- Persistent and unrelieved indigestion, whether immediately following a meal or many hours after a meal
- Discomfort or mild abdominal pain, a feeling of fullness or bloating, slight nausea, heartburn, loss of appetite, belching or regurgitation

Epidemiological Data

In areas of the world where nitrite and nitrate are found in high amounts in food and water, such as in Colombia, stomach and esophageal cancers are common, as they are also in areas of the world where cured and pickled foods are widely used, such as in China and Japan.

Prevention and Treatment

- Be moderate in the use of salt-cured, smoked, and nitrate-cured foods, and increase vitamins E and C.
- Increase iron.
- Eat a well-balanced, varied diet including good sources of the B-complex vitamins and molybdenum.
- Include good sources of selenium in your diet.
- Increase beta-carotene.
- Do not consume excessive quantities of polyunsaturated fats.

CASE HISTORY: Min Chen

Min Chen, a Taiwanese, had spent her early years eating the cured and pickled fish, meats, and other foods characteristic of her country's cuisine. When she emigrated to the United States, she continued her long-established eating habits. She ate little red meat (she had no particular taste for it), and as a result her iron stores were less than ideal.

Though she was basically healthy through her life, at about the time she turned fifty, she developed an almost constant feeling of indigestion. The pain would dissipate between meals, but every time she ate something, she became nauseated and felt a mild pain in her abdomen. It didn't get better, and in fact it got to the point where she dreaded eating.

She began losing weight and finally consulted her doctor. After completing his examination, he consulted with an oncologist who concurred with his diagnosis: stomach cancer.

Min Chen was lucky. She was operated on, and a small portion of her stomach removed. After several months she is eating normally and without discomfort. She finds she gets full a little more quickly, and on her doctor's advice she avoids cured or pickled foods, but she lives a healthy, normal life.

Dietary and Life-style Recommendations

Be Moderate in Eating Salt-Cured, Smoked, and Nitrite-Cured Foods

We have learned that in countries where the diet emphasizes salt-cured and smoked foods, there is a high incidence of stomach cancer. The culprits were discovered to be the substances used in curing those foods. Nitrites and nitrates in foods combine with amines and amides also contained in the food to form nitrosamines in the stomach. It is these nitrosamines that have been demonstrated to be carcinogenic.

Strategy   Both vitamins C and E may prevent the formation of nitrosamines in the stomach, so it is a good idea to drink orange juice or some other fruit juice rich in vitamin C when you eat foods that are rich in nitrites and nitrates.

If you like smoked or cured foods, be sure to get at least 500 milligrams of vitamin C and 200 milligrams of vitamin E in your diet or as a supplement. (See pages 321 and 322 for tables of foods rich in these vitamins.) Also, be moderate in how much of these foods you eat and read food labels to be aware of foods preserved with nitrites and nitrates.

Increase Iron

Iron deficiency has been linked to cancers of the esophagus and stomach in animal studies. It seems to make these tissues more susceptible to chemically induced cancer.

Strategy Be sure to get plenty of iron. Include several portions of iron-rich foods in your daily diet. (See table on page 309.)

Eat a Well-Balanced, Varied Diet that Includes Good Sources of B-Complex Vitamins and Molybdenum

A well-balanced diet will ensure that you get all the nutrients you need for an efficient immune system to protect you against cancer-causing agents. The B-complex vitamins and vitamin C seem to be especially important in this respect. Molybdenum, a trace mineral found in our food, seems to have a special role in preventing nitrosamine-induced esophageal and stomach tumors.

Strategy A balanced diet is one that contains two servings of protein, two to six of vegetables and fruit, four to six of bread and cereals, and two of milk and dairy products per day.

Be Sure to Get Adequate Selenium

Selenium is a powerful antioxidant that blocks cancer-causing substances in cells. Studies in humans have shown that cancer mortality rates are higher in areas where there is little selenium in the diet. The amount of selenium in food depends on where the food is produced, as the quantity of the nutrient present in soil determines how much will be found in plants and in animals that eat plants.

Strategy A safe and adequate dose of selenium is 50 to 200 micrograms per day, which is the range normally found in our daily diet. Good food sources of selenium include wheat germ, bran, tuna fish, onions, tomatoes, and broccoli. (See page 314 for table of selenium-rich foods.)

Though selenium tablets are popular as a supplement, they are not recommended. Selenium is toxic and a buildup can occur if more than

200 micrograms are consumed daily in both dietary and supplemental sources.

Increase Beta-Carotene

Many studies point to a protective role for beta-carotene against all forms of cancer, including stomach and esophageal cancers. The mechanism by which beta-carotene works is not known, but one leading theory suggests that, like selenium, it is an efficient antioxidant.

Strategy You should eat foods containing beta-carotene. It is found in dark green and deep yellow vegetables such as cabbage, spinach, carrots, broccoli, tomatoes, and Brussels sprouts. Some people advocate taking a 30-milligram supplement of beta-carotene every other day, but take care not to overdo this (or eating of foods rich in beta-carotene), as in excessive doses beta-carotene will be stored in the skin in sufficient amounts to give it a yellowish discoloration.

Although beta-carotene is converted to vitamin A in the body, you should not take vitamin A supplements. Unlike beta-carotene, which is harmless (because the body has only a limited capacity to convert it to vitamin A), vitamin A is exceedingly dangerous at doses in excess of 10,000 international units taken over periods of five to ten years.

Do Not Consume Excessive Quantities of Polyunsaturated Fats

After the American Heart Association advised people to reduce the animal fat (saturated fat) and increase the vegetable fat (polyunsaturated fat) in their diet to reduce blood cholesterol levels and the risk of heart attack, many people went overboard and consumed more polyunsaturated fat than saturated fat. This succeeded in reducing their blood cholesterol levels, but it also increased their risk of cancer. A diet high in fat of any kind puts you in a high-risk category for cancer, but polyunsaturated fats seem to be more cancer-causing than saturated ones, possibly because they impair the immune system.

Strategy Aim at equal quantities of vegetable and animal fats in the diet. (See also chapter 6 for further discussion of balancing dietary fats in the diet.)

Other Advice

If you would like further information about stomach or esophageal cancer, contact the Cancer Information Clearinghouse, National Cancer Institute, Office of Cancer Communications, 9000 Rockville Pike, Building 31, Room 10A18, Bethesda, Maryland 20205, phone (301) 496-4070.

49
Traveler's Diarrhea or Dysentery

Sometimes called "Montezuma's revenge," this ailment is caused by an infection resulting from the eating or drinking of water or food that has been contaminated by fecal bacteria or viruses. It is commonly picked up in underdeveloped nations, as well as in certain countries in southern Europe.

The contamination may arise from food prepared by cooks or other handlers with dirty hands, by drinking water that has not been properly purified, or by using dirty utensils. The problem usually lasts just a few days, and most people successfully wait it out in their hotel rooms, where they have easy access to a bathroom. Equally important is the availability of plenty of fluids to prevent such dangerous side effects as dehydration.

The leading cause of the problem is the bacteria *Escherichia coli*, which is part of the normal intestinal flora. However, when abnormally high numbers of *E. coli* are present in the intestine, the toxins produced by them prevent the intestine from absorbing water, leading to the diarrhea.

Other causative agents include *Vibrio parahemolyticus* (found in shellfish, lobster, shrimp, and crab), *Shigella*, a protozoan called *Giardiasis*, and *Salmonella*. Shigella and salmonella cause fever as well as diarrhea; salmonella and vibrio can also cause vomiting. Giardiasis causes nausea, flatulence, cramps, and diarrhea.

Although the infections are caused by bacteria, it is not a good idea to take prophylactic antimicrobial drugs when you go traveling. First, they themselves tend to cause stomach upsets; second, they can bring on yeast infections in women by killing the bacteria that tend to

290

compete with and keep down the number of yeast cells present; third, they promote the development of organisms resistant to antibiotics in the digestive system, which themselves could cause severe gastrointestinal infections at any time. Finally, they also alter the balance of bacteria in the intestines, which could have such far-reaching effects as interfering with normal blood-clotting processes, if the bacteria in the intestine that produce vitamin K should be killed. A deficiency of vitamin K would impair the normal blood-clotting processes and could lead to bruising and hemorrhaging.

Warning Signs

• The problem typically begins a few days after arrival in a foreign country, with an abrupt attack of abdominal cramps and diarrhea. It lasts for three to five days, after which normal activities may be resumed. However, it is not uncommon for a person to suffer from repeated episodes on the same journey.

Epidemiological Data

Twenty to 50 percent of all international travelers develop some degree of diarrhea. One-third of that number have to take to their beds, and 40 percent have to suspend temporarily their scheduled activities.

Prevention and Treatment

When traveling in underdeveloped countries and southern Europe:

• Do not eat food purchased from street vendors.
• Do not eat in school cafeterias.
• Eat only in restaurants that are well recommended.
• Do not eat raw vegetables (including salad vegetables); but cooked vegetables are generally safe.
• Do not eat shellfish (clams, oysters, lobsters, crabs, shrimp).
• Do not eat unpasteurized dairy products.
• Eat only fruit that can be peeled or skinned (for example, pineapple and oranges), and avoid those without skins, such as berries.
• Do not drink tap water or iced drinks unless the tap water and water used to make the ice has been boiled or chemically treated; you should also clean your teeth with the bottled or treated water. A well-known brand of bottled water is fine, but be wary of locally bottled water.

If you develop traveler's diarrhea:

- Prepare two glasses of liquids: one eight-ounce glass should contain apple or orange juice (canned), a pinch of salt, and a half teaspoon of honey; the other eight-ounce glass should be filled with boiled water and one-quarter teaspoon of sodium bicarbonate. Drink alternately from both until the diarrhea significantly lessens.
- As the diarrhea lessens, eat salted crackers, peeled fruit, and, if tolerated, some boiled milk.
- Once the diarrhea has gone, eat a bland, low-fiber diet. Such a diet should include soft foods, such as custard and other simple puddings, apple sauce, soft cooked eggs, and cereals. Gradually build up to your normal diet.

Seek help from a doctor if you have the following:

- Blood in your stools
- Vomiting
- A temperature of over 100 degrees that persists for more than three days
- More than eight bowel movements a day
- Signs of dehydration (dry mouth, decreased urine output, extreme thirst)

CASE HISTORY: Juliette Smythe

Juliette Smythe went to Greece with a group of friends. Though they opted for accommodations in a familiar Hilton hotel, they decided on their first evening to try to experience the local flavor of the town.

They dined at the hotel, but for a nightcap they ventured forth to a small bar on the waterfront. Juliette ordered ouzo, which was served in a tall glass with water. For the next few days she felt fine and stuck to well-recommended restaurants, but on her fourth night she was suddenly stricken with severe stomach cramps and watery diarrhea.

She spent the next three days in her hotel, going to the bathroom eight or nine times a day. She tried to drink fruit juice and as much bottled water as possible, and on her fourth day she improved a great deal. She was able to eat soft foods—a little cereal with pasteurized milk and an orange. She regained her strength fairly quickly, and by the sixth day she was eating normally and was able to follow her planned itinerary.

Dietary and Life-style Recommendations

Be Careful Where and What You Eat

Food purchased from street vendors is the most likely to be contaminated, while food served in clean private homes is safest. Restaurants fall in between. How good restaurants are very much depends on their standards of cleanliness, and you must use your own judgment and the recommendations of others to guide you.

Strategy   Raw vegetables, including salad vegetables, and meat and seafood are all high-risk foods. The safest foods are those that are well-cleaned and cooked, bottled carbonated beverages, beer, wine, and hot coffee and tea. Cooked foods should be eaten hot to protect against tapeworm or other parasites.

Water is not dangerous if boiled or chemically treated. This means adding three drops of halazine or iodine per quart and letting it stand for 30 minutes before drinking. Major hotels in underdeveloped countries often purify their tap water, but you should not take this for granted. Unless you are sure the water has been treated, stick to boiled or chemically treated water or bottled water, even for brushing your teeth. Beware of locally bottled water, as it is often untreated tap water, or is bottled under unsanitary conditions.

To some extent toothpaste can protect you, as it contains antibacterial substances. But you still run the risk of infection if you swallow a significant amount of water. Yogurt has no protective antimicrobial properties and will not help to prevent or cure traveler's diarrhea.

Swimmers should also beware of unchlorinated pools.

If You Get Diarrhea, Restore Your Water and Electrolyte Balance

Whenever a person suffers from severe diarrhea, he loses large amounts of water and electrolytes, both of which are crucial to the normal functioning of the body's tissues. A loss of either one will cause a person to die if allowed to continue for any length of time.

The electrolytes consist of sodium, potassium, and chloride, and diarrhea results in the loss of very large amounts of both sodium and potassium.

Strategy   By drinking mixtures of fruit juice (for potassium), a pinch of salt (sodium and chloride), and honey, you provide adequate electrolytes and water as well as a little sugar from the honey in an easily digested form (glucose and fructose).

Drinking sodium bicarbonate dissolved in water helps to settle the stomach, and provides another source of sodium. As the diarrhea subsides, you can introduce solid foods, but not until your thirst is quenched. Solids taken before this will be difficult to metabolize, and the water in them will not be readily excreted by the kidneys.

The walls of the intestines will be severely irritated by the infection, and you are better off not exacerbating this by eating high-fiber foods, so stick to soft, easily digestible foods for a few days.

When to Seek Help from a Doctor

Miles from home in foreign parts, nobody wants to go to an unknown doctor. Medical standards are low in many Third World countries, and good doctors are hard to find. However, in a life-threatening situation medical help should be sought through the local American embassy.

Blood in your stools or vomit may indicate a serious infection that will need prescription medication. A temperature over 100 degrees Fahrenheit for three days also could indicate a severe infection that needs medical treatment. More than eight bowel movements a day accompanied by a dry mouth, decreased urine output, and extreme thirst is indicative of an electrolyte and water shortage sufficient to be life-threatening. Prompt medical treatment is needed.

Strategy If you are traveling to very inaccessible areas away from doctors, it is a good idea to take a five-day supply of a strong anti-microbial drug like *doxycycline (Vibramycin)* or *sulfamethoxazole (Bactrim)*. Another drug that slows intestinal motility and gives prompt relief from mild diarrhea is *Lomotil* or *Imodium*. These can only be obtained by prescription, so discuss your trip with your doctor in advance.

Other Advice

If you take sulfamethoxazole (Bactrim) or doxycycline (Vibramycin) to relieve your diarrhea, once the diarrhea lets up, take a daily vitamin containing the Recommended Dietary Allowances to replace those nutrients lost as a result of malabsorption.

50
Underweight

Underweight is defined as being 10 to 20 pounds under the desirable weight for your height and frame size (see table on page 219). The causes of underweight may be as diverse as those leading to obesity. For instance, the hunger, appetite, and satiety signals put out by the brain may be abnormal. There may be psychological factors like those described in the chapter on anorexia nervosa and bulimia, or metabolic factors like those described in the chapter on hyperthyroidism.

A prolonged illness can also cause underweight. Such a condition may result in a lack of appetite, vomiting, diarrhea, and a high fever.

All of the kinds of underweight cited above can be corrected by appropriate therapy. However, if the condition is inherited, there may be no solution. In the same way a person who is genetically obese has difficulty losing weight, the genetically thin person may never be able to gain weight. His body's "set point" may be very low, so that when he eats more than is required to maintain his weight, the body simply burns off the calories by producing heat.

A person who is naturally underweight may be fit and active and no more susceptible to illness than anybody else. However, many have psychological problems. They often have a poor self-image. A girl may be flat-chested and feel unattractive; a boy may feel that he looks weak.

For other underweight people, health problems can be a constant worry. When you are 20 pounds underweight, you are more susceptible to infection, especially tuberculosis, but also more likely to pick up common infections like influenza and strep throat. In fact, the

Metropolitan Life Insurance Company's life-expectancy figures, calculated for ideal weights and frame sizes, show that people at the underweight end of the scale are more likely to die early. Thus, being significantly underweight is an apparent health risk.

Being underweight is dangerous if you are trying to become pregnant. Women who are underweight going into pregnancy often have a difficult time gaining the 20-plus pounds typical of a healthy pregnancy in addition to the pounds they are underweight before becoming pregnant. If they do not achieve this weight gain, there is a good chance that their babies will be underweight at birth. Such growth-retarded babies are much more likely to have birth defects, and are much more susceptible to infections.

Warning Signs

• Gradual weight loss of ten pounds or more

Epidemiological Data

Underweight tends to run in families.

Gradual weight loss is often the result of a serious illness, such as cancer, and should always be checked out by a physician.

Teenagers are often underweight owing to poor dietary habits, a desire to remain very slim, anorexia nervosa, or bulimia.

Prevention and Treatment

• Increase body weight gradually by eating a little more at each meal.
• Calculate the amount of calories that need to be consumed to cause a weight gain of one pound per week.
• Consume one to one and a half grams of protein daily per kilogram of body weight.
• Make sure that you get adequate amounts of zinc and B-complex vitamins, and cut out beverages containing caffeine.
• Try to improve your self-image.
• Avoid quack therapies claiming to offer a quick solution.

CASE HISTORY: James Spence

Jim Spence was a college professor at an Ivy League school. He was always very thin for his height; as a child he had not liked food very much, and his parents had waged a constant battle to get him to eat. In fact, he got so thin at one point that he was hospitalized for anorexia nervosa. This persisted on and off until he was about sixteen years old. After that, he ate normally, but out of obligation rather than for pleasure.

At college, exams and social obligations relegated food to last place on his list of priorities. As he moved from student to teacher, Jim's habits remained the same: if he was busy, as he often was with his research and teaching commitments, or whenever life got hectic, meals got missed.

In his middle thirties, he took up jogging. After some months he found that he seemed to pick up every cold that was going around. He went to see his doctor, who weighed him and did a complete physical. At six feet and 130 pounds, Jim was twenty pounds underweight.

His doctor explained to him that since he had not significantly increased the amount he ate since he started jogging, he was now breaking down body tissue to provide necessary energy. The more energy you use up in your daily activities, he was then told, the more vitamins and minerals you need. That's not to say that you need megadoses, but certain vitamins such as riboflavin and minerals such as iron need to be taken in larger quantities to enable the body to provide the muscles with extra energy. These nutrients are also needed by the immune system. Hence, Jim's immune system was not working at maximum efficiency and he was getting sick.

Jim started taking a one-a-day vitamin and mineral supplement containing the Recommended Dietary Allowances, and avoided missing meals. To put on weight, he followed his doctor's advice and started drinking a pint of milk a day after his run. He is still at the lower end of the ideal weight tables, but hasn't had a cold in six months.

Dietary and Life-style Recommendations

Increase Body Weight Gradually

Increase the food eaten at each meal, and eat between-meals snacks and a bedtime snack.

Strategy This can be done without adding a lot of bulk to the meal: mix butter or margarine into mashed potatoes, or add fat to vegetables; add mayonnaise to sandwiches; spread peanut butter, at 90 calories a tablespoon, on crackers, apples, or celery; have calorie-rich snacks such as nuts, dried fruits, chocolate, buttered popcorn, granola, and ice cream around the house; drink lots of milk and milk shakes; consume liberal servings of meat, bread, starches, vegetables, and desserts.

Food like broths and salads should be left out of the menu, as they provide very few calories for a lot of bulk. People who are grossly underweight tolerate butter, cream, and salad oils better than fried foods. Hence, although the latter are rich in calories, they are better avoided. A one-a-day vitamin supplement containing the Recommended Dietary Allowances is also a good idea. Be patient if your weight gain is intermittent and stops at plateaus.

Calculate How Much Food You Require to Gain One Pound a Week

See chapter 37 for specific calculations.

Here is another method. For women, the ideal weight is 100 pounds for the first five feet, plus five pounds for each inch thereafter; for men, it's 106 pounds for the first five feet, plus six pounds per inch above that height.

The amount of energy you need to keep all the necessary functions of the body going is your ideal weight times ten. Add 30 percent to that figure, and you have the energy required to sustain your activities if you are fairly sedentary. If you are active, you need to add more. (See table of energy expenditures for different sporting activities, page 336.)

Strategy To add one pound of weight a week, you need to add at least 3,500 calories a week or 500 calories a day to your diet. In a very active person, the calories needed to gain weight at that rate will be greater.

An adolescent going through a growth spurt will also need more calories, perhaps 4,000 a week, just to maintain weight. He may require 750 to 800 more calories a day to gain a pound a week.

Consume One to One and a Half Grams of Protein per Kilogram of Body Weight per Day

Underweight people have invariably lost a lot of muscle. To build muscle back up, they need two six-ounce servings of foods high in protein each day. (See page 313 for table of protein-rich foods.) If you are a vegetarian, see the chart on page 7 for advice on how to combine foods to improve the quality of their protein content.

Strategy Protein can be added to many foods without increasing the amount of food eaten. Try adding skim-milk powder to cereal, mashed potatoes, soups, gravies, baked goods, scrambled eggs, and ground meats. Try using milk instead of water in soups and instant puddings; add cheese to sauces, vegetables, and soups.

It is no use eating extra protein without exercising. Exercise turns protein into muscle. If your doctor agrees, start off slowly by going for short walks. Gradually build up their length by 15 minutes a day. Alternatively, go swimming, play tennis, or engage in other sports. Whatever you do, start slowly and remember that your body is in a weakened condition. It is also advisable to check with your doctor before starting any exercise program.

Get Plenty of Zinc and B-Complex Vitamins, and Cut Out Caffeine

Zinc and the B-complex vitamins tend to stimulate the appetite.

Strategy Make sure your diet provides the Recommended Dietary Allowances of these nutrients. (See pages 307, 318–321, and 323 for tables of foods rich in B-complex vitamins and zinc.) Also try to make your food look as appetizing as possible. Caffeine-containing beverages, such as coffee, tea, and colas, inhibit the appetite and should be avoided. (See page 300 for table of foods containing caffeine.) Another trick with appetite is to eat more quickly, as after 20 minutes of eating satiety is signaled by the brain in most people.

Other Advice

If you are a naturally thin person, you can do a lot to improve your self-image. Wear clothing and hair styles that complement slimness, always maintain good posture, get plenty of outdoor activity to improve your complexion, and build up your muscle tone by becoming physically fit.

Avoid quack therapies such as shots of vitamin B_{12} or hormones, and various forms of surgery. They either do not work or are extremely hazardous to your health.

Appendix 1 • Food Tables

ACIDIC FOODS

These foods produce acid when broken down in the body; this acid is excreted by the kidneys and contributes to the acidity of the urine.

Bacon	Crackers	Noodles
Brazil nuts	Cranberries	Peanut butter
Breads	Eggs	Peanuts
Cakes	Filberts	Plums
Cereals	Fish	Poultry
Cheese	Lentils	Prunes
Cookies	Macaroni	Spaghetti
Corn	Meat	Walnuts

CAFFEINE-CONTAINING FOODS

Caffeine has been implicated as a causal or contributing factor for several health problems, including PMS, gastrointestinal disturbances, and hyperactivity. Up to 300 milligrams per day are harmless for most people, but in amounts greater than that, this mild stimulant may make a person feel very nervous or shaky.

Food	Serving Size	Caffeine (milligrams)
Coffee		
drip	5 fl. oz.	110–164
percolated	5 fl. oz.	93–134
instant regular	5 fl. oz.	50–65
decaffeinated	5 fl. oz.	2–5
Tea		
1-minute brew	5 fl. oz.	9–33
3-minute brew	5 fl. oz.	20–40
5-minute brew	5 fl. oz.	20–50
canned iced tea	12 fl. oz.	22–36
Cocoa and chocolate		
cocoa beverage	6 fl. oz.	2–8
milk chocolate	1 oz.	1–15
baking chocolate	1 oz.	25–35
Cola drinks	12 fl. oz.	35–45

CALCIUM-RICH FOODS

Calcium is the mineral most likely to be deficient in the diet. It is well absorbed only from dairy products. It is an essential nutrient for the development of bones and teeth, and is needed for normal blood clotting and functioning of the brain, nerves, and muscles. The latest evidence also suggests that it may prevent cancer and high blood pressure.

Food	Serving Size	Calcium (milligrams)
Almonds	1 cup	500
Amaranth	4 oz.	500
Brewer's yeast	14 tablespoons	500
Broccoli	2¼ cups	500
Cheese, cottage	12 oz.	500
Cheese, sandwich	1½ to 2 oz.	500
Collard greens	1 cup	500
Custard	1 cup	500
Dandelion greens	1¼ cups	500
Ice cream	1⅔ cups	500
Kelp	1½ oz.	500
Mackerel, canned	3½ oz.	500
Milk: whole, low-fat, or buttermilk	8 oz.	500
Mustard greens	1½ cups	500
Oysters	12	500
Salmon, canned with bones	5½ oz.	500
Sardines, canned with bones	3½ oz.	500
Soybean curd	8 oz.	500
Spinach	1½ cups	500
Yogurt	¾ cup	500

CARBOHYDRATE FOODS, SIMPLE AND COMPLEX

A simple carbohydrate, such as refined sugar, contains calories but no other nutrients. However, complex carbohydrates are rich in nutrients and are essential to good health.

Simple	Complex
Cakes	Beans
Candies	Breads
Cookies	Carrots
Corn syrup	Cereals
Fruits, dried	Corn
Fruits, fresh	Crackers
Honey	Nuts
Jams	Parsnips
Jellies	Pasta
Molasses	Peas
Soda	Potatoes
Sugar, maple	Sweet potatoes
Sugar, table	Winter squash

CHOLESTEROL-RICH FOODS

Cholesterol is an essential component of every cell in the body. Our bodies make enough cholesterol to satisfy our needs, and no dietary cholesterol is required; the more found in the diet, the less is made by the body. Ideally, you should keep your dietary cholesterol to below 300 milligrams daily for lowest risk of heart attack and stroke.

Food	Serving Size	Cholesterol (milligrams)
Bacon	2 oz.	33
Beef, cooked	4 oz.	94
Butter	1 tablespoon	32
Caviar	1 tablespoon	48
Cheese, Brie	2 oz.	41
Cheese, cheddar	2 oz.	40
Cheese, processed	2 oz.	50
Cheese, Stilton	2 oz.	69
Chicken, cooked	4 oz.	109
Cod, cooked*	4 oz.	68
Crab, cooked*	4 oz.	114
Cream, heavy	1 tablespoon	21
Egg	1 medium	210
Herring, cooked*	4 oz.	111
Lamb, cooked	4 oz.	126
Liver, cooked	4 oz.	377
Lobster*	4 oz.	171
Mackerel*	4 oz.	90
Milk, whole	1 cup	34
Pork, cooked	4 oz.	126
Salmon, smoked*	4 oz.	80
Sardines, canned*	4 oz.	114
Shrimp, cooked*	4 oz.	229
Sole, cooked*	4 oz.	68
Sweetbread, cooked	4 oz.	433
Trout, cooked*	4 oz.	91
Tuna, packed in oil*	3 oz.	56
Turkey, cooked	4 oz.	92

*Foods rich in omega-3 fatty acids (see table on page 307), which are believed to negate the effects of the cholesterol present in the food.

DIETARY FIBER–RICH FOODS

Dietary fiber or roughage promotes good digestion and also helps to prevent the onset of many gastrointestinal diseases. Fiber is indigestible and passes through the digestive tract unchanged, increasing the bulk of the stool. This prevents constipation and development of diverticulosis. It also reduces the risk of developing cancer of the large intestine. Thirty to 40 grams of pectin, the fiber found in the pith of oranges, the flesh of apples, root vegetables (like turnips), green beans, and oatmeal reduces blood cholesterol levels by up to 10 percent. This is important, as a 1 percent drop in cholesterol levels reduces the risk of heart disease by 2 percent.

Food	Serving Size	Fiber (grams)
Almonds	½ cup	7
Beans, baked	½ cup	7.3
Beans, green	½ cup	2.8
Bran	½ cup	15.4
Bread, rye	1 slice	.13
Bread, whole wheat	1 slice	.4
Broccoli, cooked	1 cup	4.1
Brussels sprouts, cooked	1 cup	2.9
Cabbage, cooked	¾ cup	2.1
Carrots, cooked	¾ cup	3.7
Cereal, All-Bran	1 cup	19
Cereal, Grape-Nuts	½ cup	4.7
Cereal, shredded wheat	1 biscuit	3
Corn, cooked	1 ear	6.6
Corn, canned	½ cup	7.3
Corn flakes	1 cup	2.8
Lettuce, raw	1 cup	.75
Oatmeal	½ cup	8.4
Peanuts, roasted	½ cup	5.8
Potatoes, baked	1	3
Prunes, with pits	5 large	8.0
Raisins	½ oz.	1
Spinach	½ cup	3
Walnuts	½ cup	3.1

In general, saturated fats increase blood cholesterol levels, while poly-unsaturated fats and, to a lesser extent, mono-unsaturated fats decrease blood cholesterol levels. The average American diet is high in saturated fats. Therefore, most people should try to include in their daily diets about 2 tablespoons of a vegetable oil with a high polyunsaturated-fat to saturated-fat ratio to counteract the effects of their high saturated-fat diet.

Food (1-tablespoon serving)	Saturated (grams)	Monounsaturated (grams)	Polyunsaturated (grams)
Butter	9	5	trace
Coconut oil	11	1	trace
Corn oil	2	4	7
Cottonseed oil	4	3	7
Margarine			
hard (vegetable oils only)	5	7	2
soft (vegetable oils only)	5	6	3
Palm oil	7	6	3
Peanut oil	3	7	4
Olive oil	2	10	2
Rape oil	1	8	5
Safflower oil	2	2	11
Sesame oil	2	5	5
Soybean oil	2	4	8
Sunflower oil	2	5	7

Dietary substitutions may be made. For example, 1 oz. of walnuts is equiv-alent to 1½ tablespoons of walnut oil; 3 tablespoons of sesame seeds equal 1 tablespoon of oil; 6 tablespoons or 1½ oz. of sunflower seeds equal 1 tablespoon of oil; ¼ cup or 3 oz. of toasted soybeans is equal to 1 tablespoon of oil.

FAT CONTENT OF COMMON FOODS

Low Fat	High Fat
All fish	Duck
All shellfish	Goose
Veal, all cuts	Cold cuts
Chicken fryers and broilers*	Frankfurters
Rock cornish hen*	Beef
Turkey (not self-basting)	shell strip
Beef	T-bone steak
bottom round	club steak
top round	sirloin
eye round	chuck
sirloin tip	rib roast
roast filet	shoulder roast
rump	Porterhouse
ground round	brisket
flank steak	short ribs
minute or cubed steak	tongue

FAT CONTENT OF COMMON FOODS (*continued*)

Low Fat	High Fat
Lamb	Lamb
roast leg of lamb	shanks
lamb steaks	loin lamb chops
Pork	rib chops
lean cured ham	lamb stew
lean ham steak	Pork
All vegetables and	loin pork chops
fruit except avocados	roast loin pork
and coconuts	Canadian bacon
	bacon
	spare ribs
	salt pork
	ham hocks

*Without skin

DISTRIBUTION OF FATS IN COMMON FOODS

High in Polyunsaturated Fatty Acids	Moderately High in Polyunsaturated Fatty Acids
Safflower oil	Sesame oil
Sunflower oil	Cottonseed oil
Corn oil	Other soft margarines
Soft margarine made from	Commercial salad dressings
oils listed above	and mayonnaise
Nuts: walnuts, toasted	Fish oils
soybeans, sesame seeds	
Mayonnaise made from	
these oils	
"Butters" made from these	
seeds and nuts	
Soybean oil	

High in Monounsaturated Fatty Acids	High in Saturated Fatty Acids
Peanut oil	Meats high in fat: cold cuts,
Peanuts and peanut butter	sausages, prime cuts, etc.
Olive oil	Meat drippings
Olives	Lard
Almonds	Hydrogenated shortening
Pecans	Stick margarines
Cashews	Coconut oil
Brazil nuts	Butter and products with
Avocados	dairy fat: cheese, cream,
Fish oils	whole milk, ice cream
	Chocolate
	Bakery items
	Palm oil

HIGH-FAT FOODS

Large quantities of fatty foods should be avoided because a high-fat diet increases your risk of developing both cardiovascular disease and cancer. Animal fat is especially implicated in heart disease and strokes, and vegetable fat and animal fat both are important cancer risks.

Food	Serving Size	Fat (grams)
Almonds	1 oz.	15
Avocado	1 (10 oz.)	37
Bacon	2 slices	8
Beef, cooked, lean, or fat	3 oz.	16
Beef, corned	3 oz.	10
Beef, ground, cooked	3 oz.	13
Beef, sirloin steak, cooked, lean or fat	3 oz.	27
Buttermilk	1 cup	8
Calf's liver, fried	3 oz.	11
Cheese, blue	1 oz.	8
Cheese, cheddar	1 oz.	9
Cheese, cottage, creamed	1 cup	10
low-fat (2%)	1 cup	4
Cheese, American	1 oz.	9
Chocolate milk	1 cup	8
Egg	1	6
Ice cream, regular	1 cup	14
Ice cream, soft	1 cup	23
Lamb chop	3 oz.	31
Milk, whole	1 cup	8
Peanuts, roasted	1 oz.	14
Pork loin, cooked	3 oz.	28
Sardines	3 oz.	9
Sunflower seeds	1 oz.	14
Tuna, canned in oil, drained	3 oz.	7
Tuna salad	1 cup	22
Veal cutlet, cooked	3 oz.	9

REDUCING DIETARY FAT

Food Eliminated	Frequency of Consumption	Monthly Fat Reduction (grams)
1 oz. cream in coffee	5 times a day	900
1 serving ice cream (8 oz.)	3 times a week	168
1 slice apple pie	3 times a week	180
1 slice bread and butter	3 times a day	315
1 serving french fries (10)	3 times a week	84
1 oz. peanuts	4 times a week	144
10 potato chips	4 times a week	128
10 thin, twisted pretzels	4 times a week	48
1 tablespoon French dressing	once a day	180
1 sirloin steak (3 oz.)	once a week	108
1 lamb chop (3 oz.)	once a week	128
1 glass milk (8 oz.)	once a week	32
½ cup creamed cottage cheese	3 times a week	60

REDUCING DIETARY FAT (*continued*)

Food Eliminated	Frequency of Consumption	Monthly Fat Reduction (grams)
1 slice Swiss cheese (1 oz.)	twice a week	64
1 cup yogurt	twice a week	56
1 oz. milk chocolate	3 times a week	108
2 slices bacon	3 times a week	96

(Reprinted with permission from the American Institute for Cancer Research)

FISH RICH IN OMEGA-3 FATTY ACIDS

You should include fish in your diet at least three times a week, as the omega-3 fatty acids (eicosapentaenoic and docosahexaenoic acids) it contains seem to help protect you from heart attacks and strokes.

Fish	Omega-3 Fatty Acids (milligrams per 4 oz.)
Bass, striped sea	800
Clams, hard shell	274
Cod	229
Flounder	343
Haddock	229
Halibut	1,486
Lobster	69
Mackerel	2,171
Mussels	491
Oysters, American	583
Perch, lake	229
Salmon, pink	2,514
Sardines in fish oil	5,829
Scallops, bay	149
Scallops, sea	206
Shrimp	229
Snapper, red	686
Sole	114
Swordfish	1,029
Trout, lake	1,600
Tuna, albacore	2,400

FOLIC ACID–RICH FOODS

This vitamin is a member of the B complex; it is also known as *folacin*. It is needed for the manufacture of nucleic acids—RNA and DNA—the genetic material found in all cells, as well as for the normal metabolism of certain amino acids (the building blocks of proteins). A deficiency of this vitamin causes anemia and skin disease.

Food	Serving Size	Folic Acid (micrograms)
Apple	1 medium	5–20
Beans, green	1 cup	20–50
Beef, lean	6 oz.	5–20

FOLIC ACID–RICH FOODS (continued)

Food	Serving Size	Folic Acid (micrograms)
Bread	1 slice	5–20
Brewer's yeast	1 tablespoon	100–150
Broccoli	2 stalks	100–150
Carrot	1 medium	5–20
Cheese, hard	1 oz.	5–20
Corn	1 medium ear	5–20
Cucumber	1 small	20–50
Egg	1 large	20–50
Grapefruit	½ medium	5–20
Kidney	3 oz.	20–50
Liver	3 oz.	100–150
Milk	8 oz.	5–20
Mushrooms	3 large	5–20
Orange juice	6 oz.	100–150
Pork, lean	6 oz.	5–20
Potato	1 medium	5–20
Sesame seeds	1 tablespoon	5–20
Shellfish	6 oz.	20–50
Spinach	4 oz.	100–150
Squash	⅔ cup	20–50
Strawberries	1 cup	20–50
Veal, lean	6 oz.	5–20
Yogurt	8 oz.	20–50

GAS-CAUSING FOODS

People suffering from flatulence can be helped by omitting these foods from their diets:

Carbonated beverages
Beans and peas (try eating smaller portions or a different variety)
Cabbage, broccoli, Brussels sprouts, cauliflower (try cooking them without a lid on the pot, as this tends to reduce their gas-causing effects)
Salad vegetables and fruit
Milk, yogurt, and cheese

Specific sensitivity can also occur to carrots, raisins, bananas, apricots, prune juice, pretzels, bagels, wheat germ, pastries, potatoes, eggplant, apples, citrus fruits, and bread; omit any one at a time on a trial basis if you suspect you are sensitive to it.

GOITROGEN-RICH FOODS

Goitrogens are substances that prevent the thyroid gland from producing thyroid hormones, causing goiter (thyroid hormone deficiency) if eaten regularly in large quantities. Although these substances cannot be prevented from acting by iodine, a good supply of dietary iodine (see table of iodine-rich foods, page 309) can offer some protection against goitrogen-induced goiter. Cooking goitrogen-rich foods also greatly reduces the likelihood of goiter.

GOITROGEN-RICH FOODS (continued)

Brussels sprouts	Kelp, brown and green
Cabbage	Peaches
Carrots	Pears
Cassava (from which tapioca pudding is made)	Rutabagas
	Soybeans
Cauliflower	Spinach
Kale	Turnips

IODINE-RICH FOODS

The thyroid gland needs iodine to enable it to produce thyroid hormone (thyroxine) which controls the rate at which the cells in the body work, as well as the rate of growth and development in children.

Food	Serving Size	Iodine (micrograms)
Baked goods	3 oz.	9
Cheese	2 oz.	8
Egg	1 medium	7
Kelp	3 oz.	36
Meat	4 oz.	20
Milk	1 cup	34
Salt, iodized	1 g	74
Seafood	4 oz.	62
Vegetables	3 oz.	24

IRON-RICH FOODS

Iron is a crucial nutrient that is involved in many reactions in the body, as well as being an essential component of hemoglobin, which carries oxygen in the blood.

Food	Serving Size	Iron (milligrams)
Amaranth	3½ oz.	2.0–4
Apricots, dried	6 large halves	1.5–2
Barley	½ cup	1.5–2
Beans, cooked	½ cup	2.0–4
Beans, green	1 cup	1.5–2
Beef, lean	3 oz.	4.0–5
Berries	1 cup	.7–1.4
Bologna	3–4 oz.	1.5–2
Bread	1 slice	.3–.7
Brewer's yeast	1 tablespoon	1.5–2
Broccoli	1 cup	.7–1.4
Buckwheat	½ cup	1.5–2
Bulgur wheat, dry	2 tablespoons	.7–1.4
Carrots	1 cup	.7–1.4
Chicken, all cuts	3–4 oz.	1.5–2
Collards	1 cup	.7–1.4

IRON-RICH FOODS (*continued*)

Food	Serving Size	Iron (milligrams)
Corn grits	1 cup	.3–.7
Cream of wheat	1 cup	.7–1.4
Eggplant	½ cup	.3–.7
Figs, dried	3 medium	2.0–4
Fruits, including apples, bananas, cherries, melons, citrus, pineapple, etc.	1 piece	.3–.7
Ham	2 oz.	1.5–2
Lamb, lean	4 oz.	4.0–5
Liver, calf's	1 oz.	4.0–5
Molasses, blackstrap	1 tablespoon	2.0–4
Mushrooms	⅓ cup	.3–.7
Oatmeal	1 cup	1.5–2
Pasta	½ cup	.3–.7
Peanut butter	2 tablespoons	.3–.7
Peas, cooked	½ cup	2.0–4
Popcorn (popped)	1 cup	.3–.7
Potato	1 medium	.7–1.4
Pumpkin seeds	1 to 2 tablespoons	.7–1.4
Raisins	½ cup	4.0–5
Rice, cooked, white or brown	1 cup	.7–1.4
Tomato	1 small	.3–.7
Soybean curd	4 oz.	2.0–4
Tortilla	(approx. 6 in. diameter)	.7–1.4
Wheatena	⅔ cup	.7–1.4

LACTOSE IN COMMON FOODS

	High Amount	Low Amount	Absent
MILK	Fluid milk Evaporated milk Powdered milk	Yogurt Buttermilk	Soybean milk Nutramigen Pregestimil
MILK PRODUCTS	Ice cream Sherbet Some nondairy milks	Cheese	
MEAT, FISH, POULTRY, AND EGGS	Creamed items	Some cold cuts	All fresh forms
VEGETABLES AND FRUITS		Creamed items	All fresh or plain forms
BAKED PRODUCTS AND GRAINS	Baked with milk	Baked with cheese	French and Italian bread "Parve" goods, pasta Rice, cereals, crackers

Read the label for the presence of milk

LINOLEIC ACID–RICH FOODS

Some women with PMS may benefit from a diet high in linoleic acid. Some foods high in linoleic acid are:

Corn oil	Sesame seeds
Safflower oil	Toasted soybeans
Sunflower oil	Walnuts
Soft margarine made from the above oils	Butters made from the above seeds and nuts

Some other foods moderately high in linoleic acid are:

Cottonseed oil	Soft margarines made from the above oils
Sesame oil	Commercial salad dressings and mayonnaise
Soybean oil	Fish oils

MAGNESIUM-RICH FOODS

Magnesium is used by enzymes responsible for digesting and releasing energy from the food we eat, and is also important for muscle contraction and for maintaining blood calcium levels.

Food	Serving Size	Magnesium (milligrams)
Almonds	1 oz.	77
Avocado	3 oz.	39
Beet greens, raw	1 cup	154
Bran	1 oz.	140
Brazil nuts	1 oz.	65
Cashews	1 oz.	76
Cereal, whole grain	1 oz.	38
Cheese	2 oz.	27
Chocolate	2 oz.	167
Hazelnuts	1 oz.	53
Lima beans, cooked	1 cup	91
Peanuts	1 oz.	50
Pecans	1 oz.	41
Pistachios	1 oz.	45
Shrimp, cooked	4 oz.	58
Soybean curd	3 oz.	95
Spinach, cooked	1 cup	113
Walnuts	1 oz.	37
Wheat germ	1 oz.	96

OXALATE-RICH FOODS

This substance, if taken in large enough quantities, can lead to the formation of kidney stones in susceptible people.

Beans, baked in tomato sauce	Mustard greens
Beans, green, wax, or dried	Okra

Beets	Parsley
Blueberries or blackberries	Peppers, green
Celery	Raspberries
Chocolate	Soybean curd
Cocoa	Spinach
Collard greens	Squash, summer
Dandelion greens	Strawberries
Eggplant	Tangerines
Grapes	Tea
Kale	Watercress
Lemon peel	Wheat germ

PHOSPHORUS-RICH FOODS

Phosphorus is abundant in our diet, and deficiencies are rare. Phosphorus, with calcium, helps build strong teeth and bones. Many enzymes in the body that store and release energy from foods are dependent on phosphorus.

Food	Serving Size	Phosphorus (milligrams)
Almonds	1 oz.	126
Apricots, dried	3 oz.	102
Brains, cooked	4 oz.	389
Bran	1 oz.	257
Brazil nuts	1 oz.	169
Cereal, whole grain	1 oz.	97
Cheese	2 oz.	163–432
Chocolate, milk	3 oz.	119–206
Cocoa	1 gram	189
Fish, cooked	4 oz.	143–572
Kidneys, cooked	4 oz.	411
Liver, cooked	4 oz.	212
Milk	1 cup	226
Peanuts	1 oz.	107
Peas, cooked	1 cup	86
Walnuts	1 oz.	146

PHYTATE-CONTAINING FOODS

This is a fibrous material that binds to essential minerals in the digestive tract and reduces their absorption.

Food	Serving Size	Phytate (milligrams)
Almonds	1 oz.	366
Apple, raw	1 medium	94
Beans, green, raw	2 oz.	377
Beans, lima, raw	2 oz.	509
Brazil nuts	1 oz.	514
Bread, rye	1 slice	235
Bread, whole wheat	1 slice	163
Cereal, All-Bran	1 oz.	679
Cereal, granola	1 oz.	175

Food	Serving Size	Phytate (milligrams)
Cereal, shredded wheat	1 oz.	415
Coca, dry	1 tablespoon	94
Lentils, raw	2 oz.	248
Oatmeal, cooked	½ cup	133
Peanuts	1 oz.	214
Popcorn, popped	1 cup	37
Sesame seeds	1 oz.	1319
Walnuts	1 oz.	217
Wheat germ	1 tablespoon	244

POTASSIUM-RICH FOODS

This nutrient is essential for the proper functioning of the heart, kidneys, and muscles, for the secretion of the stomach's digestive juices, and for transmitting nerve impulses in the brain and throughout the body. Along with sodium, potassium also regulates the amount of water in the cells.

Food	Serving Size	Potassium (milligrams)
Apricots, dried	1 cup	1,273
Avocado, Florida	1	1,836
Banana	1 small	440
Beans, Lima	1 cup	724
Brussels sprouts, fresh cooked	1 cup	423
Carrots, cooked	1 cup	344
Chicken, broiled	6 oz.	483
Clams, soft	3 oz.	225
Dates, pitted	10	518
Flounder	6 oz.	1,000
Milk, skim	1 cup	406
Orange juice	1 cup	496
Potato, baked	1 medium	782
Prunes, dried and pitted	5 large	298
Spinach, chopped and cooked	1 cup	688
Sweetbreads	3 oz.	433
Tomato, raw	1 medium	300
Tuna, salt-free, canned	1 small container (3½ oz.)	327
Yogurt, plain	1 container	531

PROTEIN-RICH FOODS

Protein is essential to the body to enable it to build new tissues and to make neurotransmitters (chemical messengers in the brain), hormones, and enzymes, and to transport essential nutrients around the body in the blood.

Food	Serving Size	Protein (grams)
Beans, baked	1 oz.	13
Beef, cooked, lean or fat	3 oz.	23
Beef, ground, cooked	3 oz.	22
Beef, sirloin steak, cooked, lean or fat	3 oz.	20

PROTEIN-RICH FOODS (*continued*)

Food	Serving Size	Protein (grams)
Bluefish, cooked	3 oz.	22
Calf's liver, fried	3 oz.	25
Cheese, blue	1 oz.	7
Cheese, cheddar	1 oz.	6
Cheese, cottage, creamed	1 cup	28
low-fat (2%)	1 cup	31
Cheese, Swiss	1 oz.	8
Cheese, American	1 oz.	6
Chicken breast, cooked	3 oz.	28
Chicken drumstick, boned, cooked	3 oz.	28
Clams, raw (meat only)	3 oz.	11
Egg	1	6
Lamb chop, cooked	3 oz.	18
Lentils, cooked	1 cup	16
Lima beans, cooked	1 cup	16
Milk, whole	1 cup	8
Milk, lowfat (2%)	1 cup	8
Pork, loin, cooked	3 oz.	21
Peanuts, roasted	1 oz.	8
Salmon, cooked	3 oz.	17
Shrimp, cooked	3 oz.	21
Sunflower seeds	1 oz.	7
Tuna, canned in oil, drained	3 oz.	24
Veal cutlet, cooked	3 oz.	23
Yogurt, low-fat, fruit-flavored	8 oz.	10

SELENIUM-RICH FOODS

Selenium is essential to the health of the heart muscle and to aid vitamin E in the prevention of free radical formation, which is a possible cause of cancer. The selenium content of foods varies with the selenium content of the soil where the food was grown. However, the following list gives you some of the most reliable dietary sources of the mineral.

Food	Serving Size	Selenium (micrograms)
Beef, all cuts	3 oz.	21–46
Beef kidney	3 oz.	91–153
Beef liver	3 oz.	17–68
Bread, rye	3 oz.	18–34
white	3 oz.	15–36
whole wheat	3 oz.	32–46
Cashews	3 oz.	58
Cheese, American	3 oz.	71
Chicken, all cuts	3 oz.	12–42
Chicken livers	3 oz.	56–70
Fish, cod	3 oz.	21–39
flounder	3 oz.	29
herring	3 oz.	52

SELENIUM-RICH FOODS (*continued*)

Food	Serving Size	Selenium (micrograms)
Fish, lobster	3 oz.	19–38
mackerel	3 oz.	56
oysters	3 oz.	24–56
sole	3 oz.	13–25
tuna	3 oz.	77–119
Frankfurter	3 oz.	9–34
Ham	3 oz.	28–44
Lamb	3 oz.	15–38
Milk, skim	1 cup	12
Milk, whole	1 cup	3
Molasses	3 oz.	55–151
Mushrooms	3 oz.	9–11
Peanuts	3 oz.	33
Popcorn	3 oz.	10–28
Pork	3 oz.	15–27
Pork sausage	3 oz.	17–58
Potato chips	3 oz.	663–1,158
Rice, brown, dry	3 oz.	34
Rice, white, dry	3 oz.	6–28
Salami	3 oz.	17–58
Spaghetti, dry	3 oz.	40–64
Walnuts	3 oz.	16

SODIUM-RICH FOODS

Sodium, along with potassium, regulates the amount of water in the cells and is also essential for the proper transmission of nerve impulses and the contraction of muscles.

Food	Serving Size	Sodium (milligrams)
Bacon, broiled	3 oz.	875
Beans, baked	1 cup	862
Beans, lima	1 cup	192
Beets, canned	1 cup	378
Bread, cracked wheat	1 slice	132
raisin	1 slice	91
rye	1 slice	139
white	1 slice	127
whole wheat	1 slice	148
Butter, salted	1 oz.	282
Buttermilk	1 cup	319
Cheese, American	2 oz.	812
blue	2 oz.	900
Camembert	2 oz.	580
cheddar	2 oz.	352
creamed cottage	2 oz.	131
Colby	2 oz.	342
feta	2 oz.	632

SODIUM-RICH FOODS (*continued*)

Food	Serving Size	Sodium (milligrams)
Cheese, Gruyere	2 oz.	190
Monterey Jack	2 oz.	304
mozzarella, whole milk	2 oz.	300
parmesan	2 oz.	419
provolone	2 oz.	496
Romano	2 oz.	728
Velveeta	2 oz.	860
Chicken, cooked	4 oz.	73–98
Clams, cooked	4 oz.	137
Condiments		
garlic salt	1 teaspoon	1,850
horse radish, prepared	1 tablespoon	198
ketchup	1 tablespoon	156
meat tenderizer	1 teaspoon	1,750
MSG (monosodium glutamate)	1 teaspoon	492
onion salt	1 teaspoon	1,620
relish	1 tablespoon	125
Corn, canned	1 cup	496
Corn, sweet	1 cup	25
Corn flakes	1 oz.	287
Crab, cooked	4 oz.	1,140
Egg, cooked	1 medium	61
Fish, cooked	4 oz.	125–202
Ham, cooked	4 oz.	1,063
Liver, cooked	4 oz.	210
Lobster, cooked	4 oz.	239
Margarine, regular	1 oz.	282
unsalted	1 oz.	3
Olives, green	4 medium	384
Peanut butter	1 oz.	173
Peas, canned	1 cup	401
Pickles, dill	1	857
Pickles, sweet	1	79
Pretzels	1	269
Salad dressing	1 tablespoon	96–335
Sardines, cooked	4 oz.	938
Sauces		
barbecue	1 tablespoon	130
chili	1 tablespoon	227
soy	1 tablespoon	1,029
tartar	1 tablespoon	182
teriyaki	1 tablespoon	690
Worcestershire	1 tablespoon	206
Sausage, cooked	4 oz.	1,095
Scallops, cooked	4 oz.	302
Shrimp, cooked	4 oz.	212
Tomato catsup	1 tablespoon	201
Tomato juice	1 cup	486
Turkey, roast	4 oz.	148
Veal, roast	4 oz.	91

Theobromides are, like caffeine, members of the group of compounds called *methylxanthines*. They have been implicated in the same disorders as caffeine, which include PMS and hyperactivity. Theobromides are stimulants and will make a person very nervous and agitated if they are consumed in sufficient quantities.

Food	Serving Size	Theobromide (milligrams)
Tea	6 fl. oz.	2
Baking chocolate	1 oz.	55
Milk chocolate	1 oz.	38–52
Semisweet chocolate	1 oz.	62–139
Cocoa beverage	6 fl. oz.	65–237

TYRAMINE-CONTAINING FOODS

When eaten by some people, tyramine-rich foods cause severe migraine headaches. These foods include:

Alcoholic beverages (esp. sherry, beer, and Chianti, Reisling, and sauterne wines)
Bananas
Bologna
Broad Beans
Canned figs
Cheese, aged (including Brie, Camembert, cheddar, Emmentaler, Gouda, Gruyère, mozzarella, Parmesan, provolone, Romano, processed American, Boursault, and blue cheeses like Roquefort and Stilton)
Chocolate
Eggplant
Fish, dried (including cod and herring)
Game
Herring, pickled
Hot dogs
Liver (chicken and beef)
Meat tenderizers
Pepperoni
Pickled herring
Pineapple
Plums
Salami
Soy sauce
Vanilla
Yeast and yeast extracts
Yogurt

URIC ACID–CONTAINING FOODS (PURINE-RICH FOODS)

Foods rich in uric acid may make a gout condition worse.

125 to 700 mg per 3 oz.	40 to 125 mg per 3 oz.
Anchovies	Beans, dry
Brains	Fish
Kidneys	Lentils
Liver	Meats
Meat extracts	Peas, dry
Sardines	Poultry
Sweetbreads	Seafood
	Spinach

VITAMIN A-RICH FOODS

This vitamin is needed for the health of the skin and the epithelial tissues. It helps to maintain the structure of cell membranes and is necessary for the healthy functioning of the immune system. Vitamin A is also needed for the maintenance and growth of teeth, hair, eyes, bones, and glands. It occurs in two main forms in nature—as retinol, found only in animal sources, and as certain carotenoids, found only in vegetables. Carotenoids are one-third as potent as retinol.

Food	Serving Size	Vitamin A (I.U.)
Apricots, dried	6 halves	2,540
Asparagus	½ cup	605
Beans, green	½ cup	340
Broccoli	½ cup	2,363
Brussels sprouts	½ cup	405
Cantaloupe	½ cup	6,540
Carrots	½ cup	7,610
Corn	1 small ear	310
Egg	1 medium	590
Liver, beef	4 oz.	60,560
Milk, whole	1 cup	350
Orange juice	½ cup	270
Peach	1 medium	1,320
Peas, green	½ cup	430
Pumpkin	½ cup	8,207
Squash, summer	½ cup	410
Squash, winter	½ cup	4,305
Sweet potato	½ cup	8,500
Tomato juice	½ cup	970
Yogurt	½ cup	340

VITAMIN B₁ (THIAMINE)-RICH FOODS

Vitamin B_1 (thiamine) is needed for the metabolism of carbohydrates, for muscle coordination, and for the maintenance of nerve tissue.

Food	Serving Size	Vitamin B₁ (milligrams)
Asparagus	½ cup	.12
Beans, dried	½ cup	.13
Beef liver	4 oz.	.31
Cereal	½ cup	.10
Collard greens	½ cup	.14
Dandelion greens	½ cup	.12
Ham	4 oz.	.53
Lamb, leg of	4 oz.	.17
Lima beans	½ cup	.16
Macaroni, enriched	½ cup	.10
Milk, 2 percent fat fortified	1 cup	.10
Orange	1 medium	.13
Orange juice	½ cup	.11
Oysters	¾ cup	.25
Pork, lean roast	4 oz.	1.21

VITAMIN B₁ (THIAMINE)–RICH FOODS (continued)

Food	Serving Size	Vitamin B₁ (milligrams)
Rice, enriched	½ cup	.12
Spaghetti, enriched	½ cup	.10
Veal, roast	4 oz.	.15

VITAMIN B₂ (RIBOFLAVIN)–RICH FOODS

Vitamin B₂ (riboflavin) helps the body convert proteins, fats, and carbohydrates into energy. It is needed for building and maintaining body tissues, and for protecting the body against many skin and eye disorders.

Food	Serving Size	Vitamin B₂ (milligrams)
Asparagus	½ cup	.13
Beef, lean roast	4 oz.	.25
Broccoli	⅓ cup	.12
Brussels sprouts	½ cup	.11
Cheese, creamed cottage	½ cup	.30
Chicken, skinless	4 oz.	.21
Collard greens	½ cup	.19
Egg	1 medium	.15
Ham	4 oz.	.21
Hamburger	4 oz.	.24
Lamb, leg of	4 oz.	.31
Liver, beef	4 oz.	4.8
Milk, 2% fat fortified	1 cup	.52
Milk, skim	1 cup	.44
Milk, whole	1 cup	.41
Salmon, canned	3 oz.	.16
Sardines	4 oz.	.23
Spinach	½ cup	.11
Squash, winter	½ cup	.14
Tuna, canned	3 oz.	.11
Veal, roast	4 oz.	.35
Yogurt	½ cup	.19

VITAMIN B₃ (NIACIN)–RICH FOODS

This vitamin is found in all cells of the body and is essential for many metabolic processes, such as the conversion of food into energy, the manufacture of fat, protein metabolism, and the use of oxygen by the tissues. The term "niacin" really refers to two compounds, nicotinic acid and nicotinamide (also called niacinamide). Consuming large amounts of nicotinic acid, but not nicotinamide, can produce dilation of the blood vessels or a "flushing" effect.

Food	Serving Size	Vitamin B₃ (milligrams)
Asparagus, cooked	1 cup	1.9
Banana	1 small	.7
Beef	4 oz.	5.7

VITAMIN B₃ (NIACIN)–RICH FOODS (continued)

Food	Serving Size	Vitamin B₃ (milligrams)
Bread, enriched	1 slice	.5
Bread, whole wheat	1 slice	.8
Chicken	4 oz.	8
Corn muffin	1	1.3
Corn, sweet	1 cup	2.4
Lamb	4 oz.	5.7
Liver, cooked	4 oz.	18.2
Peaches, fresh	1 medium	1
Peanut butter	1 tablespoon	2.5
Peas, fresh or frozen, cooked	1 cup	3.2
Pork	4 oz.	5.7
Potato, boiled	1 medium	1.6
Rice, long-grain, cooked	1 cup	2.1
Swordfish, cooked	4 oz.	11.4
Tuna, canned	3 oz.	12.7
Turkey	4 oz.	8
Veal	4 oz.	8

VITAMIN B₆ (PYRIDOXINE)–RICH FOODS*

Vitamin B_6 is needed to enable one to digest and manufacture protein to replace worn-out tissues. It is also crucial to the proper functioning of the nervous system.

Food	Serving Size	Vitamin B₆ (milligrams)
Banana	1 medium	.61
Beef, cooked	4 oz.	.30
Bran flakes	1 cup	.29
Cabbage, cooked	1 cup	.10
Carrots, cooked	1 cup	.10
Fish, cooked	4 oz.	.23–.95
Grape-Nuts cereal	3 oz.	2.41
Lamb cutlets, cooked with bone	4 oz.	.14
Liver, cooked	4 oz.	.83
Milk	1 cup	.10
Oatmeal	1 cup	.29
Peanuts	1 cup	.58
Pork, cooked	4 oz.	.47
Potato, baked	1 medium	.28
Veal, cooked	4 oz.	.36

*The B-complex vitamins are vitamin B_1 (thiamine), B_2 (riboflavin), B_3 (niacin), B_6 (pyridoxine), B_{12}, folic acid, pantothenic acid, and biotin. Biotin and pantothenic acid are so widespread in foods that deficiencies almost never occur.

VITAMIN B₁₂–RICH FOODS

Vitamin B_{12} is needed for the normal development of red blood cells and for the healthy functioning of all cells, particularly those in the bone marrow, nervous system, and intestines. A deficiency causes anemia and deterioration of the nervous system.

VITAMIN B₁₂–RICH FOODS (continued)

Food	Serving Size	Vitamin B₁₂ (micrograms)
Beef, cooked	4 oz.	1–2
Cheese	2 oz.	.8
Chicken, cooked	4 oz.	1
Egg, cooked	1 medium	.8
Fish, fatty, cooked	4 oz.	5–28
Lamb, cooked	4 oz.	1–2
Liver, cooked	4 oz.	28–121
Milk	1 cup	.7
Pork, cooked	4 oz.	1–3
Veal, cooked	4 oz.	1.1
Whitefish, cooked	4 oz.	1–5

VITAMIN C–RICH FOODS

Vitamin C (ascorbic acid) is needed for the production of collagen, the intercellular cement that gives structure to the muscles, blood vessels, bones, and cartilage. It also contributes to the health of teeth and gums, and aids in the body's absorption of iron.

Food	Serving Size	Vitamin C (milligrams)
Broccoli, cooked	1 cup	140
Brussels sprouts, cooked	1 cup	135
Cantaloupe	½, 5 in. dia.	63
Cauliflower, cooked	1 cup	66
Collard greens, cooked	1 cup	87
Cranberry juice	1 cup	81
Grapefruit juice	1 cup	102
Kale, cooked	1 cup	68
Lemon juice	1 cup	112
Mustard greens	1 cup	68
Orange	1 medium	66
Orange juice	1 cup	102
Parsley, raw, chopped	1 cup	68
Papaya	1 cup, cubed	102
Pepper, raw green	1	94
Pineapple juice	1 cup	80
Spinach, cooked	1 cup	50
Strawberries	1 cup	88
Turnip greens, cooked	1 cup	68

VITAMIN D–RICH FOODS

The major function of this vitamin is to enable the body to absorb calcium, which is necessary for the development and maintenance of healthy bones and teeth.

Food	Serving Size	Vitamin D (I.U.)*
Cheese	2 oz.	.5–7.0
Egg, cooked	1 medium	28–36
Herring, broiled	4 oz.	1,003

VITAMIN D-RICH FOODS (continued)

Food	Serving Size	Vitamin D (I.U.)*
Liver, calf's, cooked	4 oz.	11.4
Milk	1 quart	400
Salmon, canned	3 oz.	428.6
Sardines, canned in oil	3 oz.	257.1
Tuna, canned in oil	3 oz.	198.9

*Ten micrograms of vitamin D are equivalent to 400 international units.

VITAMIN E-RICH FOODS

Although the role of vitamin E in our bodies is not well understood, it is widely believed to have an important role in protecting our cell membranes from wear and tear. Some evidence indicates that the vitamin can facilitate the healing of burns and wounds when topically applied. It also helps to prevent free radical formation.

Food	Serving Size	Vitamin E (milligrams)*
Almonds, raw	1 oz.	7
Coconut	1 oz.	1
Cod liver oil	1 tablespoon	3
Corn oil	1 tablespoon	12
Cottonseed oil	1 tablespoon	9
Olive oil	1 tablespoon	2
Palm oil	1 tablespoon	5
Peanuts, raw	1 oz.	5
Pecans, raw	1 oz.	6
Rapeseed oil	1 tablespoon	6
Safflower oil	1 tablespoon	5
Sesame seed oil	1 tablespoon	4
Soybean oil	1 tablespoon	13
Soybeans, dry	3 oz.	17
Sunflower seed oil	1 tablespoon	9
Walnuts, raw	1 oz.	6
Wheat-germ oil	1 tablespoon	36

*Expressed as alpha tocopherol. One milligram of alpha tocopherol is equivalent to one international unit of vitamin E. The other tocopherols are less potent.

VITAMIN K-RICH FOODS

Vitamin K is needed for the manufacture of certain substances in the liver responsible for blood clotting.

Food	Serving Size	Vitamin K (micrograms)
Asparagus, cooked	1 cup	82.7
Bacon, cooked	2 oz.	26.3
Bread, whole wheat	1 slice	4.8
Broccoli, cooked	1 cup	310
Cabbage, cooked	1 cup	87.5

VITAMIN K – RICH FOODS (*continued*)

Food	Serving Size	Vitamin K (micrograms)
Cheese	2 oz.	20
Lettuce	1 outer, 2 inner, 3 heart leaves	29.4
Liver, beef, cooked	4 oz.	104.9
Oats, rolled	1 cup	48
Spinach, cooked	1 cup	160.2
Turnip greens, cooked	1 cup	942.5
Watercress	1 oz.	16.3

XANTHINES

See tables of caffeine- and theobromide-rich foods (caffeine and theobromides are both xanthines).

ZINC-RICH FOODS

The mineral zinc is involved in the manufacture of new cells and body protein. It also aids in the proper action of insulin, helps the body's use of vitamin A, and is essential for the normal functioning of the immune system.

Food	Serving Size	Zinc (milligrams)
Apple sauce	1 cup	.2– .5
Beef, lean	3½ oz.	4.0–5.0
Bran	¾ cup	1.0–1.5
Bread, white	2 slices	.5–1
whole wheat	2 slices	1.0–1.5
Cheese, cheddar	1 oz.	.5–1
Chicken breast	3 oz.	.5–1
Clams	3 oz.	1.0–1.5
Cranberry-apple drink	8 oz.	.5–1
Egg	1 medium	.2– .5
Gefilte fish	3½ oz.	.2– .5
Lamb	3½ oz.	4.0–5.0
Liver	3 oz.	4.0–5.0
Mango	½ medium	.2– .5
Milk, whole or skim	8 oz.	.5–1
Oysters, Atlantic	3½	74.7
Pacific	3½ oz.	9.4
Pineapple juice	8 oz.	.2– .5
Popcorn	2 cups	1.0–1.5
Pork, lean	3½ oz.	4.0–5.0
Potato, cooked	1 medium	.2– .5
Puffed wheat	1 oz.	.5–1
Rice, brown	1 cup	1.0–1.5
white	1 cup	.5–1
Tomato	1 medium	.2– .5
Tuna	3 oz.	.5–1
Wheat germ	1 tablespoon	1.0–1.5

Appendix 2 · Special Dietary Guidance

Age (years)	Weight (kg)	Weight (lbs)	Height (cm)	Height (in)	Protein (g)	(RE)² Vitamin A	(mcg)³ Vitamin D	(mg) Vitamin E	(mg) Vitamin C	(mg) Thiamine	(mg) Riboflavin	(mg equiv.) Niacin⁴	(mg) Vitamin B$_6$	(mcg) Folacin	(mcg) Vitamin B$_{12}$	(mg) Calcium	(mg) Phosphorus	(mg) Magnesium	(mg) Iron	(mg) Zinc	(mcg) Iodine
Infants																					
0.0–0.5	6	13	60	24	kg × 2.2	420	10	3	35	0.3	0.4	6	0.3	30	0.5	360	240	50	10	3	40
0.5–1.0	9	20	71	28	kg × 2.0	400	10	4	35	0.5	0.6	8	0.6	45	1.5	540	360	70	15	5	50
Children																					
1–3	13	29	90	35	23	400	10	5	45	0.7	0.8	9	0.9	100	2.0	800	800	150	15	10	70
4–6	20	44	112	44	30	500	10	6	45	0.9	1.0	11	1.3	200	2.5	800	800	200	10	10	90
7–10	28	62	132	52	34	700	10	7	45	1.2	1.4	16	1.6	300	3.0	800	800	250	10	10	120
Males																					
11–14	45	99	157	62	45	1,000	10	8	50	1.4	1.6	18	1.8	400	3.0	1,200	1,200	350	18	15	150
15–18	66	145	176	69	56	1,000	10	10	60	1.4	1.7	18	2.0	400	3.0	1,200	1,200	400	18	15	150
19–22	70	154	177	70	56	1,000	7.5	10	60	1.5	1.7	19	2.2	400	3.0	800	800	350	10	15	150
23–50	70	154	178	70	56	1,000	5	10	60	1.4	1.6	18	2.2	400	3.0	800	800	350	10	15	150
51+	70	154	178	70	56	1,000	5	10	60	1.2	1.4	16	2.2	400	3.0	800	800	350	10	15	150

Age (years)	Weight (kg)	Weight (lbs)	Height (cm)	Height (in)	Protein (g)	(RE)[2] Vitamin A	(mcg)[3] Vitamin D	(mg) Vitamin E	(mg) Vitamin C	(mg) Thiamine	(mg) Riboflavin	(mg equiv.) Niacin[4]	(mg) Vitamin B6	(mcg) Folacin	(mcg) Vitamin B12	(mg) Calcium	(mg) Phosphorus	(mg) Magnesium	(mg) Iron	(mg) Zinc	(mcg) Iodine
Females																					
11–14	46	101	157	62	46	800	10	8	50	1.1	1.3	15	1.8	400	3.0	1,200	1,200	300	18	15	150
15–18	55	120	163	64	46	800	10	8	60	1.1	1.3	14	2.0	400	3.0	1,200	1,200	300	18	15	150
19–22	55	120	163	64	44	800	7.5	8	60	1.1	1.3	14	2.0	400	3.0	800	800	300	18	15	150
23–50	55	120	163	64	44	800	5	8	60	1.0	1.2	13	2.0	400	3.0	800	800	300	18	15	150
51+	55	120	163	64	44	800	5	8	60	1.0	1.2	13	2.0	400	3.0	800	800	300	10	15	150
Pregnant[1]					+30	+200	+5	+2	+20	+0.4	+0.3	+2	+0.6	+400	+1.0	+400	+400	+150		+5	+25
Lactating[2]					+20	+400	+5	+3	+40	+0.5	+0.5	+5	+0.5	+100	+1.0	+400	+400	+150		+10	+50

[1] Pregnant and lactating women are well advised to take iron supplements as recommended by their physician.
[2] 1 RE = 5 IU
[3] 1 mcg = 40 IU
[4] One mg equivalent is equal to 1 mg of niacin or 60 mg of tryptophan (tryptophan can be converted to niacin by the body).

Reproduced from Recommended Dietary Allowances, 9th ed. (1980), National Academy of Sciences, Washington, D.C.

THE U.S. RECOMMENDED DIETARY ALLOWANCE

These are the nutrients that must appear on a food-packaging label, together with the FDA daily recommended amounts for each.

Nutrients that *Must* Appear	The U.S. RDA	Nutrients that *May* Appear	The U.S. RDA
Protein (g)	65	Biotin (mcg)	300
Vitamin A (RE)	1,000	Vitamin D (IU)	400
Vitamin C (mg)	60	Vitamin E (IU)	30
Thiamine (mg)	1.5	Vitamin B_6 (mg)	2.0
Riboflavin (mg)	1.7	Folic acid (mcg)	400
Niacin (mg)	20	Vitamin B_{12} (mcg)	6
Calcium (mg)	1,000	Pantothenic acid (mg)	10
Iron (mg)	18	Phosphorus (mg)	1,000
		Iodine (mcg)	150
		Magnesium (mg)	400
		Zinc (mg)	15
		Copper (mg)	2

THE BALANCED DIET

The best way to ensure a balanced diet for an adult is to eat the following daily:

Category of Food	Portions per Day
Dairy foods (includes milk, yogurt, unsalted cheese)	2 cups
Protein foods (meat, poultry, fish, eggs, beans)	two 3–4-oz. servings
Fruits	4 pieces
Vegetables	3 cups
Breads, cereals, pastas, and rice	4 slices or cups

THE BLAND DIET

Foods in a bland diet are low in fat, fiber, acid, and spices. Bland diets are usually followed by people with gastrointestinal conditions that would be made worse by certain foods.

Recommended Foods	Foods to Avoid
Milk, cream, cheese, buttermilk, yogurt, malted milk	Fried or fatty foods
Cottage or cream cheese or other soft milk cheese	Smoked and preserved meat and fish; pork

THE BLAND DIET (continued)

Recommended Foods	Foods to Avoid
Butter or margarine	Pastries, preserves, candies
Vegetables: potatoes, peas, squash, asparagus tips, carrots, tender string beans, beets, spinach (these vegetables can be puréed if necessary)	All raw vegetables and all cooked vegetables except those listed under Recommended Foods
Boiled, poached, or scrambled eggs (scrambled eggs should be prepared in a Teflon pan or double boiler)	Alcoholic beverages and carbonated drinks except when prescribed by your physician
Orange juice, ripe bananas, avocados, baked apple (without skin), apple sauce, canned peaches, pears, apricots, white cherries, stewed prunes, other fruit juices (if tolerated)	All fruits except those listed under Recommended Foods
	Pepper and other spices; vinegar, ketchup, horseradish, relishes, gravies, mustard, pickles
Roast beef and lamb; broiled steak, lamb, or veal chops; stewed, broiled, or roast chicken; fresh tongue; liver; sweetbreads; baked, poached, or broiled fish	
Milk- or cream-based soups	
Bread, cereals, and pasta; white bread and rolls, crackers, refined cereals	
Custard, Junket, ice cream, tapioca, rice, bread or cornstarch pudding, gelatin desserts, sponge cake, plain cookies; prune, apricot or peach whip	

GLUTEN-FREE DIET

Food Category	Foods Containing Gluten	Foods Without Gluten
Grains	Wheat (including wheat cereals, breads, potatoes, malt, Postum, breaded products, thickened sauces, gravies, soups, beer, ale) Rye Oats (though oatmeal is tolerated by some people) Barley Most products made from the above	Corn (including corn meal, corn flakes, grits, hominy, popcorn, corn chips) Rice (Cream of Rice, Rice Krispies, rice flakes, puffed rice) Millet (tapioca) Buckwheat (kasha)
Vegetables and fruits	Cream soups	Clear soups Fruit and vegetable juices Fruit ices Fruit whips Potato chips

GLUTEN-FREE DIET (*continued*)

Food Category	Foods Containing Gluten	Foods Without Gluten
Nuts and beans	Bean soups thickened with flour	All types of nut butters
Dairy foods	Some ice cream Cheese spread Malted milk	Milk, cheese, cream Plain yogurt Custard
Meat, fish, and poultry	Breaded, made with filler Canned (read label)	All fresh, frozen, and un- processed meat, fish, and poultry Eggs, meringues Clear meat soups
Fats and oils	Salad dressings thickened with wheat starch	Oils, margarines, butter Other salad dressings
Miscel- laneous foods	Postum Gravies and sauces Mixed infant dinners Junior dinners that contain flour thickeners	Hard candies Coffee, tea (avoid instant types) Arrowroot Jellies, jams, syrups, hon- ey, carbonated bever- ages, cocoa, olives, pickles, salt, pepper, spices, herbs, vinegar, wine

THE LOW-SALT DIET PLAN

The following is a day's menu of foods low in sodium:

BREAKFAST	Juice or grapefruit Egg or unsalted cottage cheese Toast with unsalted butter or margarine Cooked cereal (prepared without salt) Milk (whole or skim) Tea or coffee
A BROWN-BAG LUNCH	Sliced chicken, lettuce, tomato, alfalfa sprouts on whole wheat bread Raisins and unsalted nuts Apple Canned fruit juice, coffee, tea, or milk
A COFFEE-SHOP/ SHORT-ORDER LUNCH	Hamburger on bun with lettuce and tomato Tossed salad with vinegar and/or oil (not salad dressing) Soda pop or flavored milk Fruit gelatin

THE LOW-SALT DIET PLAN (*continued*)

A DIETER'S LUNCH Unsalted crackers or bread
Tossed salad with vinegar and/or oil (as above), but
without diced cheese and assorted canned vegetables such as those served at salad bars
Melon half with unsalted cottage cheese
Fruit juice, coffee, tea, skim milk (limit use of
sodium-based artificial sweeteners to two pack-
ets per day)

EVENING MEAL Broiled codfish
Broccoli with lemon juice
Saffron rice (homemade without salt)
Dinner roll
Unsalted butter or margarine
Tossed salad
Fruit compote
Coffee, tea, or milk

TO MINIMIZE NUTRIENT LOSSES DURING COOKING

Foods	Suggestion	Reason
All foods	Cook with a minimum of water	Water-soluble nutrients (B-complex and C) are leached out in water
Milk in glass bottles	Keep away from light	Riboflavin is light-sensitive
Cut cabbage, greens, cut citrus	Keep wrapped airtight	Vitamins C and A are air-sensitive
Potatoes, cabbage, leafy greens	Place ready-to-cook vegetables in steamer	Vitamin B_{12} and thiamine are destroyed

FOOD EXCHANGE LISTS

The foods in the exchange lists that follow are grouped according to their
nutrient similarities: vegetables; fruits and juices; starch (breads, cereals,
beans); protein; milk; and fat. Within each list, foods are described in specific
quantities or units. The term *exchange* is used because a serving of food
within a list can be exchanged for another food within the same list. For
example, on the fruit list, you can exchange 10 cherries for one half cup of
orange juice, should you prefer the orange juice. Or you can make two exchanges, in a case where 10 cherries and one half cup of orange juice would
equal a whole medium apple (since half an apple equals 10 cherries and half an
apple also equals one half cup of orange juice). The total number of servings for
each calorie level is given in the table on page 332.

FOOD EXCHANGE LISTS (*continued*)

List 1: Free Foods (unlimited quantities allowed)

Bouillon	Gelatin, unsweetened	Chicory
Clear broth	Lemon, Lime	Chinese cabbage
Coffee	Mustard	Endive
Tea	Pickle, sour	Escarole
	Pickle, dill	Lettuce (all kinds)
	unsweetened	Parsley
	Vinegar	Radishes
		Watercress

List 2: Vegetable Exchanges (½ cup cooked or 1 cup raw)

One exchange of vegetables contains about 5 grams of carbohydrate, 2 grams of protein, and 25 cal.

Asparagus	Catsup (2 tbsp.)	Peppers (red or green)
Bean sprouts	Cauliflower	Rutabaga
Beans (green or wax)	Celery	Sauerkraut
Broccoli	Cucumbers	Summer squash
Beets	Eggplant	Tomatoes—1 cup raw
Brussels sprouts	Mushrooms	½ cup cooked
Cabbage (all kinds)	Okra	Tomato or vegetable
Carrots	Onions	juice—6 oz.
		All leafy greens

List 3: Fruit Exchanges

One exchange of fruit contains 10 grams of carbohydrate and 40 cal.

FRUITS

Apple—½ med.	Fruit cocktail, canned—	Pineapple—½ cup
Applesauce—½ cup	½ cup	Prunes, dried—2
Apricots, fresh—2 med.	Grapefruit—½ small	Raisins, 2 tbsp.
Apricots, dried—4	Grapes—12	Strawberries—¾ cup
halves	Honeydew melon—⅓	Tangerine—1 large
Bananas—½ small	(7″ dia.)	Watermelon—1 cup
Blueberries—½ cup	Mango—½ small	cubed
Cantaloupe—¼ med.	Nectarine—1 small	
(6″ dia.)	Orange—1 small	JUICES
Cherries—10 large	Papaya—⅓ med.	Apple, Pineapple—
Dates—2	Peach—1 med.	⅓ cup
Figs, dried—1 small	Pear—1 small	Grapefruit, orange—
		½ cup
		Grape, prune—¼ cup

List 4: Starch Exchanges (cooked servings)

One exchange of starch contains 15 grams of carbohydrate, 2 grams of protein, and 70 cal.

FOOD EXCHANGE LISTS (*continued*)

List 4: Starch Exchanges (cooked servings) (*continued*)

BREADS
Any loaf—1 slice
Bagel—½
Dinner roll—1 (2″ dia.)
English muffin—½
Bun, hamburger or
  hot dog—½
Cornbread (1½″)—
  1 cube
Tortilla (6″ dia.)—1

VEGETABLES
Beans or peas (plain)
  cooked—½ cup
Corn—⅓ cup or
  ½ med. ear
Parsnips—⅔ cup
Potatoes, white—1
  small or ½ cup
Potatoes, sweet or
  yams—¼ cup
Pumpkin—¾ cup
Winter squash—½ cup

CRACKERS
Graham (2½″ sq.)—2
Matzoh (4″ × 6″)—½
Melba Toast—4
Oysters (½ cup)—20
Pretzels—8 rings
Rye Krisps—3
Saltines—5

CEREALS
Hot cereal—½ cup
Dry flakes—⅔ cup
Dry puffed—1½ cups
Bran—5 tbsp.
Wheatgerm—2 tbsp.
Pastas—½ cup
Rice—½ cup

DESSERTS
Fat-free sherbet—4 oz.
Angel cake—1½″
  square

List 5: Protein Exchanges (cooked weight)

One exchange of lean meat contains 7 grams of protein, 3 grams of fat, and 55 cal.

Beef, dried, chipped—
  1 oz.
Beef, lamb, pork, veal
  (lean only)—1 oz.
Cottage cheese, un-
  creamed—¼ cup

Poultry without skin—
  1 oz.
Fish—1 oz.
Lobster—1 small tail
Oysters, clams,
  shrimp—5 med.

Tuna, packed in
  water—¼ cup
Salmon, pink,
  canned—¼ cup
Egg—1 med.
Hard cheese—½ oz.
Peanut butter—2 tsp.

List 6: Milk Exchanges

One exchange of milk contains 12 grams of carbohydrate, 8 grams of protein, and 80 cal.

Buttermilk, fat free—1 cup
Yogurt, plain, made with nonfat
  milk—¾ cup

Skim milk—1 cup
1% fat milk—7 oz.

FOOD EXCHANGE LISTS (continued)

List 7: Fat Exchanges

One exchange of fat contains 5 grams of fat and 45 cal.

Avocado (4″ dia.)—⅛
Bacon, crisp—1 slice
Butter, margarine—1 tsp.
French dressing—1 tbsp.
Mayonnaise—1 tsp.
Roquefort dressing—2 tsp.

Thousand island dressing—2 tsp.
Oil—1 tsp.
Olives—5 small
Peanuts—10
Walnuts—6 small

FOOD PORTIONS ALLOWED FOR DIFFERENT CALORIE LEVELS

The table below shows the total number of servings allowed for each calorie level for the food exchange lists on pages 329–332. At all levels the protein intake will be adequate and vitamin and mineral supplements should not be necessary if selections are made from a variety of foods.

LIST	Number of Portions Allowed for Various Calorie Levels			
	1,000 Calories	1,200 Calories	1,500 Calories	1,800 Calories
List 1—Free Foods	...............................Unlimited.............................			
List 2—Vegetable Exchanges	2	2	2	2
List 3—Fruit Exchanges	3	3	3	3
List 4—Starch Exchanges	3	5	7	9
List 5—Protein Exchanges	6	6	7	7
List 6—Milk Exchanges	2	2	2	3
List 7—Fat Exchanges	2	2	6	7

A 1,500-CALORIE MEAL PLAN

For a person following a 1,500-calorie meal plan, the exchanges may be allotted as follows:

Basic Plan	Sample Menu	Free Foods
Morning		
List 3 (1 portion)	½ small grapefruit	Coffee, artificial
List 5 (1 portion)	1 medium egg	sweetener
List 4 (2 portions)	1 slice whole wheat bread and 1½ cup puffed cereal	
List 7 (1 portion)	1 tsp. margarine	
List 6 (1 portion)	1 cup (8 oz.) skim milk	
Noon		
List 5 (2 portions)	½ cup tuna (in water)	Lettuce, pickles,
List 4 (2 portions)	2 slices bread	lemon juice,
List 7 (3 portions)	2 tsp. mayonnaise and 1 tsp. oil	vinegar

A 1,500-CALORIE MEAL PLAN (*continued*)

Basic Plan	Sample Menu	Free Foods
List 2 (1 portion)	3 slices tomato	
List 3 (1 portion)	½ cup diced pineapple	
Evening		
List 2 (1 portion)	½ cup string beans	Lettuce, radishes,
List 5 (4 portions)	4 oz. chicken (no skin)	soy sauce,
		parsley
List 4 (2 portions)	½ cup mashed potato and	
	4 oz. fat-free sherbet	
List 7 (2 portions)	2 tsp. margarine	
List 3 (1 portion)	2 dates	
Snack		
List 6 (1 portion)	8 oz. skim milk	Coffee
List 4 (1 portion)	1½ in. square	
	sponge cake	

Appendix 3 • Other Information

BLOOD CHOLESTEROL LEVELS

Numerous studies have determined that cholesterol levels over 180 milligrams of cholesterol per 100 milliliters of blood put you at an increased risk for heart disease. However, if your cholesterol level is within a few points of those in the table, your extra risk is probably low. All the same, you should follow the guidelines in chapter 6 and try to reduce your cholesterol count to 180 or less.

	White Males	White Females not on Hormones
AGE (YEARS)	BLOOD CHOLESTEROL (mg/100 ml)	BLOOD CHOLESTEROL (mg/100 ml)
0–4	154.6	156
5–9	154.9	163.7
10–14	157.6	159.6
15–19	149.9	156.6
20–24	166.5	164.1
25–29	182.2	170.7
30–34	192.2	175.4
35–39	201.3	184.3
40–44	206.5	193.0
45–49	212.2	202.5
50–54	212.7	217.7
55–59	213.9	230.5
60–64	213.0	230.8

BLOOD CHOLESTEROL LEVELS (*continued*)

AGE (YEARS)	White Males BLOOD CHOLESTEROL (mg/100 ml)	White Females not on Hormones BLOOD CHOLESTEROL (mg/100 ml)
65–69	212.6	232.8
70–74	208.2	228.5
75–79	204.9	231.0
80+	206.6	222.1

SOURCES OF NUTRITION INFORMATION

The Food and Drug Administration
5600 Fisher's Lane
Rockville, Maryland 20857

The U.S. Department of Agriculture
Food and Nutrition Information Center
USDA National Agricultural Library, Room 304
10301 Baltimore Boulevard
Beltsville, Maryland 20705

The USDA Extension Service:
consult your local telephone directory

The Department of Health and Human Services
Health Services Administration
The U.S. Public Health Service
Washington, D.C. 20852

The U.S. Government Printing Office
Pueblo, Colorado 81009

The American Society for Clinical Nutrition
9650 Rockville Pike
Bethesda, Maryland 20014

The American Medical Association
Department of Foods and Nutrition
535 North Dearborn Street
Chicago, Illinois 60610

The American Dietetic Association
430 North Michigan Avenue
Chicago, Illinois 60611

The Nutrition Foundation
888 17th Street, N.W.
Washington, D.C. 20006

STRESS MANAGEMENT TECHNIQUES

Here are some suggestions on managing your stress:

1. Learn yoga, deep breathing, meditation, or progressive relaxation exercises. Set aside a few minutes each day (for example, a work-break in the midafternoon) when you can practice these.

2. Engage in vigorous aerobic exercise (jogging, brisk walking, swimming) for 20 to 30 minutes, three or more times a week.

3. Join a social group outside your family or work, and then make time for it.

4. Avoid setting impossible deadlines or goals. Make a realistic list of tasks for each day, and tackle them one by one.

5. Don't let yourself be constantly interrupted or distracted. Learn to ignore the telephone, or turn on your answering machine.

6. Find a quiet place where you can spend a few minutes alone each day.

7. When tension mounts, excuse yourself for a few minutes of meditation, deep breathing, or a walk around the block.

8. Avoid constant clock-watching. Allow yourself enough time to get to meetings or other obligations.

9. Try to keep hostile feelings in check by expressing them. If someone or something makes you angry, voice your feelings in a calm, rational manner.

10. Learn to avoid situations that make you tense or angry. If you can't stand waiting in lines at the bank, for example, go at times when the bank is not busy.

11. Cultivate a supportive network of people with whom you can share your feelings and ideas.

12. Take up a hobby or activity you enjoy.

13. Avoid turning to alcohol or cigarettes to relieve tension. The effects of both are temporary and end up increasing tension.

14. Make sure you get enough sleep.

15. Avoid taking work home. If this seems impossible, consider whether you are managing your life effectively.

16. Plan at least one vacation a year during which you can truly escape.

17. Learn to manage your finances so that you can avoid constant worry about bills.

18. Try something new occasionally—a different type of ethnic food, a new route to work, a visit to a new art exhibit.

19. Acquire a pet, especially if you live alone. The undemanding devotion of a cat or dog can make living in a frustrating and often hostile world more tolerable.

20. Accept your limitations. Every now and then, make a list of your accomplishments and the positive aspects of your life.

(Used by permission of G. S. Sharpe Communications Inc.)

SUBSTANCES NOT ESSENTIAL TO HEALTH

The following substances are claimed by faddists to be essential components of the diet; in fact, none are essential. They are also not vitamins.

Substance	Facts and Fallacies
Carnitine, or "vitamin B_T"	Used in fat metabolism, but made by the body from lysine
Bioflavenoids, or "vitamin P"	Not useful for treatment of any human condition
Choline	Found in all cell membranes, this does *not* combat atherosclerosis
Para-aminobenzoic acid (PABA)	Part of the folic acid molecule
"Vitamins" Q and U	No function in humans
Nucleic acids (RNA and DNA)	No evidence exists that these prevent aging
Laetrile, or "vitamin B_{17}"	No function in humans, and does *not* combat cancer
Pangamic acid, or "vitamin B_{15}"	There is no evidence that this has any effect on any human disorder, including heart disease, aging, fatigue, diabetes, cancer, glaucoma, schizophrenia, allergies, breathing problems, or inflammation of the liver

CALORIES USED PER MINUTE OF EXERCISE

ACTIVITY	CALORIES BURNED Weight: 115–150 lbs.	Weight: 150–195 lbs.
Aerobic dancing	6–7	8–9
Basketball	9–11	11–15
Bicycling	5–6	7–8
Golf	3–4	4–5
Jogging (5 mph)	9–10	12–13
Jogging (7 mph)	10–11	13–14
Rowing machine	5–6	7–8
Sexual intercourse	4–5	5–6
Skiing (downhill)	8–9	10–12
Skiing (cross country)	11–12	13–16
Swimming	5–6	7–10
Tennis (doubles)	5–7	7–8
Walking (2 mph)	2–3	3–4
Walking (4 mph)	4–5	6–7

Note: 3,500 calories burned = loss of 1 pound of body weight
(Reprinted with permission from *Rx Being Well*, July/August 1986.)

Index

337